New Women's Writing in African Literature
24

Editor:	*Ernest N. Emenyonu* Department of Africana Studies University of Michigan-Flint, 303 East Kearsley Street, Flint, MI 48502, USA
Assistant Editor:	*Patricia T. Emenyonu*
Associate Editors:	*Simon Gikandi* Department of English Language & Literature, University of Michigan, 7609 Haven Hall, Ann Arbor, MI 48109-1045, USA
	Francis Imbuga Literature Department, Kenyatta University, PO Box 43844, Nairobi, Kenya
	Nnadozie Inyama Department of English, University of Nigeria, Nsukka, Nigeria
	Emmanuel Ngara Office of the Deputy Vice-Chancellor, University of Natal, Private Bag X10, Dalbridge 4014, South Africa
	Charles Nnolim Department of English, School of Humanities University of Port Harcourt, Rivers State, Nigeria
	Ato Quayson Pembroke College, Cambridge CB2 1RF, UK
	Nana Wilson-Tagoe SOAS, Thornhaugh Street, London WC1H 0XG
Reviews Editor:	*James Gibbs* 8 Victoria Square, Bristol BS8 4ET, UK james.gibbs@uwe.ac.uk

African Literature Today

1-14 were published from London by Heinemann Educational Books and from New York by Africana Publishing Company

Editor: Eldred Durosimi Jones
  1, 2, 3, and 4 Omnibus Edition
  5 The Novel in Africa
  6 Poetry in Africa
  7 Focus on Criticism
  8 Drama in Africa
  9 Africa, America & the Caribbean
  10 Retrospect & Prospect
  11 Myth & History

Editor: Eldred Durosimi Jones
Associate Editor: Eustace Palmer
Assistant Editor: Marjorie Jones
  12 New Writing, New Approaches
  13 Recent Trends in the Novel
  14 Insiders & Outsiders

Backlist titles available in the US and Canada from Africa World Press and in the rest of the world from James Currey, an imprint of Boydell and Brewer

ALT 15 Women in African Literature Today
ALT 16 Oral & Written Poetry in African Literature Today
ALT 17 The Question of Language in African Literature Today
ALT 18 Orature in African Literature Today
ALT 19 Critical Theory & African Literature Today
ALT 20 New Trends & Generations in African Literature
ALT 21 Childhood in African Literature
ALT 22 Exile & African Literature
ALT 23 South & Southern African Literature
ALT 24 New Women's Writing in African Literature
ALT 25 New Directions in African Literature

Note from the publisher on new and forthcoming titles

James Currey Publishers have now joined Boydell & Brewer Ltd. *African Literature Today* will continue to be published as an annual volume under the James Currey imprint. North and South American distribution will be available from The University of Rochester Press, 68 Mount Hope Avenue, Rochester, NY 14620-2731, USA, while UK and International distribution will be handled by Boydell & Brewer Ltd., PO Box 9, Woodbridge IP12, 3DF, UK.

ALT 26 War in African Literature Today
ALT 27 New Novels in African Literature Today
ALT 28 Film & African Literature Today
ALT 29 Teaching African Literature Today

Guidelines for Submission of Articles

The Editor invites submission of articles or proposals for articles on the announced themes of forthcoming issues:

Ernest N. Emenyonu, *African Literature Today*
Department of Africana Studies, University of Michigan-Flint
303 East Kearsley Street, Flint M148503, USA
email: eernest@umflint.edu
Fax: 001 810 766 6719

Submissions will be acknowledged promptly and decisions communicated within six months of the receipt of the paper. Your name and institutional affiliation (with full mailing address and email) should appear on a separate sheet, plus a brief biographical profile of not more than six lines. The editor cannot undertake to return material submitted and contributors are advised to keep a copy of all material sent. Please note that all articles outside the announced themes cannot be considered or acknowledged and that articles should not be submitted via email. Articles should be submitted in the English language.

Length: articles should not exceed 5,000 words

Format: three hard copies of all articles should be submitted, double-spaced, on one side only of A4 paper, plus on disk. Disks may be formatted for IBM or P.C. but please label all files and disks clearly.

Style: UK or US spellings. Direct quotations should retain the spelling used in the original source. Italicise titles of books or plays.
Use single inverted commas except for quotes within quotes.
Notes and Works Cited should appear at the end of the text.
Avoid subtitles or subsection headings within the text.

References: to follow series style (Surname date: page number) in brackets in text. All references/works cited should be listed in full at the end of each article, in the following style:
Surname, name/initial. *title of work*. place, publisher, date
Surname, name/initial. 'title of article'. In surname, name/initial (ed.)
title of work. place of publication, publisher, date
or Surname, name/initial, 'title of article', *Journal*, vol. no.: page no.

Copyright: it is the responsibility of contributors to clear permissions where appropriate

Reviewers should provide full bibliographic details, including the extent, ISBN and price, and submit to the reviews editor
James Gibbs, 8 Victoria Square, Bristol BS8 4ET
james.gibbs@uwe.ac.uk

Dedication

This issue of
African Literature Today
is dedicated to
Professor Eldred Durosimi Jones
& Marjorie Jones

With this journal for almost 35 years,
they provided unparalleled devoted leadership
to the cause of African literature

New Women's Writing in African Literature
24

A Review

Editor:	Ernest N. Emenyonu
Assistant Editor:	Patricia T. Emenyonu
Associate Editors:	Simon Gikandi
	Nnadozie Inyama
	Francis Imbuga
	Emmanuel Ngara
	Charles Nnolim
	Ato Quayson
	Nana Wilson-Tagoe
Reviews Editor:	James Gibbs

JAMES CURREY
OXFORD

AFRICA WORLD PRESS
TRENTON, N.J.

James Currey
is an imprint of Boydell & Brewer Ltd
PO Box 9, Woodbridge, Suffolk IP12 3DF, UK
www.boydell.co.uk
and of Boydell & Brewer Inc.
668 Mt Hope Avenue, Rochester, NY 14620, USA
www.boydellandbrewer.com

Transferred to digital printing

1 2 3 4 5 13 12 11 10 09

British Library Cataloguing in Publication Data
New women's writing in African Literature : a review. –
(African literature today ; 24)
1. African literature – 20th century – History and criticism
2. African literature – women authors – History and criticism
I. Emenyonu, Ernest N.   II. Emenyonu, Patricia T.
896'.099287'09049

ISBN 978-0-85255-524-8 (James Currey paper)

Typeset in 9/11 pt Melior
by Long House Publishing Services, Cumbria, UK

Contents

Notes on Contributors   ix

EDITORIAL ARTICLE
New Women's Writing: A Phenomenal Rise   xi
   Ernest N. Emenyonu

ARTICLES

Season of Desert Flowers: Contemporary Women's Poetry
from Northern Nigeria   1
   Aderemi Raji-Oyelade

Eagles in the Age of Unacknowledged Muse:
Two Major Writers in Contemporary Nigerian Literature,
Akachi Ezeigbo & Promise Okekwe   21
   Femi Osofisan

To Trans-emote a Cosmos: Yvonne Vera's Holistic Feminist
Vision in *Butterfly Burning*   43
   Chimalum Nwankwo

Representations of the Womanist Discourse in the Short Fiction of
Akachi Ezeigbo & Chinwe Okechukwu   55
   Ijeoma C. Nwajiaku

Calixthe Beyala Rebels Against Female Oppression   69
   Tunde Fatunde

Ken Bugul's *Le Baobab fou*: A Female Story about a Female Body   77
   Ada Uzoamaka Azodo

From Liminality to Centrality: Kekelwa Nyanya's *Hearthstones*
– A Case in Point   91
   Monica Bungaro

'Submit or Kill Yourself ... Your Two Choices': Options for Wives
in African Women's Fiction   104
   Helen Cousins

Exile & Identity in Buchi Emecheta's *The New Tribe*   115
   Clement Abiaziem Okafor

A Failed Sexual Rebellion: The Case of Ama Ata Aidoo's *Anowa*   130
   Iniobong Uko

'To Write Beyond the "Fact"': Fictional Revision of Southern
African Women in History by Yvonne Vera & Lauretta Ngcobo   138
   M.J. Daymond

Usurpation & the Umbilical Victim in Zulu Sofola's *King Emene*   156
   Azubuike Iloeje

Rage in the Cage of a Page: Commitment of Southern African
Protest Poetry by Women   168
   Simiyu Barasa

BOOK REVIEWS

Margaret Macpherson: Stephen Gray (ed.), *The Picador Book of African Stories*   174

Robert Fraser: Véronique Tadjo, *As the Crow Flies* trans. Wangui wa Goro   176

Margaret Macpherson: Moses Isegawa, *Abyssinian Chronicles*;
Violet Barungi (ed.), *Words from a Granary: an anthology of short stories
from Ugandan Women Writers*   178

Ernest N. Emenyonu: Debo Kotun, *Abiku*   182

Wole Ogundele: Abubakar Gimba, *Footprints*; Kris Obodumu, *Die a Little*   183

Atuki Turner: Four novels from Uganda   187

Kari Dako: Jacqueline Bardolph (ed.), *Cross/Cultures 47, Telling Stories:
Postcolonial Short Fiction in English*   190

Wumi Raji: *Little Drops I & II: an Anthology of Contemporary Nigerian
Short Stories*; Sola Adeyemi, *Goddess of the Storm & Other Stories*   192

Kari Dako: Sam Aryeetey, *Home at Last*   195

Kari Dako: Stephanie Newell, *Ghanaian Popular Fiction: 'Thrilling
Discoveries in Conjugal Life' & Other Tales*   196

Pietro Deandrea: Kofi Anyidoho & James Gibbs (eds), *FonTomFrom:
Contemporary Ghanaian Literature, Theatre & Film*   197

James Gibbs: Stephanie Newell, *Marita: or the Folly of Love: A Novel by A. Native*   199

James Gibbs: Books received   204

Index   205

Notes on Contributors

Ada Uzoamaka Azodo is Adjunct Associate Professor of African Studies and French Studies at Indiana University of Northwest. She is co-author of *Emerging Perspectives on Ama Ata Aidoo* (1999).

Simiyu Barasa is a graduate of Egerton University, Njoro, Kenya, currently pursuing a career in Theatre Arts.

Monica Bungaro teaches African literature and culture, critical theory and gender studies at the Universities of Birmingham (England) and Florence (Italy). Her articles have been published in *The Atlantic Literary Review*, New Delhi (2002) and *Africa, America and Australia*, University of Turin, Italy (2002).

Helen Cousins teaches literature at Newman College, Birmingham (England) specializing in African women's writing and feminism.

Margaret J. Daymond is a Professor of English and Fellow of the University of Natal, Durban, South Africa. She is the author of *South African Feminisms: Writing Theory and Criticism 1990–1994* (1996) and *Women Writing Africa: Southern Region* (2003).

Tunde Fatunde is a Senior Lecturer in the Department of Foreign Languages, Lagos State University, Nigeria where he teaches Sociology of African and Afro-Caribbean literatures written in French. As a playwright, he has written and staged plays both in Nigerian pidgin English and in French.

Azubuike Iloeje is a Senior Lecturer and Head of the Department of English, University of Calabar, Nigeria.

Ijeoma C. Nwajiaku teaches in the Department of Languages at the Federal Polytechnic, Oko, Anambra State, Nigeria. She is currently working on her doctoral dissertation, which focuses on contemporary Nigerian female writing.

Chimalum Nwankwo is a Professor of English at North Carolina State University, Raleigh (USA). He has published several collections of poetry. The latest, *The Womb in the Heart and Other Poems* (2002) won the prestigious Association of Nigerian Authors Poetry Prize for 2002.

Clement Abiaziem Okafor, formerly Chair of the Department of English, University of Nigeria, Nsukka, currently teaches in the English Department, University of Maryland Eastern Shore. He is the author of *The Banished Child: A Study of Tonga Oral Literature* published by the British Folklore Society.

Femi Osofisan is Professor of Theatre Arts, University of Ibadan, Nigeria. A versatile and prolific award winning poet and playwright, his works are widely read in educational institutions in Africa and elsewhere in the world. He is currently the General Manager and Chief Executive of the National Theatre, Igamu, Lagos.

Aderemi Raji-Oyelade is a Professor of African and African-American Literatures in the Department of English, University of Ibadan, Nigeria. His articles have appeared in *Research in African Literatures*, *Wasafiri*, *Glendora Review* and *Position*, among others.

Iniobong Uko is a Senior Lecturer in the English Department at the University of Uyo, Nigeria. She is currently a Visiting Assistant Professor in the Department of Africana Studies, University of Michigan-Flint. Her major areas of research are African literature, African-American literature and women's studies in which she has published journal articles.

Ernest N. Emenyonu

The rapid upsurge of writing by African women in the last two decades of
the twentieth century was a most striking phenomenon in the development of modern African literature. It was not only apparent in the
quantity and variety of output but also in the quality and craftsmanship of
the writing. There have been remarkable innovative stylistic experimentations as well as thematic expansions into uncharted waters, alien
domains and incursions into hitherto taboo subjects. The trend is
continent-wide and it is not peculiar to any one region of Africa. It
embraces women of all ages. In 1994 for instance, Hafsa Muhammad Buba,
a sixteen-year-old Muslim schoolgirl from Maiduguri, Nigeria, published
an exciting 265 page novel, *Peeping into Destiny*, while still in secondary
education at Queen's College, Lagos, making her to date the youngest
female novelist of her country. The novel took her three years to write and it
was said that she often asked the advice of her classmates in the course of
writing, and as often had many of them chip in to recopy her hand-written
drafts before sending them to be typed. *Peeping into Destiny* made history
in Nigeria: Hafsa was young, female and from the North. But it was also an
achievement that highlighted the great strides being made by women
generally in literary creativity in the second half of the twentieth century.

The dawn of the twenty-first century brought with it a new literary
awareness in Africa: African female writers have come a long way from
the 1960s when the few women that published fiction could be counted
on one's fingers and they were hardly noticed by critics or if noticed at all,
were not taken seriously. At the end of the twentieth century, it was no
longer out of place to talk about generations of female African writers, or
categorize female authors as 'established' or 'emerging'.

In an incisive article, 'Female Writers, Male Critics' (*ALT* 13, 1983),
Femi Ojo-Ade drew attention to a critical imbalance and apparent lack of
objectivity in the appreciation of the works of female African writers as
well as in the image of womanhood depicted in African fiction written by
men. Two decades later, ALT 24 is celebrating a rapid rise in African
women's writing that builds on the works studied in the earlier volume

Women in African Literature Today ALT 15 (1987). This creativity is
evident not only in the dominant European languages but also in indigenous African languages. By the exit of the twentieth century, the whole
world had taken note. Nadine Gordimer, a female writer from South
Africa had won the Nobel Prize for Literature in 1991. Two years later, the
African continent lost a leading female writer – Flora Nwapa of Nigeria. A
novelist, short story writer, and poet, Flora Nwapa held in her hands on
her death bed on 17 October 1993, the first printed copies of her three new
plays – *The First Lady, Two Women in Conversation* and *The
Sychophants* (sic). A pioneer African female novelist, she had published
poetry and short stories before revealing her talents as a playwright,
albeit, at the tragic end of her career. The three plays showed her at her
most pungent in her devastating condemnation of African male oppression and denigration of womanhood. No area escaped her rage – domestic
violence, child marriage, polygyny (especially the notion of marrying four
wives and loving them equally), and what to her was female enslavement
in the name of marriage. No one saw her final pronouncement: 'Marriage
as a modern institution should be abolished from the face of the earth'
coming. No one could have imagined that three decades earlier when
Efuru was published. It only goes to show how far Flora Nwapa, who
resisted the label 'feminist' for much of her career, had changed over time.

The phenomenon of female change was not limited to creative artists.
African women scholars too, were no longer satisfied to have somebody
else define for them the aesthetics of female writing, or patronizingly
describe for them the dynamics and intrinsic realities of being a woman in
the African socio-cultural and political environment. African female creativity has moved rapidly alongside with advanced and authentic scholarship by African female intellectuals and a heightened female initiative
in entrepreneurship in the publishing industry. These gains, these
achievements, these conquests, far from diminishing have instead grown
profusely with time. This volume is a tribute to the immense endeavours
of female African creative artists, scholars and publishers in the second
half of the twentieth century.

Three essays in this volume focus on three established women writers
– Buchi Emecheta, Ama Ata Aidoo and Zulu Sofola. This is not a contradiction of the theme of 'New Women's Writing in African Literature'. It is
instead intended as a mirror on continuity and legacies. Emecheta, Aidoo
and Sofola are of the first generation of writers whose vision and creativity helped to define and project female aesthetics and cultural experiences which inspired not only their peers but also the second generation
of female writers. They also represent female African writers whose
works were essentially interpreted within the framework of Western
feminism. Emecheta, possibly the most prolific female African writer to
date, has in her most recent novel, *The New Tribe*, shifted vision and
focus from the women on the African continent or African women trans-

ported into the Western world by sheer force of circumstance, to a new generation of Africans (male and female) who are citizens of the Western world because they were born there to migrant parents. The focus now is on a new generation, and a new social reality. Are these steadily growing new inhabitants Africans or are they 'a new tribe of the Western hemisphere'? This is the crux of the inquiry in 'Exile and Identity in Buchi Emecheta's *The New Tribe*'.

The article on Aidoo was chosen as an opportunity to revisit Aidoo's fiction from the perspective of African feminist discourse which seeks to 'deconstruct imperialistic images of the African, rejecting liminal and negative images of women' prevalent in the fiction by men. African women scholars who take exception to interpreting the works of African women writers within the context of Western feminism, justify their position with the explanation that the African feminist struggle includes the survival of the female as well as the male in the African society. The preferred term *womanism* makes room for accommodation between the sexes, as they embrace rather than separate from each other after mutual understanding.

The article on Zulu Sofola gives this journal the opportunity to pay tribute to the memory of a great female African zealot, mentor and pioneer. Zulu Sofola died in 1995 during sabbatical leave in the United States. She was the first published female playwright in Nigeria as well as the first female Nigerian (possibly African) professor of theatre and dramatic arts. Her memorable 1986 article, 'The Bogey of African Writers' Language Limitation on the Creative Process: The Core of the Matter', showed her to possess one of the earliest voices to interrogate the critical issues of aesthetics and originality in African Literature. It is hoped that history will accord her the place she so richly deserves in the growth and development of African literature in the twentieth century.

It is evident from the dialogue and discourse in the following chapters that far from singing divergent and discordant notes, first generation female African writers and their emerging successors of the second generation, continue to visit and revisit the common issues of being female in Africa, the third world, and, defining reality from the perspective of the African woman.

WORKS CITED

Buba, Hafsa Muhammad. *Peeping into Destiny.* Lagos: Tisons Publishers, 1994.

Nwapa, Flora. *Conversations.* Enugu: Tana, 1993.

—— *The First Lady.* Enugu: Tana, 1993.

Ojo-Ade, Femi. 'Female Writers, Male Critics'. In *ALT* 13, London: Heinemann, 1983.

Sofola, Zulu. 'The Bogey of African Writers' Language Limitation on the Creative Process'. In Emenyonu, Ernest (ed.) *Literature and Society: Selected Essays on African Literature.* Oguta: Zim Pan African Publishers, 1986.

African Theatre
edited by Martin Banham
James Gibbs & Femi Osofisan

Reviews Editor Jane Plastow
Associate Editors Eckhard Breitinger, John Conteh-Morgan,
Hansel Ndumbe Eyoh, Frances Harding, Masitha Hoeane,
David Kerr, Amandina Lihamba, Olu Obafemi & Ian Steadman

African Theatre, an annual publication, provides a focus for research, critical discussion, information and creativity in the vigorous field of African theatre and performance. *African Theatre* also carries reports of workshops, a review section and the text of a previously unpublished play from an African writer.

'An exciting development...' – *Research in African Literatures*

RECENTLY PUBLISHED
African Theatre in Development
'...a "must have" for anybody interested in issues relating to theatre and development in Africa.'
– Sola Adeyemi in H-AfrLitCine@h-net.msu.edu
'...a valuable source on the latest developments in theatre in Africa.' – H.net book review
African Theatre: Playwrights & Politics
African Theatre: Women (Guest Editor: Jane Plastow)
African Theatre: Southern Africa (Guest Editor: David Kerr)

FORTHCOMING
African Theatre special issue
Soyinka: Blackout, Blowout & Beyond

CONTRIBUTIONS ARE INVITED FOR
African Theatre: Young People & Performance

Material should be sent for consideration to:
The Editors, *African Theatre*
8 Victoria Square, Bristol BS8 4ET
Fax: 44 (0) 117 974 4137

James Currey Publishers 73 Botley Rd, Oxford, OX2 0BS, UK
Africa World Press 541 W. Ingham Avenue, Suite B, Trenton, NJ 08638, USA
David Philip 99 Garfield Rd, Claremont 7700, South Africa

> Season of Desert Flowers:
> Contemporary Women's Poetry
> from Northern Nigeria

Aderemi Raji-Oyelade

Preamble: the virgin text

The chance discovery of a slim book of poetry led inextricably to a study of an emergent body of a relatively unknown or unrecognized tradition of female poetry written in English in Northern Nigeria. On 29 April 1997, while attending a reading culture campaign in Kaduna, Kaduna State, I visited an open shop of stationery close to the city's central post office where stale, appropriated or stolen and certainly secondhand books were cheaply sold. There, I found, in a rather new and neat state, a copy of a text entitled *The Genesis and Other Poems* written by Hauwa M. Sambo. My curiosity in this newly found poet became even more pronounced when I discovered that the lady who was seated next to me hours later inside the British Council auditorium where the reading symposium took place was herself the author of the collection. I proceeded to engage Sambo in a long discussion on the nature of writing, the condition of the woman, her idea of writing, as well as her vision as a female author living in the North. Her responses were so short and frank that I began to wonder if the writer were not pushing her modesty to the point of shyness. But the noted modesty did not becloud the expression of her ideological disposition; when for instance I tried to know how she has been responding to the male literary tradition, Sambo replied, 'I'm not a feminist if that's what you mean.' About an hour after that brisk statement and after I had pointed at some feminist-oriented ideas in her *Genesis*, she responded, insistently, 'I'm neither a feminist nor against feminism.' That same evening, a participant at the workshop who I would later come to recognize as Ibrahim Sheme, gave me a copy of a freshly published collection by Nana Aishatu Ahmad – *Vision of the Jewel* – for possible review.

Long after that double discovery and chance encounter, I continued to wonder if that equivocal utterance by Sambo is not an apt representation of the ambiguous vision of the Northern Nigerian female writer operating in a patriarchal sphere where the superiority of the male is a given on account of religious and cultural permutations, and where the notion of women's visibility and participation in the social order is viewed with a reactionary squint. Do all female poets in the North have the awareness of the hegemonic hang-on of the male gaze which perpetually threatens? With what ideology do they respond to the politics of exclusion and suppression practised by patriarchy, sustained by religion and protected by state? How different is the female poet's aesthetics of presentation from mainstream Nigerian poetry, especially related to works written by male writers from the North? These, I believe, are the questions which would be frequently posed in varying degrees of emphasis to open discussions on the incidence of women's exclusion from the canon, the nature of women's writing/poetry, the condition of the female person, and the aesthetic as well as the critical energies of the female imagination.

Behind the veil, or veiling and the nature of silence

In an essay entitled 'Female Voices in Poetry: Catherine Acholonu and Omolara Ogundipe-Leslie as Poets', and published in 1989, Obi Maduakor axiomatically commented on what can be called the zero presence of the female voice in Nigerian poetry:

> It is in the area of poetry that the Nigerian female writers are still trailing languidly behind the men folk on the literary scene. (75)

Before Acholonu and Ogundipe-Leslie, the first notable female writer to produce a volume of poetry was Mabel Segun (*Conflict and Other Poems*); and with others like Phabean Ogundipe, Francesca Yetunde Pereira, Ifi Amadiume and Flora Nwapa, the first slim body of Nigerian female poets established an ethereal presence, almost silhouetted to a critical enterprise which favoured and found connection with a literary tradition dominated, controlled and patronised by men. It is noteworthy that the first group of women who tried their hand on poetry were university-educated Southerners at a time when most of Northern Nigeria privileged Arabic education over Western education and in a culture where the character of 'woman' and the notion 'poetry' meant a contradiction of association.

Poetry written in English by women from the northern axis of the country is indeed a very young and developing tradition in the broad dynamism of contemporary Nigerian literature. By 'northern axis', I refer to the mass of land naturally separated from Southern Nigeria by a combination of physical geography and colonial history. Literally speaking, 'Northern Nigeria' is a reference to the entire trough and bulk of land above the Rivers Niger and Benue; it is also the savannah space occupied by various ethnic nationalities, with the Hausa and the Fulani in the majority, governed by colonial British authority in the nineteenth century and designated until 1914 as 'the Northern Protectorate'. It is paradoxical to note that the writing and recitation of poetry was a popular activity among women in the pre-colonial empire of Usman dan Fodio and one prominent female poet during this glorious period greatly influenced by Arabic literary tradition was Nana Asmau, daughter of the emperor.[1]

Collections of poetry by women are a rarity until the second half of the 1990s. To be precise, the last four years of the twentieth century witnessed the publication of works which has given significant leverage to the activity of the Northern Nigerian female writer as poet. Therefore, the criticism of such a very young tradition is generally, or at best, a tentative one not only because the field is still sparsely populated by both critics and writers but also because definitive and precise theoretical viewpoints would be *too* anticipatory of the unfolding tradition. However, one of the central, and as yet enduring, statements contained in Lloyd Brown's book *Women Writers in Black Africa*, is the treatment of women's writings in African literature as the 'other voices, the unheard voices, rarely discussed and seldom accorded space in the repetitive anthologies and the predictably male-oriented studies in the field'.(3) Brown's observation is as valid now as when it was made over 20 years ago, especially if it is applied to developments in regional and specific national literatures across the continent.

The historical fact of the absence of the female writer, and especially the poet, is sufficiently highlighted in *Creative Writing, Writers and Publishing in Northern Nigeria*, an IFRA publication written in parts by Abba Aliyu Sani and Jibrin Ibrahim, and Emmanuel B. Omobowale. According to the authors, Zaynab Alkali's *The Stillborn* (1984) was 'a milestone in northern Nigerian women's writing in English' (3); it was to Northern Nigeria what Aminata Sow Fall's *Le Revenant* was to Senegalese literary history as the first novel written by a woman within the specified culture. As recently as 1997, Sani and Ibrahim insist almost with a certain valid declaration that the writing of poetry in English is alien to the few female writers in the North:

> Among the female authors from northern Nigeria, who use English as a medium of communication, there are no short story writers, no poets, no critics and only one dramatist. There are also no authors who specialize in children's books, except those who write folktales. (3-4)

It is an obvious point that contemporary Northern Nigerian literature, in the tradition of several other regional and national literatures in Africa, is largely dominated by men. From available records, not more than five out of about sixty-six publications have been ascribed to women between 1973 and 1995. Apart from Zaynab Alkali and perhaps, Stella Oyedepo, all the other prominent or notable authors are male: they include Labo Yari, Ibrahim Tahir, Mamman Vatsa, Muhammed Sule, Adah Ugah, Abubakar Gimba, Jip Ubah, Mu'azu Maiwada, Ibrahim Malumfashi and Olu Obafemi.[2] A few women writers have, however, been represented in a major anthology of Northern Nigerian writing – *Vultures in the Air: Voices from Northern Nigeria*, edited by Zaynab Alkali and Al Imfeld and published by Spectrum in 1995.[3] Using 'the deafening silence' of women writers in Senegal before the publication of Aminata Sow Fall's *Le Revenant* in 1976 as specific focus, Christopher Miller inferred that beyond explaining the reasons for the late emergence of writing by African women, the implications and consequences of that lateness need to be examined:

> The belated emergence of women writers raises a large number of questions concerning the relation of literate culture to patriarchy, the control of literary production, and the process of canon formation outside the boundaries of first-world canons. (247)

A couple of pages later, Miller writes about the 'lag in critical attention' noting that there is a general apathy or disinterest in the criticism of works by women. (257)

In the context of modern Nigerian literary tradition, women's writing from the North is subject to double invisibility and double repression. It can be said without contradiction that the 'absence' of women in the nation's conventional history is only equalled by the lack of interest in works produced by writers, whether male or female, from the North. There is no gainsaying the fact that if creative writing in Northern Nigeria, derived from and greatly influenced by, Arabic literary tradition, is considered to be in a state of insignificance, and if women's literature in the country is generally under-represented, works produced by *women from the North* are overtly and unceremoniously ignored and repressed by the conventional critical practice of earlier African male scholars. In the traditional history of our literature, the inclusion of efforts by pioneer writers from Northern Nigeria, both male and female, has been negligible.

Drawing upon the theoretical assumptions of psychoanalysis and Marxism, Jon Stratton argues in *The Virgin Text: Fiction, Sexuality and Ideology* that bourgeois culture is constructed in such a way as to privilege man over woman, that the woman is an object, a 'fetishistic' body controlled by another, and a subject of denials including sexual desire:

> In the lived world it is women who occupy the site of social order, the site of 'reality' – that is, the family. The illusion is that this is, let us say, a desirable site; that it is the site of power and that women occupy it voluntarily. ... The repressed reality is that women are constructed into this position. Within the sexualized, fetishistic system males are constructed as the fixers and females as the fixed. Thus while both males and females are a part of a single system, it is in fact males who are the real realisers of society. It is males who embody the site of power. (1987: viii–ix)

The condition or the popular image of the Northern Nigerian woman can be roughly defined as the veiled part of experience and being, arguably that which is neither seen nor heard. By inference, the patriarchal image of the woman is that which is configured by A.J. Griemas and J. Courtes as *non-being* and *non-appearing*, that is FALSE, in the cardinal permutation of 'states of being' provided in 'The Cognitive Dimension of Narrative Discourse' (1976: 440). The woman is perpetually under the veil, locked away from sight and protected from herself by the religio-cultural straitjacket of the *purdah*, the convenient Islamic tradition of keeping the woman in blissful obscurity.

Describing women as the muted group contained and which subsists in the dominant (male) group, Elaine Showalter notes that there is a mutual wild zone of exclusive male and female experience where misunderstanding/ignorance occurs; as it were, the greater possibility of misunderstanding in gender relationship is the male assumption that the female imagination is controlled by trivia and that female experience lacks value.[4] In the next few pages, I shall attempt to place critical value on the developing tradition of poetry by women by using representative texts to establish the point of a liminal visibility through the 'veil' of repression or non-beingness that has long been cast on the figure of the woman and the female author in that part of the country.

Beyond the purdah, or the veil of visibility

The recent relative visibility of contemporary writing in English from the North is made possible by strategic recourse to the immediacy of the newspaper medium, the brief enthusiasms of spasmodic magazines and journals and indeed, most significantly, by the momentary zeal of publisher-writers like Labo Yari, Joseph Mangut, Ibrahim Malumfashi, Nana Embaga and most recently the sustained interest of Ibrahim Sheme. Currently a research fellow with the Sheu Musa Yar Adua Foundation, Sheme has been for many years political, literary and art editor of the *New Nigerian* newspaper; he has used his most popular literary column, *Write Stuff*, to re-present established writers and introduce new writings, a substantial number of them by women, especially from the North.

In 1995, Ibrahim Sheme established a publishing outfit called Informart, to nourish the creative yearnings of potential and prospective authors all of whom, for the strategic but implicit reason of its establishment, are Northerners.[5] The Informart list includes fiction and poetry like Sambo's *The Genesis and Other Poems*, and *Disaster in the House*; Suzanna Onus's *The Turning Wheel* and *Waves of Emotion*; Nana Aishatu Ahmad's *Vision of the Jewel* and *Voice from the Kitchen*; Fatima Usara Hassan-Tom's *Eyes of Darkness* and *A Flight Heavenwards*; Hannatu Tukur Abdullahi's *She Talks, He Talks*; Binta Salma Mohammed's *Contours of Life*; Aishatu Gidado Idris's *Rabiat*; Bello Musa Dankano's *A Season of Locusts*; Mohammed Garba Wala's *The Icons*; Hawwa M. Allurawa's *The Weeping Heart*, and Ibrahim Sheme's *The Malam's Potion* and a collection of stories, *Brides & New Brooms*, edited with Hadiza Lantana Ampah. Apart from the Sheme factor, there have been other individual and institutional efforts to get works by relatively unknown writers published. For instance, Stirling-Horden Publishing has produced two titles of Cecilia Kato, a female poet from Kaduna, the central region of Northern Nigeria, while Maria Ajima from Benue had her first collection of poems – *Cycles* – published in Britain, a year before Hauwa Sambo's *Genesis*, through the support of an in-law and family friend.

Between 1996 and June 2000, about eight volumes of poetry appeared, at least three are forthcoming while a substantial number of manuscripts are undergoing completion and anticipating publication. Notable among contemporary female poets writing in Northern Nigeria now are Maria Ajima, Hauwa Sambo, Nana Aishatu Ahmad, Binta Salma Mohammed, Hadiza Ampah, Cecilia Kato, Hannatu Tukur Abdullahi, Angela Miri, and Vicky Sylvester Molemodile. It is instructive to note that most of these poets had been writing very early in their school days before getting published. That has always been the story of writing but in the case of the female author, and the Northern female author in particular, the prospects of publication are indeed very bleak. The female poet has less than half the chance of being patronized of a male poet. The majority of emergent female voices can be located within the Maiduguri–Zaria–Kano–Jos creative axis with significant efforts from Makurdi, Gombe and Abuja areas. Of them all, Nana Ahmad (Mogaji) had perhaps the first most significant introduction to the reading public in *Voices from the Fringe* (1988), the anthology of new Nigerian poets edited by Harry Garuba. But the female author who holds the honour of being the writer of the first published single volume or collection of poems from the North is Maria Ajima with her *Cycles* (1996). It is also important to add that in the same year of her debut as published poet, Ajima achieved national recognition when her prose work, *The Survivors*, won the Association of Nigerian Authors/Spectrum Prize. This, to speak metaphorically, marked the season of migration away from obscurity, invisibility and the syndrome of the symbolic 'purdah' in Northern Nigerian Literature. The 'desert' of contemporary Nigerian literature is alive with bouquets of female poetry.

In our sisters' gardens, or desert flowers represented

Published by Janus, London, Maria Ajima's *Cycles* (1996) is the first volume of poems to be written by any female author in English from across the Rivers Niger and Benue. By the time of its publication, the author was an active member of the Association of Nigerian Authors having attended her first meeting of the national conference in 1988. Currently, Maria Ajima is a director of the Benue State Water Resources and Sanitation Agency. *Cycles* is a collection of poems dedicatory and philosophical in parts; it is most significantly the poet's contemplation on the cycle of human existence covering such themes as those of life, love, motherhood, intimacy and death. The second collection, *Speaking of Wines...* (1998), reinforces the focus of the poet on ordinary human experience as well as her concern for socio-political issues and the condition of the woman.

Taken together, Ajima's collections have a poetic style that is expository as it is contemplative. *Cycles* comes across with such a disarming simplicity that understanding is determinate; but beneath that simplicity is the elegance of a voice commenting on the poetic process and struggling to establish her womanness in the patriarchal sphere. The first title poem of the collection reflects on and expresses awe at the repetitive course of natural seasons imagined as feminine to which 'Man' relates as 'being higher':

> And nature always repeats 'erself
> And it is a cycle
> The flowering plant
> The aging tree
> The flowing stream
> The blowing air
> Seasons round –
> All and all else is cycles
> Man the being higher too
> Cycles all seasons round! (1996: 1)

The next eight poems including titles such as 'The Muse', 'Under Compulsion to Write', 'Acknowledgement' and 'Dreams' form the sequence of the poet's idea about the nature and function of writing. In 'Time of the Muse,' Ajima signifies 'Night' as the appropriate and most inspirational moment to write and ends by saying,

> Poetry is weaving an image of life
> That's all, or is it? (1996: 7)

The other two unmarked but noticeable movements in *Cycles* are the motherhood sequence and the love sequence which seem to complement the authorial thematic intention of the collection. From 'A Mother's Prayer' through 'She's Majestic But Does Not Know' to 'The Unknown Guest', the poet eulogizes the mother who is the archetypal 'crown for every man called man' (29) and writes about the 'queenly' condition of pregnancy, the agony and joy of birthing, and the final welcome of a child into the home (28–34). The next four pieces, which follow, are poems touching on the sensual feelings of the poetic persona (35–38). The definition of love, the sense of parting, the dual act of amorous persuasion and rejection, and blissful love are the main subjects treated with a high degree of intimacy in this collection. In 'Love,' the persona simply submits:

That is all I ask of you
And the rest will follow
Just like rain after the storm
An endless cycle
Loving me, Loving you! (1996: 37)

There are other poems tinted with gestures of love, poems that bear the intimate personal feelings and experiences of the poet in her relationships with friends, family and the larger society. There are poems like 'Three Old Ladies,' a remembrance of the impact made on the poet in early life by three of her aunts; 'Missing Her', which comments on the spiritual bonding between mother (Ajima) and first daughter (Inori); 'Lady Niobe,' a poem based on the Greek legend of the daughter of Tantalus who lost all her children to the vengeful offsprings of Leto, but which documents contextually the agonies of an African woman at the death of her only child; and 'For Those With Lovers And Those With "Ruwanido"' a poem for lonely and envious hearts.

Perhaps the most significant poem that reflects the political conscience of the poet is 'The Beautiful Ones Had Sprouted' dedicated to Dele Giwa.[6] This is the story of a volatile moment in Nigeria's recent history characterized by the retroactive imprisonment and murder of prominent citizens by the military regime of the day. Told in the folkloric and allegorical tradition, it talks about the uprooting of the 'sons' (the beautiful ones) from the land by their own fathers under the helpless watch of the mother 'constrained/By age old tradition.' The poem is also a call to arms, for justice:

Tell it to the heavens
Sacrilege has been committed
Let this complacence
This slumber
Of a great nation
Burst like a water fall
For how long
Oh my people
Will you shrug your shoulders at calamity... (1996: 23)

This poem can in fact be related to others like 'Joblessness and Despair,' which bears the poet's concern for the socio-economic shortcoming of her country, and 'Second Generation' which refers to the sociopolitical repercussions of the ostentatiousness that marked the oil boom period of the Nigerian nation in the 1970s.

I have chosen to discuss Maria Ajima's *Cycles* in very broad terms because I think it is a significant representative collection with an unmistakable feminine tone especially in its portrayal of the issues of motherhood, sisterhood, and the vagaries of love so intimately addressed by the poet. The poem 'Woman' best stands as the coda for the feminist sensibilities of the poet:

Woman
Love and tenderness needing
Care and watering,
Evergreen youth
Ageless mind.
Woman,
Battered,
Swayed,
Grow stronger! (1996: 55)

Ajima's second collection continues the creative, feminist and political concerns of *Cycles*. The promising title of that collection – *Speaking of Wines* – draws especial attention to the author's romantic notion of the poetic activity. Apart from 'Water Falls', 'Speaking of Declarations', 'The Artist and the Word', and 'The Muse, Music and Flowers,' other notable poems in this collection include 'Freedom Songs', 'A Song for Kudi, Bisoye, Suliat and Lorritha Jaja' dedicated to women who died in the struggle for the democratization of governance in Nigeria, and 'In Times Like This' which delineates, in spite of its wordiness, the main characters and players in the nation's recent experience of military dictatorship. But so ingeniously, it is in this same poem that the poet returns the reader to the notion of cycles in nature and life:

I speak
Of the theory of cycles
...
The very fate of man
Is attuned to change
Permanence remains an aberration (1998: 42)

The other remarkable thing to say about Maria Ajima as poet is that in relying heavily on her personal experience, she draws on her intense romantic relationship with her husband to buttress her belief in the tradition of marriage and the complementary affiliation of man and woman. 'Love Elicits Love (From a wife to a husband)' and 'Jupiter and Juno' (in *Speaking of Wines...*) are texts which directly represent this point with relative exactitude.

Hauwa Sambo's *The Genesis*, coming soon after *Cycles*, takes on a related but separate significance. Slim as it is, the collection is the documented evidence of the first female voice from the core North of contemporary Nigerian poetry. It is one of the first remarkable utterances which attempts to subvert, albeit unwittingly, the conception of the modern Northern Nigerian female writer as incapable of poetic imagination. *The Genesis* is also the consolidation of the attempt to lift the veil of female invisibility within the literary canon of contemporary Nigerian writing. As Sambo stated in a conversation, to the (Northern) Nigerian society, a woman writing poetry especially is a foster child of silliness: 'people including my relatives used to tell me, 'this is foolishness... How can a woman sit down and write?'' Sambo literally sat down to write in 1986 and by 1987, a couple of her poems got published in *Today*, a newspaper based in Kaduna.

The twenty-one poems which make up *The Genesis* treat themes similar to those observed in Maria Ajima's work. In the first and title poem, Sambo draws a portrait of the blissful and tranquil character of Nature as directly opposed to the destructive capability of mankind:

> Before me is the best of beauty
> A place we have all sought...
> A place fraught not by danger
> ...
> Sending myriads glints from the surface of the blue lake
> So calm and gentle... (1996: 7)

In a romantic sense reminiscent of the pastoral poetry of William Wordsworth, the poet symbolizes Nature as 'the old Nurse' (11), 'the living poem(s)' and indeed, the 'mother of all' (26). 'Of Poems and a Poet' is Sambo's reflection on the functional content of poetry; more especially, it deals with the nationalistic possibilities/uncertainties of the writer's conception of her country as a land fit for 'elegies', 'dirges', 'odes', or 'ballads'. In 'Love Task', the poet addresses imagined sisters on the complexity and facade associated with the choice of a male partner in marriage:

> bear in mind that rich men get poor
> slender men get fat
> handsome men get ugly
> and virile men get tired.
> With these in mind
> The choice of a husband is an easy task. (1996: 16)

The other 'nuptial' poem in this collection is 'All I Need', a succinct expression of a woman's need in a prospective suitor, but which can also be read against the backdrop of personal expectation from a community governed by faith and truth:

> All I need in this world is
> A heart that loves and cares
> ...
> An eye of beauty
> And a tongue of truth. (1996: 24)

Other personal poems in *The Genesis* include dedicatory ones like 'Glorious Child' in direct reference to Sambo's first daughter, Yasmin, 'Ancient Law Giver' for the disciplinarian father of the poet, and the critical 'Learn' in which the poet succinctly attacks the phenomenon of the imitation of Western pop culture by African youth. 'Rose of Ophelia' is the poet's most intense craving for emotional love while 'Love in Heaven' appreciates the divine mercy of God for man:

And all his works with mercy doth embrace
That blessed angels he sends to and fro
To serve to wicked man
To serve to his wicked foe. (1996: 22)

The poem with the most political overtone is 'We Shall Survive (for Farida Mustapha).' Written after the unfortunate death, during a police–student clash, of Miss Mustapha, an undergraduate student of Ahmadu Bello University, Zaria, and coinciding with Commonwealth Day of 1987, the poem is a bold song of protest seeking the echoes and prayers of freedom:

As we survived the wombs of our mothers
So shall we survive this hostile environment
Avenging the loss of those before us
Fighting for those yet to come
And like a ream in a bottle we shall always rise. (1996: 20)

Sambo's second collection is yet unpublished; in parts, it contains her early poems on her husband and her experience in Benue State where she spent her national service year after graduating from the University of Maiduguri between 1994 and 1995.

After Sambo, Nana Aishatu Ahmad (Mogaji) was the second female poet from the core North to publish her work in a single volume. But more significantly, she was one of the first to gain national recognition in 1988 when her poem was included in the historical and prestigious anthology of 100 new Nigerian poets edited by Harry Garuba and sponsored by the Association of Nigerian Authors. Ahmad's two collections entitled *Vision of the Jewel* (1997) and *Voice from the Kitchen* (1998), attest to the poet's sustained commitment to the art of writing. From the few commentaries available on Ahmad's poetry, and by the comparative standard of her second collection, I believe that she is a serious writer straining for wider relevance. Abba Aliyu Sani notes that the poems in *Vision of the Jewel* 'manifest a keen lyrical sense, an intensely emotional style and a predilection for the familiar, the everyday',[8] while Aderemi Bamikunle laboured, albeit successfully, to establish the aesthetics of the simplicity of language in *Voice from the Kitchen*.[9]

The full title of Ahmad's first collection is *Vision of the Jewel. A Collection of Poems Heralding the Birth of Gombe State.* Apparently, all of the twenty-two poems in this collection are based on the poet's reflection and her representation of the people's expectation on the moment of the creation of Gombe State at the peak of the populist, internal balkanization of Nigeria by the ruling military junta of the day. From text to text, the new state is envisioned as the 'beautiful bride', 'our bride', 'the jewel', 'a queen', and the 'noble' land. Gombe is the one whose elegance 'is beyond the reach of arts', the one for whom the persona 'laughed with tears of joy'. In 'I Dreamt of the Bride' (1997: 11).

The sense of nationalism, or rather patriotic *stateism*, is undoubtedly pervasive in Ahmad's collection. A sizeable number of the poems can be noted as dedications to primary individuals who partook in the process and the euphoria of the state's creation. 'Immortalised Hope' expresses the poet's gratitude on behalf of the people to the Head of State, 'our august guest', who signed the enabling decree; the poem also declares the people's full support for the General who made the 'priceless manna' possible:

> You are peerless in our eyes
> Our trumpets shall sound to none but you
> Unto you our drums shall beat. (1997: 13)

Such overt declarations are also found in 'The Captain', probably for the first military governor/administrator, 'Chief of Chiefs', for the paramount ruler of Gombe and 'State Matron', that is the first lady of the new state. The poet also has thoughtful words for other administrators, civil servants, politicians and commoners in poems like 'Fountains', 'Servants of the People', and 'Masters of the Rostrum'. One particular poem which directly sounds a note of caution against the economic destruction of the new state is the one in which the poet warns the clan of contractors:

> When you contract,
> Remember not to make her the dwarf
> That much admires the tall but contends with fate
>
> When you contract,
> The motive should not be to fatten your accounts
> For that will bear long days of pain. (1997: 33)

Ahmad's poetry is deeply significant not only for being the first to express so fully a robust sense of nationalism and patriotism, however parochial; hers is also the first deliberate attempt to effect a consciousness for style and poetic language. In *Voice from the Kitchen*, there is ample evidence of artistic development in the wider, intense thematic concern as well as in the mature diction of the poet. The intimate voice of a lyrical poet is felt throughout the text containing seventy-five poems with an average of fifteen lines. Ahmad's poetic maturity is reflected in the way the text is controlled by a lyrical deftness of repetitive phrases, parallelism and a great deal of measured rhythm.

The collection is divided into three thematic parts namely 'Adversity', 'Elegy', and 'Memories'. In spite of the overarching attempt to locate the domain of performance in the domestic sphere, that is, *the kitchen*, the collection is the poet's textual representation of social and political anguish, sometimes a scathing reaction against blinding oppression and betrayal and indeed a clamour for a just and humane world. In 'Let Me Open My Tear-Filled Heart', Ahmad seeks to …

> present these solemn voices
> Crying for justice
> To reign supreme in this universe. (1998: 14)

The title poem, the author's first proclamation of her feminine personality, reads like an acceptance of the traditional role of women as managers of the kitchen, 'the only key/To men's heart' (16). But the poem also contains flares of the irrepressible spirit of the woman oppressed physically and economically:

> The ever ardent fire
> Burning beneath my pot
> Like flames of regression
> Kindled within us
> By the cruelty and scorn
> Of those who mock our cries with snores (1998: 16)

The subtle reaction against patriarchy which is also echoed in 'Wizardry' (Let me break this silence/My lips were sealed for ages) is complemented throughout the first part of the collection in the poet's frontal reaction against socio-political oppression of man, woman and nature. Poems like 'Guided Missile', 'Sword in the Song', 'Vivid Azure', 'Agony' and 'This Patched Land' bear testimony to Ahmad's sensitivity to public issues. In what reads like a disturbing advertisement for the feminine personality, the poet says in 'Honour':

> I am the goal of princes
> I kill and emerge stronger
> I exalt and dash to pieces my darlings
> I am a gown
> Strife and struggle are my price. (1998: 68)

The essential lyricism and the poet's consciousness of self and others find further representation in the second section which is predominantly an expression of grief at the death of loved ones, and in the third section containing the poet's memories of love, affiliation and other intimacies. In 'Remarkable Day', Ahmad reflects on her wedding day described as divinely ordained. The subsequent poems dedicated to 'M.B.' are apparently for the poet's love for whom she wished a radiant and everlasting communion. (79–86) 'Co-Wife' is the poet's radical reaction against the phenomenon of the other woman, the co-wife in the patriarchal harem of traditional African and Islamic societies. She addresses the wife:

> Don't give her the chance
> To intrude into your peace
> Break you to pieces
> And plant bitterness amidst sweetness. (1998: 87)

Nana Aishatu Ahmad is indeed a very promising voice, an emergent 'desert flower' in the developing field of contemporary Northern Nigerian poetry. The feminine author's ideological disposition against patriarchy is perhaps felt more in her work compared to the writings of Ajima and Sambo. Yet it can be noted that Ahmad, like others, would be quick to react against the suggestion of a feminist colouring in her poetry. As in

Sambo's comment quoted earlier, Ahmad manages to show her anguish against male superiority and in the same breath, the poet relates to the domination with a measure of philosophical ambiguity and religious serenity. In the last poem in *Voice from the Kitchen*, the poet submits herself to the wheel of destiny:

> I know not what my fate will be
> But fervently pray that:
> I will live this life without stain
> And leave this world without a sore
> And go to the next with much in store. (1998: 94)

The other three poets whose works have been published to date are Cecilia Kato, Binta Mohammed and Hannatu Tukur Abdullahi. Kato is perhaps the most prolific of all the female poets writing now in Northern Nigeria. Her first collection *Victims of Love* (1999), which is a representation of her life and others in the complexities of love – was quickly followed by another entitled *Desires* (1999; pub. 2000). Kato has completed two other collections awaiting publication by Stirling-Horden; the titles are 'Rebirth' and 'A Budget for Women.' The first collection is divided into three parts, 'Visions', 'Chat', and 'Victims of Love'. The poems are mainly dedicatory poems written for her teacher (Professor Ebele Eko), husband (John), children, female friends and idols like Lady Diana, the late Princess of Wales. Kato's concern for the woman is found in her exhortatory poem, 'Woman':

> Take a good look at life
> Tread its leopard path
> And chew its bitter kola
> Swallow its sweet juice with open eyes
> And dance the ballroom dance of its endless marvels
>
> Look life straight in the face
> Point accusing fingers at it
> Call its diverse names
> According to its star groupings (1999: 30)

From her literary offerings, Kato can also be arguably described as the most radical female poet to date in terms of her free-flowing, yet gripping, poetic diction as well as her daring commentary on the socio-political and religious situation of her home state, Kaduna. Kato is a Christian from Kagoro in Kaura, Kaduna South. She considers herself a minority poet in the predominantly Muslim North. Interestingly, her writing has a liminal difference from the works of other female poets in the North, and more precisely, she reacts doubly against patriarchy as well as against the ethnic imperialism of Hausa–Fulani hegemony. Her revolutionary personality can be read in the *Desires* poems including 'Soldiering Tongue', 'My Neighbour Thanked Me with a Bullet', 'The Dirge', 'Burukutu Song', 'Waje Fought the War Too', and 'Oh North' where she poetizes:

There are two families in the North
Brought together by geographical accidents
And historical manipulations
Of letters read to our ancestors
Who thumb-printed
Agreements in head nods
A long time ago. (2000: 31)

In 'My Kind of Poem', Kato signs the manifesto of her creative intention:

I like to write a poem
that talks to the castigated heart of man
that peels blocked minds
and opens myopic eyes suspended in the air

I like to write a poem
That spits venom against time's oppressive hands (2000: 3)

Binta Mohammed, author of *Contours of Life* (1999) is from Kano State where she teaches at the Bayero University. Before *Contours* was published, Mohammed had been fully involved over a decade in several literary activities in Kano and had participated in various programmes organized by the Association of Nigerian Authors. Perhaps one of the reasons for Mohammed's recent, if not late, publication is her sense of modesty and the conviction that she needed a longer period to refine her poetic talent. In 'Irresistible Impulse', the poet seems to comment on her attainment of voice, her emergence from literary obscurity:

I no longer
Feel shy and, anyway, when working
Or playing what else is there to
Do but write. (1999: 37)

Saleh Abdu notes in *Contours* (1999) the evidence of a 'civilized poetic tone that complains, without doing so, against the abandonment and disappointment of a world malignantly measured to satisfy men.'[10] This is indeed a faithful reading of the collection. There is the subtlety of a mature voice behind the seemingly simple lines of Mohammed's poetry. Divided into two sections, the collection deals with the old familiar themes of female subjugation and dimensions of socio-political turmoil in the country. The first section, 'Politics of Life' focuses on national problems such as fuel crisis, inflation, coup d'etat, and the pains of disunity and other broken dreams; the second section, 'Salt of Life,' deals with more personal issues; it is here that the feminine self comes to the fore whereby the poet concentrates on issues of spinsterhood, beauty, affection, hopes, deceit, disappointment, solitude, dream, courtship, supplication and virtual, faithful love, portrayed from poem to poem in approximately that order. In 'Deceitful Designs' and 'Black Monster', the poet reflects on aspects of male deception through the agonizing voice of a woman:

And when harmony was reborn
I must erase your memories
Your romantic heart, the most
Deceitful of them all (1999: 25)

I mistook him for a saint
As I had never known a rogue
I thought he was an angel
As I had never seen one (1999: 46)

'Virtual Reality' is the poet's representation of a woman's critical observation of the virtues of a man in courtship; it reads like a letter from the
deepest recesses of a woman's mind telling of her fragile and once bitten
heart and almost preferring certain solitude to uncertain affection.
Therefore, she prays:

I can no longer find peace in the
Music of love – though I know
Peace will come, the Angel of
Dawn will come. (1999: 49)

Hannatu Tukur Abdullahi's *She Talks, He Talks* (1998) is to date the most
stylistically sustained work of poetry by any Nigerian female poet to fore-
ground the woman question in contemporary, postcolonial African
society. The form of the address noted in Mohammed's poetry becomes
the enabling aesthetic fount upon which the entire network of
Abdullahi's text is drawn. Essentially, *She Talks, He Talks* is composed as
a pair of a dozen and one poems deliberately dialogic in design with one
utterance of poem by the female persona counterpointed by another by a
responding male voice bearing a rhetorically taunting question mark.
Hadiza Ampah's perceptive interpretation of Abdullahi's poetic effort is
worth noting as an important gynocritical commentary from one who
essentially belongs to the literary tradition:

[The collection] illustrates how a woman spends the best part of her life in
drudgery as an appendage to a man. Not only that, it shows how the rights of the
woman are being increasingly infringed upon. The woman sets the pace,
provokes thoughts and actions, and the man reacts, carrying along the mild
conflict of sexes, ages and a battle of strength between the feminine and the
masculine. (1998: 6–7)

In the first pair of poems entitled 'Starlet/*Starlet?*, the woman's physical
endowments are presented first as marks of her tenderness and goodness,
with the response by the male persona challenging the representation and
instead drawing the image of the woman as a Circe-like figure, a wraith, a
temptress and indeed an inscrutable entrapment for the unwary male:

Voice of a nightingale
Soothing the heart
Voice you will love to choose (1998: 10)

She sings to him the rhymes of the dark
Dogs warn him with so loud a bark

He listens not, his mind astral
He follows her accepting her betrothal (1998: 11)

The woman's declarative voice in 'Gentle Soul' provokes the taunting response of the man in *'Gentle Soul?';* the man imagines the woman as a lying and weak personality who spews nothing but unreason, the one whose arrival into his life brings grief, following the universal myth of the Creation story. The woman's argument that man is unloving with a capacity for irresponsibility in 'Licensed' (re-echoed in 'Prodigal Husband'), meets a rather caustic and proud retort in the corresponding poem:

> He is now spare
> He no longer cares
> Her pains she has to bear
> Like an unloved deer
> For he has another dear (1998: 17)
>
> *If I could think of a worse name*
> *I would crown you without shame*
> *I have seen enough and the worst of you*
> *Give me a break, I have had my due.* (1998: 18)

On and on, the critical dialogue is executed between pleading, accusatory and regretful tones, the woman always the tender voice and the man acting macho, until the drama reaches a counterpoint in 'Out' where the woman establishes a sense of personal assurance to challenge the male persona on equal terms:

> I can see why you are shouting
> I know why you talk so loud
> My mind has now settled so I can laugh
> ...
> Is it because she beats your ego?
> Or because she can make a General quiver?
> Ha! it's because you were once her baby. (1998: 26)

A round of mere rhetorics by the female voice follows the man's challenge of a state of equality, equal opportunity and responsibility, stressing the universal and traditional task of the woman. Finally, she submits in 'Sine Qua Non':

> I really feel for you
> O Superior Gender
> ...
> We are interdependent
> There is nothing we can do
> Because we have no other. (1998: 42)

The feminist reader would note in this text the vacillation of the female voice which is as disappointing as it is unfortunate for the psychological liberation of the modern Nigerian woman. The dialogue ends with the patronizing voice of the man lending credence to my earlier observation about the ambiguous nature of much of Northern Nigerian *feminine* poetry. Even though Abdullahi's text or any other work by the Northern Nigerian female poet can not be claimed as the result of the radical feminist imagination, it is important to note the significance of *She Talks, He Talks* as a useful exposition of the 'subtle but steady stir towards self-reassessment among educated Hausa–Fulani men and women'.[11] In the collection, the dialogic possibility of conflict in gender relations is practically explored to reproduce an actual textual exchange between the female poet and a male correspondent whose identity remains anonymous.[12]

An ending

I would like to conclude this article with the observation that female poetry written in English in Northern Nigeria is developing a character all of its own, and yet an adjunct to the complementary contribution of other Southern female poets in the male-dominated literary field of modern Nigerian writing. The main preoccupation of many of the poets includes a romantic concern for the environment, a predisposition towards celebrating motherhood, sisterhood and womanhood, a subtle critique of patriarchy and religion, two broad factors of their suppression, and most clearly an essentially experiential representation of the vagaries of love. The reader will find in much of the female poetry, as evidenced in most of these collections, a robust tendency to reflect on the psychological aspects and implications of love or the absence of love between man and woman. Aesthetically speaking, much of the literary work from this region is marked by simple poetic diction sometimes inventive and successful, and sometimes commonplace and uninspiring. However, the fact of the emergence of the female poet in Northern Nigeria over a decade after the publication of Mabel Segun's *Conflict and Other Poems* (1985) is a positive sign of things to come, in the growth of a virile tradition of Nigerian poetry written by women.

NOTES

1. Acclaimed as the first female poet in Northern Nigeria to commit her thoughts to writing, Nana Asmau wrote numerous poems in Ajami, the Hausa version of the Arabic language.
2. In the IFRA Occasional Publication No. 11, the definition of the 'Northern Nigerian' author is a rather permissive and elastic one; the state of origin is the sole means of differentiating the Northern from the Southern writer. The example of Olu Obafemi, Stella Oyedepo, and Segun Oyekunle is very instructive. By virtue of being indigenes of Kogi and Kwara States, part of the original geographic expression called 'Northern Nigeria', the authors are designated as Northerners whereas they share common cultural affinities with Southern writers of Yoruba extraction.

3. Perhaps the first major anthology of its kind, *Vultures in the Air* is an odd collection of short stories and poems, thirty-seven in all, by writers of Northern origin including contributions from two Southerners: Gabriel Ajadi, an Ogbomoso man teaching at the University of Ilorin and Obi Iwuanyanwu, a Southern Igbo from Umuahia who had spent some time in the North and was teaching at University of Jos at the time the anthology was being compiled. Notable among the female voices are Zaynab Alkali, Aishar Umar and Binta Mohammed.

4. See Elaine Showalter, *The New Feminist Criticism*, p. 262.

5. The only notable writer on the list of Informart Literary Series who is not an indigene of Northern Nigeria is Suzzana Onus who has spent most of her life in the North. Onus is from Edo State in the midwestern part of the country. She currently resides and works in Abuja where she moved from Kaduna.

6. Dele Giwa, one of the most brilliant Nigerian investigative journalists, was killed on 19 October 1986, with a letter bomb sent by men suspected to be agents of the ruling military junta headed by General Ibrahim Babangida.

7. In personal dialogue with the poet, Hauwa Sambo reflected on the psychological predicament of the typical Northern Nigerian female who, for cultural as well as religious reasons, is almost prohibited from making her views known in and to the public.

8. See Sani's preview of Ahmad's first collection in 'Introduction', n.p.

9. Bamikunle's attempt to integrate Ahmad's work within the larger framework of the Wordsworthian ideal of the language of poetry is commendable; but the comment that the poet is 'the second serious female poet in the Northern states...' ignores the presence and effort of Hauwa Sambo, who arguably got her collection, *The Genesis and other poems*, published before *Vision of the Jewel*. See Bamikunle, 'Foreword', p. 8.

10. See 'Foreword' to Mohammed's collection of poems, p. v.

11. See 'Publisher's Note', *She Talks, He Talks*, p. 4.

12. In conversation, Hannatu Abdullahi vows not to reveal the identity of the male writer of the corresponding poems to her original work. I observe that this is the second of such texts in which a 'literary couple' would collaborate to produce a collection in modern Nigerian writing; the first is *Voices: A Collection of Poems*, almost equally shared by Temilola Abioye (f) and Tade Ipadeola (m) (Ibadan: General Graphics Ltd., 1996). The difference here is that the right to name the male author is denied in Abdullahi's work.

WORKS CITED

Primary materials

Abdullahi, Hannatu T. *She Talks, He Talks*. Kaduna: Informart, 1998.
Ahmad, Nana A. *Vision of the Jewel*. Kaduna: Informart, 1997.
—— *Voice from the Kitchen and other poems*. Kaduna: Informart, 1998.
Ajima, Maria. *Cycles*. London: Janus Publishing Company, 1996.
—— *Speaking of Wines...* Makurdi: Fambi, 1998.
Mohammed, Binta S. *Contours of Life*. Kaduna: Informart, 1999.
Kato, Cecilia. *Victims of Love*. Ibadan: Stirling-Horden, 1999.
—— *Desires*. Ibadan: Stirling-Horden Publishers, 2000.
Sambo, Hauwa M. *The Genesis and other poems*. Kaduna: Informart (c.1996).

Secondary materials

Abdu, Saleh. 'Foreword'. *Contours of Life*. Kaduna: Informart, 1999: iv–v.
Ampah, Hadiza. 'Foreword'. *She Talks, He Talks*. Kaduna: Informart, 1998: 6–7.
Bamikunle, Aderemi. 'Foreword'. *Voice from the Kitchen*. Kaduna: Informart, 1998: 8–11.
Brown, Lloyd. *Women Writers in Black Africa*. Westwood, Conn.: Greenwood, 1981.
Garuba, Harry (ed.). *Voices from the Fringe: an ANA Anthology of New Nigerian Poetry*. Lagos: Malthouse Press, 1988.
Griemas, A.J and J. Courtes. 'The Cognitive Dimension of Narrative Discourse'. *New Literary History* 7.3 (1976): 433–47.
Maduakor, Obi. 'Female Voices in Poetry: Catherine Acholonu and Omolara Ogundipe-Leslie as Poets'. In Otokunefor and Obiageli Nwodo (eds) *Nigerian Female Writers: A Critical Perspective*. Lagos: Malthouse, 1989: 75–91.
Miller, Christopher L. *Theories of Africans: Francophone Literature and Anthropology in*

Africa. Chicago and London: The University of Chicago Press, 1990.

Sani, Abba Aliyu, *et. al. Creative Writing, Writers and Publishing in Northern Nigeria.* IFRA Occasional Publication No. 11. Ibadan: IFRA/African Book Builders, 1997.

Showalter, Elaine (ed.). *The Feminist Criticism: Essays on Women's Literature and Theory.* New York: Pantheon, 1985.

Stratton, Jon. *The Virgin Text: Fiction, Sexuality and Ideology.* Sussex: Harvester, 1987.

Eagles in the Age of Unacknowledged Muse: Two Major New Writers in Contemporary Nigerian Literature Akachi Ezeigbo & Promise Okekwe

Femi Osofisan

I In the most arid desert – such is the miracle – are plants which grow resiliently green. Everywhere around them drought and death abound, but always these plants remain lush with water, and in due season they even burst into colourful flowers.

It is this drama of struggle and endurance, of heroic affirmation against the forces of despair and annihilation that seems to have reproduced itself in the desert land of contemporary Nigerian literature, and the image springs effortlessly to mind especially, when we pause to examine the works of two of our most recent writers.

The present state of literature in our country is of course no secret any longer to anybody who cares to know. After the corruption, profligacy and gross incompetence of our governments during the oil boom years of the 1970s, and the inevitable collapse of our economy that followed, the publishing industry, like most enterprises, virtually folded up.

The readership market shrank drastically, in the wake of growing poverty and mass unemployment. Books became rare on the bookshelves, and rarer still the bookstores which displayed them. The international publishers – and particularly Heinemann which had founded the flourishing African Writers imprint and had so laudably promoted our writing – shut down or sold out their stock and fled back to Europe.

The local publishers, never very adventurous in the first place or much interested in the area of general publishing, kept even more exclusively to the narrow but fairly lucrative market of educational books. In despair, would-be writers, desperate to be heard, resorted to the expedience of vanity houses or self-publishing ventures. And the result now is that, for both established and budding writers, it is not so much the talent nor the quality of the output that counts to get into print any more, as the ability to find the money by themselves. Hence it is to me an amazing phenomenon to witness the sheer number of works which keep coming out almost every week to swell our reading list.

As I see it, we can never pay sufficient tribute to all these writers who, out of sheer desperation, or guts, or the irrepressible need for self-promotion, risk all they can to get into print. It is even more impressive when one realizes that most of these writers are young persons who are unemployed, or are just managing to eke out a living on menial, badly-paid jobs. The goddess of literature, it seems, is so attractive, that self-appointed votaries will follow her, even in their rags, and eagerly sacrifice themselves.

I have had occasion, elsewhere, to salute this stubborn determination by our contemporaries to continue to publish, and hence ensure that the voice of the Muse continues to be heard in the land. Unappreciated generally, and unacknowledged, the creative genius nevertheless refuses to be stifled.

Naturally, in these strenuous circumstances, the results are not always successful. They cannot be, given the enormous costs of publishing, the near absence of editing services, and also, sometimes, the low level of education of the people involved. Such is the impatience and eagerness of the young authors to get into print and establish their names, that they are quite often unwilling to go through the necessary apprenticeship and training required to hone their skills. Thus many books come out with several avoidable errors, mostly relating to the feeble control of language and a murderous assault on grammatical laws. Especially for those who publish themselves, the lack of intermediary editorial processes is too obviously a painful need. This is why the quality of the output is so frequently uneven, and sometimes even embarrassing.

But all the same, what impresses me, in spite of these shortcomings, is how the aspiring talents refuse against all odds to be daunted. They go on searching for and creating new outlets in the form of chapbooks and magazines; they form various literary associations where they read to one another; they doggedly pursue potential sources of patronage, even in spite of repeated, even predictable, disappointments.

Once in a while – following a very rare and infrequent turn of luck – one or other of these writers strikes gold, so to say, in the form of a sudden access to the international market. This happens when he wins an international literary prize, and is then adopted by a major publisher in the world market.

This is paradise at last! For a writer who is still struggling to be recognized on the home front, and is unable to find a publisher, you can imagine what an incredible boon this means! From now on, his life changes completely. He is now faced with the possibility at last of realizing his dreams; of doing what he loves most henceforth, and getting paid for it. He will travel and discover the world; he will be the toast of literary salons; his works will be reviewed in the best journals; he will acquire fame. Such has been the career of the young Helon Habila, perhaps our most famous example, who won the Michael Caine Prize in 2001 and was immediately absorbed into the Penguin family. But there are also Okey Ndibe, Akin Adesokan and a few others.

These names we celebrate enthusiastically, as is only to be expected. We throw parties for them, out of admiration and envy. Envy because, as with footballers, the dream of all of us is to enter into the glamour of the international market. So these writers become our heroes, and we begin to follow their career with avid curiosity.

All this is quite normal no doubt. But the problem, as I am beginning to suspect, is that this craving for the foreign may well be a mask for something more insidious in our contemporary make-up. I fear that this fascination with foreign awards and endorsement may just have induced in us a surreptitious disease of self-deprecation, if not even a general complex of inferiority.

Indeed, it is beginning to look as if we have returned to the climate of those pre-Independence and immediate post-Independence years, in which we never seemed capable of appreciating our own achievements, unless and until they had been duly sanctioned by some authorities in Europe. Thus we will not honour our proven heroes, it seems, unless the foreign critics give them a corresponding stamp of approval. And if they live among us, but have not won any foreign prizes, none of the writers we ourselves know to have demonstrated remarkable talent will receive more than a cursory attention from our local commentators. Flowers may bloom in the desert, but it is obviously not the donkeys that say so.

This, I suspect, must be the reason why the two writers I wish to talk about here have so far been given relatively scant notice in recent evaluations of our literary output. Whereas by both the quantity of their works, and the quality of their imagination, the two writers have more than earned their right to be considered among our major writers, they are quite surprisingly still regularly confined to the margins of discourse, even as we ourselves have ironically continued to pile them with awards.

II In fact, there are extremely few writers today, among the new literary generation, whose achievement even comes near either that of Akachi Ezeigbo, or of Promise Okekwe. This is more amazing, when one observes that both are Igbo women, and married, and are full-time professionals – that is, 'victims' of the usual burdens and constraints associated with the social and traditional roles they have to fulfil. But in their curriculum vitae is a daunting list of titles which even their male counterparts must find humbling. Akachi – and I am deliberately using their first names here, in order to distinguish them from their husbands – is a full scale university professor, and the current head of the English department at the University of Lagos. Among her publications are four books of literary criticism, thirty-one critical essays, three collections of her own short stories, two books for children, and three full-length novels! A collection of stories for children is also due to be out soon. This is a formidable output by any scale of measuring.

Promise, who is at least a decade younger, is a tireless and amazing book-churning machine, with two collections of short stories, three books of drama, four collections of poetry, *ten full-length novels*, and twenty-seven children's books! Already completed also, and waiting to be published – I happen to know – are another novel and a book of poetry. All this at the age of 34!

Please notice that I have put emphasis here on *full-length* novels. Most often, as Buchi Emecheta complained at the last ANA meeting in Asaba (November 2002), the books being passed around by our writers as novels are nothing more in fact than pamphlets. But not so with these two women. Not only have they written authentic novels, but both also have started this unprecedented tradition in our bookshelf, of writing trilogies, a tradition which, you remember, Chinua Achebe had tried with only unsustained success to initiate.

It is interesting exploring the similarities between these two prolific, and immensely gifted writers, apart from their both being Igbo and female. Both are graduates, with doctoral degrees from the nation's premier university at Ibadan. Both live and work in chaotic Lagos, indeed within a kilometre of each other in the Yaba-Akoka neighbourhood. Akachi has been living in Lagos most of her adult life: she first came to the city to continue her studies shortly after the collapse of Biafra, and after her first degree, was posted to the north for her NYSC year. After this, she taught school in Kaduna for two years, and then returned to Lagos with her husband in 1977. She has never left since. Promise arrived in Lagos after undergraduate studies in Calabar, a short stint as Public Relations Officer with the Federal Road Safety Commission in Abeokuta, and graduate work in Ibadan. She has been working since as a banker in the city.

What does this say about their thematic concerns or sources of inspiration? We shall look at this presently. But it is perhaps interesting to point out here that this is one of the occasions when the usual criterion of age that we use to categorize our writers does not seem to work. By that criterion, these two women should belong to two different generations, Akachi to the second generation after Zulu Sofola (along with names like Zaynab Alkali, Ifeoma Okoye, etc), while the younger Promise should be placed among the third generation (alongside people like Ogaga Ofowodo, Remi Raji, Onookome Okome, Maik Nwosu, etc). But this classification would be meaningless here, for although Akachi can be said to have begun to gain notice when her entry won the second prize at the NBC Short Story Competition in 1975, it was only recently that she came into prominence. Her first book, a collection of short stories titled *The Buried Treasure* (Vista Books) only appeared in 1992 in fact, the same year that also saw the publication of Promise's first book, an anthology of short stories entitled *Soul-Journey into the Night* from Kraft Books. It is obvious therefore that both women actually began to publish the same year, and should be studied together.

There is something significant, I think, to be said also about both of these women being successful writers, in the sense of earning enough financial remuneration from their publications. The usual song of lament that we hear from other writers, about their books not selling, and therefore of their not being able to recover the investments they put on the books, is definitely not the case with either Akachi or Promise. Commendably, the two women have perfected strategies of recuperating their money, and making publishing a profitable adventure for themselves – Akachi through well-planned book launchings from which, she proudly announces, she never fails to realise enough money to cover her costs; and Promise, operating from the vantage point of being her own publisher and someone intimately involved in the trade, from knowing the right levers to pull for successful marketing.

Another point to note is that their books are always well produced, with good layout, and attractively designed covers. All these no doubt add to the qualities which have enabled the two writers to become our most assiduous prize-winners. Akachi has in her kitty the 1st Prize of the 1994 WORDOC Short Story Competition, the 2001 ANA/Spectrum Prize, and was in that same year the first winner of the Zulu Sofola Prize for Creative Writing. In addition, she has enjoyed writing fellowships in London, Cambridge and Pietermaritzburg in South Africa.

Promise's hoard of awards is even more impressive: in 1999, both the ANA/Cadbury Prize for Poetry and the ANA/Spectrum Prize for Literature; in 2000, the ANA/Spectrum Prize for Literature again, as well as the ANA/Okigbo Prize for Poetry in Africa; and in 2002, both the ANA Prose Prize, and the ANA/Matatu Prize for Children's Literature. She too has enjoyed writing fellowships in America, Germany and lately, Japan, and given public readings as well in Spain, Romania, Zimbabwe, Togo, and Ghana.

It was therefore not surprising that, at the last ANA convention, both women were again prominent among the award winners. Promise won the very first ANA/NNDC Prose Prize (dedicated to Saro Wiwa) for her novel *Hall of Memories*, and also, under the pen name of Ada Iloekunanwa, the ANA/Matatu Prize for her children's book, *The Street Beggars*. Akachi, whose novel, *Children of the Eagle*, received honourable mention for the ANA/NNDC Prize, was awarded the first Flora Nwapa Prize for Women's Writing for the overall quality of her work. Pertinently, the judges admitted to using the award to 'recognize a writer who has shown an unusual dedication to creative writing over the years ... (and) for her commitment and perseverance in writing and reflecting on her people's history and destiny. She has shown that being a woman should not exclude her from creatively working to understand her world.'

It can be seen therefore how belated it is, the kind of homage that one is paying in this essay to the two women. Readers who by now are familiar with the periodic surveys I make of our writing must be no doubt disappointed at this extended lapse. I plead guilty, with only the extenuating excuse that my routine obligations in my present employment have kept me shamefully away for this long from the active currents of productivity in the field. Let us hope therefore that this essay goes a little way in form of compensation.

It will be impossible, of course, in an essay like this, to cover the prolific output of these two writers. What I will do therefore is restrain my discussion to what I consider the major part of their work, which in this case happens to be their trilogies. In looking at these, I hope to be able to reveal at least the most salient points about their styles and techniques, and their most important pre-occupations.

III   The three books which make up Akachi's trilogy are *The Last of the Strong Ones* (1996), *House of Symbols* (2001), and *Children of the Eagle* (2002). From Promise, we have *Hall of Memories* (2001), *Zita-Zita* (2002), and *Fumes and Cymbals* (2002). The structures of these books already begin to reflect the dissimilarities in their authors' conception and purpose. Akachi's books are more of a trilogy in the traditional understanding of the genre, that is, three books which are interrelated, but which can be read independently one of the other. Each is therefore a complete story by itself, such that, even though it is the same family from the same village that we are dealing with, it is a different generation of it that is in focus from book to book.

With Promise however, the three books are more or less like different sections of the same extended story. In fact it is probably the problem of length that obliges the author to separate the story into three books. The main characters that we meet in the first book are the same central figures in the last book, although their children come more and more to the fore as the story progresses. Hence the books have to be read in the sequence in which they were written, for without acquaintance with the first one, it would be almost impossible to understand the second, or the one that follows it. Besides, and far more here than with Akachi, there are constant cross-references backwards from the later books to the former ones, a technique that may bewilder a reader not forewarned. That is perhaps why the three books are designed to be enclosed in one single jacket and purchased together as one complete body of work, collectively titled *Tomorrow's Yesterday*.

But it is in their authorial ambitions, particularly, that the two women are to be distinguished one from the other. Akachi is a 'womanist', in the sense which female writers from Africa love to define their own form of feminism against the fiery, anti-male catechism of their Euro-American sisters. Her intention, we observe, is to tell her people's story, the same familiar goal of 'finding where the rain began to beat us', that we recall only too well from the works of Achebe and his unfortunately less-gifted heirs. As Akachi puts it herself in the very last pages of the Epilogue to

The Strong Ones, 'The work of mending and binding broken minds and bodies has no end for those who desire to preserve a tradition and bring a people back to life. That is our task. That is our desire' (154).

But that ostensible declaration is only a half-mask, a strategic disguise for her real intentions. For Akachi is not out merely to clone Achebe. Indeed, what makes her venture of cultural retrieval especially unique and interesting is that, far from imitating her male predecessors, her real target in fact is to de-authorize their versions of history and identity politics, that is – as it were – to stand Achebe and Achebeans on their head! Fuelling her desire to write is a deep-seated compulsion, not just to present the female version of past and present history, but also, to dismantle and undermine the prevailing male perspective, by substituting a carefully selected (and equally partisan) anthology of female counter-narratives. And, as if we do not know this already in her first books, she finally allows Nnenne, her alter ego, to tell us of her ambitions in the last novel in the trilogy, *Children of the Eagle*, in the form of a revealing encounter with her grandmother. This was after the old woman had just recounted to her the legend of Okorigwe and his extraordinary exploits and was expecting her to be impressed. Listen however to what follows:

> 'But are there no female heroes-heroines?' I asked my grandmother. 'Was there no female Okorigwe?'
> She laughed. 'I do not remember any female Okorigwe,' she replied. I was not satisfied with her answer, but I didn't say so to her. However I told myself that I would go in search of a female Okorigwe because I was convinced she existed. If she did exist, then I must find her. I must excavate her and bring her to the limelight like her male counterpart. *But if indeed she did not exist, then I would invent her...*' (*Children* 329, my emphasis)

Akachi's whole agenda in her novels can be said to have been summarized in those lines. Continuing on the following page, she elaborates:

> ... my people's belief [is] that things in the universe stand in pairs, that if something stands, another like it stands next to it to complement it. Therefore, there should be a female Okorigwe. But, what I heard or came up with were stories about witches, jealous co-wives, wicked stepmothers, incorrigible liars, temptresses, adulterous women and wretched widows. I also heard a few stories about empty-headed paragons of beauty in distress, crying to be rescued. And, of course, there were stories about virtuous women who could not *crush an ant*.
> When I became older ... I realized, through experience and intuition, that no female Okorigwe existed because society completely wiped off all traces of her existence, leaving a blank, an empty space ... So I took full responsibility for celebrating her in writing.' (*Children* 330–1, emphasis as in original text)

This is more or less what Akachi's books are about – that is, a search for 'female Okorigwes'. They are the four 'strong ones' in her first novel, the ones whose biographies become emblematic of the entire history of the Umuga community in the period that white imperialism comes to establish itself in Igboland – the same period in fact that Achebe

presented to us through Okonkwo. Again, still writing back to her male
predecessors, her next book, which covers the succeeding generation to
that of the Okonkwos, is captured for us through the story of another
matriarch, daughter of one of these 'strong ones', whose cognomen,
appropriately enough, is 'Eaglewoman'. Finally, in the third book, we see
another generation, the present post-Independence and post-Biafran generation, and symbolized again in the portraits of Eaglewoman's daughters.

That is why the male characters in her works are always in the margins
of the narration, even a positive one like Osai (Josiah Obidegwu Okwara),
Eaglewoman's immensely supportive husband and the assistant district
officer (ADO) of Atagu local government council in *Symbols*. It is the
wives (*alutaradi*), the daughters (*umuada*), the mothers, the priestesses,
the *oluada* (women's representatives) of the village and their *obuofo* (the
inner council), that interest Akachi, not the husbands or sons or chiefs,
except of course when they are acting as obstacles to the women's self-
fulfilment. Always Akachi foregrounds the heroism of women in their
encounters with men and patriarchal traditions; it is their very resistance
that shapes them into figures of legend.

Indeed, Akachi's grand design is to establish these women as the
spawn of a single, transcendental female breed, of a mysterious primordial kernel of radiance and strength that is identified only with women.
Thus, having created her charismatic heroines in her first book, she
ensures that all the subsequent women that follow are not just their
daughters or granddaughters, but in fact their *reincarnations*. In her
vision therefore, there is only one original source of true feminity, an
essence of goodness – aptly symbolized by the eagle – which combines
toughness with compassion, aggressiveness with grace, and combative-
ness with creativity, and is the recurrent and redeeming energy of society
in every age. This fact, deliberately hidden or erased by a conspiracy of
male historiography, must be unmasked, and it is her ardent personal
agenda to do so.

IV   But not so, it seems, with Promise Okekwe. No less belligerent, her
programme lies however in a different direction to Akachi's. Her targets
seem to stretch further beyond the theme of gender discrimination and
encompass the broader area of social injustice in general. Thus the women
in her works have no special privilege merely because of their feminity,
nor can they lay any exclusive claim to virtue or villainy. They are as much
prey as predator; as much the hunters as the hunted. And so, even though
a number of them are given prominence in her narration, as is to be
expected, so also are a number of men, who are painted with equal
diversity. In her works, the gender never really matters: the writer's sympathy is with all the oppressed everywhere, against the human predators.

As I pointed out earlier, the three books in her trilogy are not three separate stories, but rather broken segments of the same single extended tale. This involves primarily three women, their husbands and other male liaisons, and their offspring up to the third generation. The link between the women is the country's head of state, his Excellency Michael Igini, to whom two of them, Aku and Afiadu, are married at different times, and for whom the third, Zita-Zita, refusing the offer of marriage, nevertheless has a son. All three of them eventually get separated, in one way or another, from Igini: Aku, the first wife, leaves him when she discovers his affair with Zita-Zita, who was her maid; Zita-Zita herself is abandoned when, stung by her conscience, she refuses to marry Igini and displace her mistress as First Lady in the State House. And Afiadu, having been married just to compensate the frustration caused by Zita-Zita's rejection, becomes the victim of a loveless marriage, and is abandoned to unbearable loneliness. It is the search by these women for love and fulfilment, and the sometimes traumatic consequences of this search, that forms the core of Promise's story.

Yet it is clear that, although she depicts the sufferings and passions of her three protagonists convincingly, and with great sympathy and sensibility, she does not present them primarily as the victims of gender prejudice or of patriarchal society. Promise, unlike Akachi, is not a combatant 'womanist' out to replace his/tory with her/story. In fact, to tell the truth, she does not appear to be in the main interested either in the emotional and psychological drama that their desperate situations create. First of all, the agony is not limited only to her female characters, for such male figures as Captain Black, or his follower 'Friendly' Kenneth, suffer from disjunction as much as Afiadu or Akwaeke; while women like Cecelia Briggs, Lori Menakaya, or Lady Vivian Ede are just as ludicrous or depraved as Big Zaak, Toni Johnson and Shabbir Idris who are male. Similarly her gallery of attractive personae is just as gender-blind, including female figures (Fierce Mary, Ngomma, Aku, etc) as well as male (Onyeoma, Vincent Mapo, J.K Shakpa, Dr Gabriel, Frederick McDermot, etc).

Then, even more striking, is the impression one gets from her style of narration, that these personal experiences of hurt are for her only of tangential interest – that her real intent in fact is to lead us to something else, something *behind* them, deeper than individual pain, something that reflects the wider picture of society's tragic anomie. Whereas Akachi leaves us in no doubt in her books about where the body is buried, that her concerns are about the restoration of women's rights, the characters in the works of Promise, and the story she tells, seem always to be just a clever excuse to expose the terrible condition of our crisis-laden society. Uppermost in her mind, beyond the injustices meted to the women, are the corruption and inadequacies of our ruling class, and the suffering of the common people. On virtually every page therefore, running alongside her main story, is a sustained commentary about the government's criminal mismanagement, about its consequences for the people, and the need to sanitize the country. It is the mark of her mature craftsmanship that all this is so artfully done, that it rarely becomes obtrusive, as it usually is in most works of political pleading.

Part of the reason why she succeeds so well with this strategy of trenchant but oblique criticism, is the cast she has deliberately created to tell her story – that is, women who are married to, or are at least intimately connected with, men who are at the centre of the nation's politics, and who themselves are endowed with a restive social conscience. It therefore becomes logical that, as Promise tells their story, and embeds it within the context in which it happens, she naturally has to tell us the parallel story of the country and of its misadventure in the hands of its rulers. Thus the politics fits neatly into the narration, and does not sound awkward or forced.

The other device she employs – and one I consider to be really courageous – is to situate her story in the very context of immediate history. There is nothing new or extraordinary of course in this use of history as a template for artistic imagination. Indeed, so frequently is this done by our writers in Africa, that most of our literature has been described as 'factions', that is, the recreation of actual history through the disguise of fiction. Akachi's novels for instance are located at precise junctions in our political history, from the period of colonial incursion and Christian evangelization in Igboland (*The Strong Ones*), to the immediate period afterwards, the 1940s and 1950s, when Christianity and western education had taken root (*Symbols*), and then to the 1990s, when memories of pre- and post-Biafran conflict were still vivid (*Children of the Eagle*). But you will find her still using pseudonyms for actual places and public figures, in order, perhaps, to avoid controversy and direct reference. Thus for instance, the city of Lagos is referred to as Lagoon City, Enugu is Coal City, Ibadan is Ibaland, and Kaduna is Kada City in *Children*, so thinly disguised really, that one wonders why she bothers at all. Besides, as I said above, it is the cultural problems chaining women down that are her major *bêtes noires*, not the political crises.

V   But what is unique about Promise is the degree to which she is willing to dispense with the veil of fiction, and literally call a spade by its name. So angry and so passionate is she about contemporary events in our country, that she will not take refuge in safe but opaque allusions or vague innuendoes. For her, fiction is virtually the same as this evening's newspapers; it is about the wounds of this very morning, this afternoon, still bleeding, sizzling, hurting; and her characters are almost the very people we meet daily and recognize on the streets and in State House. Remark for instance the degree to which we are able to make immediate recognition of these events which occur in her trilogy – Dimka's coup d'état and the assassination of Murtala Mohammed; Obasanjo's ascension to power; the military regime, and its eventual transition into a civilian arrangement; the assassination of journalist Kaltho; Gani Adams and the OPC phenomenon; the bloody Hausa–Yoruba clashes in Idi-Aba in Lagos; the workers' strike, led by Adams Oshiomole against the fuel price hike; the Ikeja bomb explosions and the rescue operations which followed, and so on. All these events, with very slight attempt at camouflage, form a backdrop to her story. And then, of course, there is the direct naming of Aso Rock, the official residence of Nigeria's Head of State. But the most daring instance undoubtedly is the assassination of former Justice Minister Bola Ige, whose name is of course not directly mentioned, but whose identity is never in doubt because of the other facts she supplies, such as dates and places. The intention of this writer, as I read it then, is to trap us, the readers, in the very marrow of the story, to get us so profoundly implicated, both morally and emotionally, in the drama she narrates, such that we feel that it is our story and our situation, not a remote fantasyland or just a titillating tale. We are meant thereby to be induced into a sense of guilt or outrage, our conscience pricked to the point where we are challenged, not just to begin to reflect deeply about the society we live in, but perhaps also to want to do something about it.

This would be a difficult assignment at any time for a writer to give herself. But what in others would be perfect material for a tedious or humdrum performance, Promise rescues from banality by the sheer luminous power of her imagination and narrative style, and transforms into a scintillating tale.

One of her strengths is her obvious love of people, her interest in the egregious human cast that make up the population of a generation and of our hybrid modern community. Hence we see her trying to draw as many characters as possible into her canvas, with every corner of the narration populated and talkative, like one of those prints by Bruce Onobrakpeya. No one, it seems, is without importance – again and again Promise is breaking off from the main story to fill us with details about even characters we would normally regard as secondary to the story. Like one of our West African markets, the universe of her imagination is always busy, always buzzing with diverse voices and anecdotes, evoking echoes that go back to Chaucer or Rabelais or Tristram Shandy. That is why her story is a millipede with a thousand legs and manifold shells; whereas with Akachi, it is like an excursion through a room of female bronzes.

This aspect of characterization marks an area of vivid difference between the styles of Akachi and Promise. Akachi tends to focus on paradigmatic grand figures, who become symbols of feminine strength and grace, and of resistance against male chauvinism. Other characters with whom they interact are occasionally interesting of course – such as the girl Lois, or the afflicted Diribe of Eaglewoman's household – but they appear and disappear only as much as they serve the career of the main figures. Akachi's books are usually an assemblage of the (auto)biographies of selected powerful women, for whom she as writer then assumes the role of chronicler or diarist. Hence she is necessarily selective: 'Like palm wine,' she says, in the voice of the self-appointed raconteur of *Children of the Eagles*, 'I tap my memory and the memory of my family to invoke the spirits of my ancestors, to call them to life... My approach, therefore, will involve identifying key occurrences, tracing the patterns they create in the lives of my subjects and establishing the way and manner in which they influenced their lives and achievements. Perhaps the mouth should not talk about everything the eyes see or the heart knows, but it ought to talk about everything that is necessary' (*Children* 86–7).

Driven by this kind of mission, for which affirmations must be unambiguous and counter-refutations persuasive, it is not surprising that the technique Akachi has chosen for her narration is one that can be described as either elegantly neo-classical, or timidly conventional. Alternating fluidly between the third-person voice of the narrator, and the first-person voices of the characters as each is made to tell her own story, Akachi writes simple, straight-forward, and limpid prose, occasionally embellished with proverbs and Igbo expressions, but devoid of overtly self-conscious or eccentric stylistic experimentations. Her style is therefore for the most part free flowing, with well-harmonised syntactic sequences, and ordered phrases.

This same preference for uncomplicated lucidity can be seen even in the personality of the characters that fill her cast. Although her heroines are fully-rounded, three-dimensional characters, they are for the most part devoid of complex emotional traumas or psychological obsessions, just as the men and women who oppose them are driven by clearly discernible passions. Thus the couple at the centre of the story of *Symbols*, for instance, are a happy couple, in contrast to other chronicles of domestic life that we know, which are invariably crisis-ridden. And because of this, the tensions in their life, and hence the drama which Akachi narrates, comes not from their own disagreements, but rather, from their collisions with external forces – from Eaglewoman's former unsuccessful suitors, and from Soronje, a former bosom friend now turned implacable enemy; and for her husband Osai, from Moses, Soronje's husband, a jealous and spiteful kinsman.

For the most part, what we have is a delightful tableau of Eaglewoman as she climbs steadily to success, of her domestic and commercial activities, her generosity of spirit, her emotional trauma and triumphs as she copes with the expected rites of motherhood, such as pregnancy, childbirth and child loss, her husband's near fatal illness, and so on. We also see how the couple is sustained by a faith built on a peculiar synthesis of Christianity and traditional spiritual forces, represented by the healer and mystic Ezenwayi.

Ironically, it is this successful crafting of portraits – portraits of female prototypes, of historical collisions, and of environments and landscapes – that makes Akachi's achievement somewhat vulnerable. Thus it is not surprising for instance, to come across readers, and usually younger women too, who claim that *Symbols*, which can rightly be considered her masterpiece, is 'uninteresting', or 'tedious to read'. This is to be understood obviously against the background of their antecedents and their expectations. Children of the age of globalization, their tastes have been moulded largely by imported pulp and Western paraliterature, whereas *Symbols* is short in suspense and fast-paced dramatic action, in the kind of stuff, that is, that popular fiction offers, and to which they are addicted. Instead, the book's strength is in vivid description, in the effortless way it captures the palpable rhythms of domestic life, and the deep, nostalgic ethos it evokes of traditional and recent, contemporary life. *Agon*, 'conflict', is not really the purpose or central attraction of this big, ambitious book, as rather, its sweeping, profound reach for roots, its exploration and recapturing of the tenors of traditional life in transition to modernity.

VI   But I do not want to be misunderstood here. It is not that Akachi is totally blind to, or silent about, the political tensions amidst which her characters operate. The community of Umuga after all, where virtually all her books are located, is a society in violent flux, still trying to come to terms with modernity brought by the forceful incursion of European culture and religion. In *Strong Ones* for instance, two concurrent accounts make up the story – on one hand, the biographies of these four powerful women, Ejimnaka, Onyekozuru, Chieme, and Chibuka, through which the author celebrates their productive individualism and wilful independence, and rejection of patriarchal domination; and on the other, the story of the community's inevitable confrontation with the white imperialists, and their superior fire power. This story of the coming of colonialism and Christianity to a part of Igboland may be stale, but it is not mute. The chapters dealing with the ensuing war and the people's courageous resistance, then with their defeat and the terrible consequences, are among the most moving in the book.

Nevertheless, what is obvious is that it is the role of these four strong-willed and attractive heroines that is constantly foregrounded. Because of them, the parallel adventure of history takes a back seat. Hence in *Children*, where you have a reunion of a widow and her five daughters, political events such as the Biafran war feature prominently, but still, the main discussions and conflicts repeatedly revolve around the issue of women's rights, especially the right to own land and property:

> My sisters and I realized that women were not expected or permitted to own land in our culture even when they pay for it with their own money. If land is bought with a woman's wealth, the real owner of the land is her husband, if she is married. It is viewed as a misfortune to have a family populated by daughters, without a son.' (*Children* 94–5)

It is in this book particularly, among her trilogy, that Akachi most forcefully pursues her crusade for female emancipation, and articulates the need to assert the equal and complimentary partnership of the sexes in all social and political relationships. With four passionate, well-educated young women as protagonists, and with the chief narrator among them being an accomplished university professor of literature this time, the protesting voices are quite formidable, and their own personal stories of success (and failure) not only illustrate, but become concrete models for, Akachi's ideological catechism.

But in my view, it is precisely because of this plurality of voices that the argument becomes too noisy, the feminist agenda too loud, for the power of conviction not to slacken. That is why *Symbols*, which is content to demonstrate rather than argue, to illustrate rather than sermonize, remains my favourite of the trilogy. Eaglewoman, just by being herself, is eloquently persuasive of the majestic possibilities of womanhood: although she does not have her daughters' intellectual credentials, she is obviously more accomplished, more capable and resilient, more dignified and more *womanly*, than any of them turns out to be. She does not have to verbalize her qualities to the reader; the very process of her journey through life – her coping with daily chores and challenges, of making choices at moments of adversity; her social relationships; her constant reflections on all these and all the banal details of how she makes it to prosperity, to become a *'Tree that grows money'*, in a transitional Igbo society are enough by themselves to present a positive and convincing portrait of 'womanity' as Akachi wishes us to understand it.

This is where her strength lies: for Akachi, unlike Promise, is an enchanting painter of portraits. In the tradition of the omniscient narrator, she weaves freely in and out of the minds of her characters, especially Eaglewoman, but her itinerary, like that of the late nineteenth-century naturalists, is like that of a camera walking leisurely and lovingly through space. Again and again, she shows that she has an eye for those telling details which mark out a situation for drama, lyricism or suspense:

> With a growl, the door of the bread room opens as Eaglewoman gives it a determined shove. She is astonished at the damage the harmattan has done to the doors in the house. Or could it be that the wood is of inferior quality, probably not from the iroko tree which everyone except, of course, the Local Government Authority knows is the best type of wood. She lights two *Tilly* lamps, pumping gently to build up pressure. The room brightens, bathed in light. Seconds later, the room swarms like a beehive. Hands flutter and plunge into bowls and tins; feet glide across the room, propelled by nimble bodies. Peals of laughter hit the air like a house of many bells...' (*Symbols* 108)

This is quite unlike Promise, who tends to rush breathlessly through tortured memory and psychotic disturbance, with little room for the details of location or physical description, beyond the minimum required for symbolism, contrast or emphasis. With Akachi it is just the opposite. Her canvas is so cleverly designed that the people, places, and even domestic pets (the dog Bana, the parrot Icheoku), that she describes come palpably alive and familiar, such that we almost see them. With deft touches of her brush, she is able to capture the little gestures in which the beauty of human relationships are often graphically summarized; or the caprice and voluptuous cruelty of children (little Nnenne prodding Diribe's swollen crotch, or stubbornly enduring the *okosa* punishment); or the mystery of spiritual transcendence (Ezenwayi's interventions).

But sometimes the message is not so much in what is said, as what is left, simmering, in the subtext. Examine closely for instance the following passage, and then try to uncover the sheer wealth of *unspoken* stories behind the details:

> Akuchukwu, the water vendor, stands at the open door smiling at Eaglewoman. Behind her short and rotund figure tower two women who ply the same trade with her. Their drab working clothes are slightly wet from water that spilled from their pots. Gingerly, they step over the threshold one after the other, holding firmly to the clay pots they are carrying balanced on huge banana stem pads on their heads. They pour the water into a huge pot in which Eaglewoman stores drinking water. This is water from Okpara Anyanwu – Son of the Sun – the life-giving spring which babbles over stones and warbles among ancient rocks and forests like a songbird. The three women put their pots down and chat a little with Eaglewoman. They ask after her children and crack a joke or two about the harmattan, about its relentless onslaught which blisters heels, cracks lips, peels the skin, giving off white flakes ... Then they set out on yet another trip to Okpara Anyanwu, clutching the leftover loaves Eaglewoman gave them. They pause to hide their money in their *ajiego*, money belt, which they retie around their waists. Adjusting their *wrappa*, they retrieve their pots and walk away, still laughing from their jokes...' (*Symbols* 114)

This prompts Eaglewoman into empathy:

> There are many other women involved in water vending, she ruminates, her heart going out to them. In spite of the hardship, they struggle on, making numberless trips to Okpara Anyanwu or Otaru, in the thick of darkness, in the small hours, at dawn, in the heat of the noon and afternoon. At all hours, the human chain formed by these women, broken at numerous points, can be seen stretching from Atagu Country Headquarters, down and along the main roads, the footpaths to the steep slopes of the beautiful Otaru and princely Okpara Anyanwu ... The world is full of pain, she thinks, but who could decipher these women's pain, seeing how cheerful and witty they are? When lizards press the ground with their bellies, who could tell which of them is afflicted with bellyache?' (*Symbols* 114–15)

This is far more effective, in my opinion, in calling attention to the difficult plight of women, than the intellectual ruminations of the sisters in *Children*. It is, to repeat, one of Akachi's strengths, this ability to fill her canvas with minute but telling details, and then to provoke, through them, an affective response, either in terms of compassion or of philosophical insight. Furthermore, notice how, in order to lend an acute note of immediacy to the action, the narration always moves along in the present tense, a strategy that helps to shore up the excitement, and place the reader directly in the narrative's running context.

VII   But if Akachi writes like an inspired sociologist and chronicler, with naturalist grace and temper, Promise's approach is from the opposite end of the fountain, where the poet-dramatist and mythopoeist of surrealism resides and sings from. Indeed the poetic intent manifests itself right from the first pages of the book, where her opening chapters are conceived more or less like prose poems and incantatory prologues.   Then the chapters are arranged in each book along the letters of the alphabet, moving from A to Z, like a pilgrimage through the full gamut of her imagination. (Of course this can be controverted, since the story does not really end at Z, as I earlier pointed out, but in fact continues in the next book. But that's another matter for now.)

Reading Promise, the impression one gets is that it is the poetry of the passage that counts even more than the narration itself. Her aim is obviously to convey both the affective and auditory impact of the moment, rather than merely its physical context, of which there is sparse description anyway. Her paragraphs ring always with a sonorous concern for the sound, rhythm, and weight of words, for the pauses and paces that make for emphasis, tempo and pitch – for the cadences, that is, of speech and song and melody, all the familiar secrets of oral poets. This reach for orality shows in the constant mingling of prose and verse, in her frequent recourse to short sentences and phrases, one-line paragraphs, song snippets, sound effects, repetitions, onomatopoeia, and so on.

Sometimes this is used to accelerate the scene's momentum and increase the suspense, such as those chapters of *Fumes*, when Frederick is being driven off to an unknown destination by kidnappers, and the prose breaks into frequent staccato fragments; or earlier on, when the dreaded Achikwu masquerade approaches, and she tries to convey the gathering terror it brings, by arranging her syntax into short, breathless clauses and dramatic exclamations:

> The fireballs had multiplied. Their innumerable sparks dazed everyone in Onyeoma's house. All the doors leading to the various rooms in the house were tightly shut. Tightly. And the people inside the rooms were trembling. Trembling.
> *Achikwu* was close. *Achikwu* was almost at the front of Onyeoma's house.
> Stamping feet! The felling of trees! Thud! Thud! Sparks and sparks. It was like an earthquake in hell. Gbim! Gbim! Dim! Dim!
> No voice. Only the sound of destruction. The tim, tim of anger and the noise of silence deadening throbbing hearts. Then the guttural, aching, penetrating the ears in righteous anger ...
> Ekenma nwa Ogwugwu
> Ekenma nwa nmuo
> Does mother hen swallow eggs?
> Does a man kill the one whose death will be his responsibility?
> Ekenma nwa Ogwugwu
> Ekenma nwa nmuo
> Does a crocodile eat its own flesh?... (*Memories* 57–8)

It is a device she also uses to convey pathos, as for instance in that moment when Zita-Zita is forced by Afi's cruelty to part again from her son, just after meeting him for the first time after their long separation. As she tries to comfort the young child, he too bursts into tears, and the text continues as follows:

'Wipe away your tears.'
He did
New tears replaced the erased ones
Tears against tears
Tears sympathizing with tears
She let go and stood to her full height
But he had not yet learnt to let go
He would learn in time
Oh he would learn that one never gets all one asks for in life
That sometimes those who love you can bring you so much sorrow and misery.
He would learn. (*Zita-Zita* 135)

Most often however, this device of mingled prose and versification is used to express the inner thoughts of a troubled mind, and is therefore not surprisingly the one chosen by the author for the scenes in which Zita-Zita features. Driven to insanity by an accumulated experience of misfortunes, this woman, whose much-scarified face seems an apt metaphor for her tragedy-ridden life, is always carrying on a series of internal dialogues, arguing either with her troubled conscience, or with people who are dead already, especially her late husband.

On a different occasion again, it is to impress us with the depth of the dedication that Aku inspires in the handicapped children, that the narration breaks from prose, and reads like a litany or psalm:

Their sorrow kept them alive.
Their spirit laughed in their pain knowing they have the panacea.
Their hearts became calm as they worked.
Their labour filled the aching time.
While others talked shop, they laboured silently.
While others beat their chests, they worked in quiet corners.
During the harvest,
Others reaped in hundreds
They reaped in thousands.
Moths hung on other people's proceeds stored away for life.
They planted their proceeds in many people's hearts.
Theirs multiplied in the hearts of all those they gave them to.
Aku believed all these to be true.
She sang it into their ears.
She instilled in them the urge to dream dreams.
And she made them work seriously on their dreams. (*Zita-Zita* 140–1)

At such moments, the lines are hardly distinguishable from poetry. Unlike Akachi's composed and rational prose, Promise's pages are mostly a string of broken fragments, of rambling shards of memory linked only by the fact that they emanate from the same demented source. In Akachi, the narrator is a level-headed, methodical intelligence, a skilled biographer chosen by her subjects for her power of eloquence and discernment, and we see her carefully sifting through her material and sorting out the pertinent details in linear, chronological sequence. But in Promise, the central character is for the most part Zita-Zita, the delirious widow of Igini, whose broken mind is constantly wandering between the past, the present and the future in one confused flux of anamnesis.

As a foil to her, we have Aku, the committed activist, who grows, from catering to the handicapped, to become a cabinet minister. But notice that her dreams too are conveyed to us not through direct statement, but metaphorically, through poetic imagery:

> She stood at the balcony of her duplex and looked beyond the people eating and drinking and making merry over her so-called fortune. She saw tomorrow, a haggard woman with fallen breasts, sunken cheeks and flatulent belly. She gazed at her as tears flooded her eyes and she knew she was ready for the job. All that was soft and wise in her went out to welcome tomorrow and prepare for her a food [fit] for a queen. Out of her abundant resources, she knew she would do her best to ensure that the hungry would not only eat but that they would work and laugh a lot. (*Fumes* 119–29)

It is through poetic imagery too, that Promise casts her vision of the future, and she calls it 'Beautiful'. It is a city, and it is also a woman, and Raphael, Igini's grandson through Zita-Zita, seems the one destined to create it. Repeatedly it comes to him in the form of an attractive woman, talking to him, inspiring him to dream. And not surprisingly therefore, it is to him that the seeking women from Ibadan, after days and nights of fasting and prayers following the death of Uncle Sam, come for guidance.

VIII   There are a few more points I wish to discuss about these two women writers. One concerns their use of humour, and the other their attitude to sex, and to Christianity, and the last, their optimism. It is striking in fact how closely, in these areas, they seem to share analogous perspectives, in spite of their differences on other matters. Compare the following passage from Akachi:

> She does not have many clothes on her – just a loose blouse and a *wrappa*. He removes both and soon she is naked, her stomach bulging a little, not having fully shrunk after her third experience of childbirth. She shifts a little, lies on the bed, waiting for him. She realizes that her heart is beating fast though she knows it is not from excitement on account of what is about to take place ... .he strips himself, dropping his trousers and vest on a chair, on top of her clothes. He climbs in, lies next to her. He strokes her smooth flank, allowing his hand to travel upwards ... Bending his head, he sucks her breasts, one after the other, filling his mouth with her warm milk ... She holds him with the tenacity of a climbing plant encircling a tree. (*Symbols* 316)

to the following, where the younger Promise dares to be more earthy, more lushly explicit:

> Galvanized by the maestro's music playing in his enamoured loins, he helped

her out of all she wore ... For them, lovemaking was not just an act of giving and receiving pleasures, it was not even an art for they allowed what they felt at the time they felt it to ferry them across raging seas. And the experience was usually terrific. His great member, a beautiful piece of God's art of the finest quality had just embraced her lovely, tasteful, clitoris. His wild fingers grabbed her gorgeous breasts and played the cymbals and tambourines with her haughty nipples which pushed and pushed their way into his glutinous lips. ... She yelled her gratitude at his crazy thrusts and she came in chains of multiple ecstasies. (*Fumes* 438)

This reads, unfortunately, like some of the worst of salacious kitsch, especially with the gushing adjectives. Curiously, her usual assurance tends to flag in the grip of Eros. However, what I am trying to get at is the fact that, in both women novelists, as in most of our contemporary writing, the customary diffidence and traditional squeamishness about the matter of sex are over. 'These are things we do not normally talk about overtly, except perhaps in proverbs, riddles and proverbs,' says one of the women who come to visit Nnenne and her sisters at their homecoming in Umuga. 'But,' insists Nnenne, 'we should talk about these things – as you put it...This is the only way to learn, to be aware.' (*Children* 113–14)

Both writers believe not only in the healthy benefits of a good, reciprocal sexual relationship, but also in the power of physical sex for therapeutic ends. In the passage above, for instance, Akachi's Eaglewoman is healed out of a prolonged phase of depression only when her husband, desperate to revive her spirits, makes love to her. But this is not to say, all the same, that either writer is in favour of infidelity or unbridled extramarital sex: indeed, there seems to be such a concern in both women to present a chaste ideal, that the universe of their plays is soaked in the ethics of moral correctness. Thus the torrid scene just cited above from *Fumes* is a prelude to the violent and tragic end of the sybarite Michael Junior, and his mistress Nora. Their death through *magun*, the dreaded Yoruba taboo against marital infidelity, whose efficacious power Promise seems to accept without question, becomes a potent admonition against lascivious living and illegitimate liaisons.

Always the accent in the two women is on good marital relationships, especially in Akachi. Vociferous as she is for the empowerment of women, and against their marginalization in a male-dominated society, she is not for all that an iconoclast or phallophobist. She protests and denounces, but her goal is negotiation, compromise, reconciliation. Hence her preference is for dialogue, 'nkolika', and her advocacy for women's rights does not lead her into a hatred of men. On the contrary: 'I tell myself constantly,' she declares, again in the voice of Nnenne, 'that the love of a good man together with a stable home is a form of refuge for a woman ... A hard-working woman needs a sweet loving man to lean on.' (*Children* 351). And in an interview with Anthonia Makwemoisa (*Journal of Cultural Studies*, 3,2:500), Akachi elaborates on this: '... in this part of the world, it is still important for one to marry... We are not radical feminists... There are still values we want to observe here....I don't want to be someone who scatters or destroys things... I believe in marriage, in having and raising children. I believe in the family... I don't believe in discarding our cultural values and replacing it (sic) with an alien one. For me, globalization means accepting what I have and marrying it with what is coming from outside.' Promise, it is certain, cannot agree more: throughout the trilogy, she continuously celebrates the fulfilment of her positive heroine, Aku, cuddled in the loving arms of Frederick McDermott. Indeed, his disappearance for days during the kidnap episode is the only real crisis that she suffers in the story.

Probably then, it is this staid and upright climate of the books that is responsible for the relatively limited use of humour that one finds in them. Both women seem to me to be too earnest and too sober about their mission to be able to surrender to the free and unbridled exuberance of laughter. Although they do present some funny passages and extraordinary personalities – such as Promise's autodidact Captain Black with his grandiloquent turns of phrase and colourful speech, or Aguba-Juku, the notorious drunkard – these characters are in the end mere clichés, programmed foils in the calculated web of the plot. What I miss are passages of raw fun and ribald joke, of rib-cracking, rambunctious laughter, such as you find in the Tutuolans.

IX   But never mind, there are other compensations. One of these is their open, and non-doctrinaire, attitude to traditional culture. Considering the fact that both writers are practising Christians – Akachi a Protestant, and Promise a Roman Catholic – the degree to which they have managed to remain sensitive and sympathetic to our lore and customs is, to say the least, fascinating. Akachi by overt proselytizing, and Promise by covert suggestion, are sometimes unsparing in their criticism of Christianity and in the role it played in the erosion of certain elements of our culture. Unapologetically therefore, Promise subtly blends the role of masquerades and ancestral spirits into the fabric of her narration in *Memories*. In Akachi, the Irish priest, Father O'Brien, comes in for harsh condemnation in *Strong Ones*, for sowing religious division and fratricidal hatred among the people of Atagu community; while, significantly enough, Okwudiba, one of her emblematic matriarchs, never uses anything brought to the land by the foreigners. Even more tellingly, the strain of anti-Christian resentment comes out in one moment when Eaglewoman admires the *uri* patterns on one of the women:

> Her body is adorned with the most intricate and beautiful *uri* patterns Eaglewoman has ever seen. For a moment she remembers the intimate hours her mother had shared with her and her younger sister in their childhood: hours spent pleasurably as Aziagba patiently and painstakingly explored her daughters' bodies ... tracing imaginable figures, lines and circles with her nimble fingers wielding a curved *uri* knife, leaving behind unbelievably lovely

designs ... But that was long ago, before they became church people, Christians.

Eaglewoman wonders why the church condemns, as sinful and immoral, women's desire to adorn the body with *uri* and other forms of adornment: *uhie, nkisiala, nki, nja* and *jigida*. What is sinful or immoral about it? (*The Last of the Strong Ones* 87)

Nevertheless Akachi must be credited for not staying with this one-sided view of things, but trying as much as possible to give a balanced picture. Therefore, even as she condemns what she considers to be the deleterious effects of colonialism and Christianity, she also is fair enough to point out the benefits we have derived from them. Aziagba's escape to the church, in order to save her twins from death, is perhaps the strongest instance of this positive side of Christianity. All the same, she keeps her eyes open: 'The Christian faith, which most of us adhere to,' she makes one of her characters declare, 'does not say we should forget or abandon our culture. It does not instruct us to dishonour our past or erase the memory of our rich history and tradition.'

Conciliation in Akachi; anger and horror in her younger sister – whatever the difference in their temperaments, or chosen modes of expression, both authors never end their works in despair. With all the scenes of pain and suffering, loss and deprivation, violence and villainy that abound on their pages, the women seem more determined to help us climb out of the chaos into a better world, a world of hope. Akachi's strong women are models of struggle and resistance, and of triumph against formidable odds; their stories are meant to serve as empowering models for her readers, particularly the younger women. Promise's Zita-Zita yields for a while to overpowering temptation, and is made to pay cruelly for it; but in the end, it is her grandson who is destined to bring light to the benighted nation. And even though the consummate 'people's leader', Uncle Sam, is assassinated, there is always still the shining example of Aku, a saint no doubt, whose unshakeable commitment to the ideals of selfless service and generosity, and whose refusal to be cor-rupted, should be an inspiration to us all. Thus the novels end invariably with the announcement of a new birth, or a swelling pregnancy, or the dawn of a new effort of exploration.

There are flaws in the books of course, some even embarrassing where they relate to avoidable solecisms. Promise is often careless indeed with her writing, and her poetic ambition sometimes leads to overly swollen prose or inappropriate tropes. Akachi is sometimes blind, or deliberately indulgent, to the *hubris* of her matriarchs, and sometimes she disappoints our expectations when the mythical resonance she is aiming at fails. Nnenne's musings read more like academic essays sometimes. But these flaws are more than compensated by the imaginative reach of the authors and the amplitude of their conception. And I am willing to take on anybody who dares dispute that *Hall of Memories* and *House of Symbols* are among our ten best books of the last decade.

Let's raise our glasses then – these women are the new eagles in our sky! They are splendidly on wing, and will soar to unexpected horizons, whether we wish it or not. By their output, they have established themselves already among the masters. Indeed Akachi herself announced their triumphant arrival in her last book. Towards the end of *Children*, the sisters are suddenly struck by the fact that the Eagle occurs in several cognomens in their community, far more often than the other birds like the parrot, the hawk, and the ostrich. They begin to speculate on the reason for this phenomenon, till one of them suggests an answer:

> 'I think it's because the eagle is the most intelligent in the world,' Obioma answers. 'It's an amazing bird and can soar higher than any other winged creature. Eagles are said to see three times better than human beings.'
> 'Hey, we are the children of *the eagle*!' Amara cries... (*Children* 191, emphasis in original script)

That jubilant cry we should all take up now and shout to the wind.

WORKS CITED

Ezeigbo, Akachi. 1996. *The Last of the Strong Ones*. Lagos: Vista Books.

—— 2001. *House of Symbols*. Lagos: Oracle Books.

—— 2002. *Children of the Eagle*. Lagos: Vista Books.

Okekwe, Promise. 2001. *Hall of Memories*. Lagos: Oracle Books.

—— 2002. *Zita-Zita*. Lagos: Oracle Books.

—— 2002. *Fumes and Cymbals*. Lagos: Oracle Books.

To Trans-emote a Cosmos
Yvonne Vera's Holistic Feminist Vision
in *Butterfly Burning*

Chimalum Nwankwo

Striving to mediate the multiple confluence of disparate cultures, the African writer has translated or has transliterated indigenous reality into the ruling colonial language with varying success. These efforts have encompassed the ambitious and parochial experimentation of Gabriel Okara in *The Voice*, the daringly, part elegant, part quaint modes of expression in Okot p'Bitek's works and the sure-footed dexterities of Chinua Achebe. Amongst those high points are other efforts in the use of an alien colonial English tongue to capture the vanishing, moribund and still evolving realities of Africa. Only the professional translator or transcriber knows the difficulties involved in such efforts at transfer of culture many of which have concentrated on the language, with all its semantic possibilities, and its nuances. I have come to the tentative conclusion that perhaps there have not been as many successes as failures because most of the efforts have not really taken into full consideration the fact that what needs to come into play is the more elusive and more difficult aspect of the struggle, and that is the struggle to go beyond language to include a more overt effort to *trans-emote the cosmos*.

I would also like to add that the writers have fared very much better in dealing with this difficult technical situation and its cultural and political ramifications than have their numerous critics and commentators, anxious to be in print as serious interpreters of African cultural productions. Those who have failed have done so mostly because they do not have the foggiest notion of what a single word in these original African languages means. Some of those who have succeeded have done so only as part of the massive and fraudulent game of trial and error involved in dealing with many things African. This situation rides on the credo of anything goes, anything we can get away with, powered by the woolly and equally fraudulent politics of the current state of interpretations called Post-modernism, a plural method spinning out of the intrinsic wildness of Deconstruction. So critics have engaged in a murky exercise of transfer of culture without any *compatible* systematic lamps. They have at best translated without trans-emoting the cosmos of the production, grafting scions without the requisite test of compatibility of the new parent.

What does *to trans-emote the cosmos* mean? To trans-emote the cosmos means going beyond surface meaning into those zones of reflection involving the reasons behind the generation of a specific reality by any people. Words are already finished vehicles. But like the vehicles of technology, there are reasons behind the parts or characters of the construction of words and idioms and ideas.Those reasons are the x factors which trigger the feelings behind the words. In other words, what is emoted is only possible because of the totality of properties contributing to the formation of what will do the emoting. We are looking here at the marriage of the ontological and the linguistic. The critic of the translated consciousness, which is what African literature and other such literatures are, is definitely less aware of the complexity of this issue than the writer who is the translator of that consciousness. While Soyinka thinks the reason for this technical miscarriage between critics and writers is because 'critics have now outstripped the productivity, i.e. the writers' (Petersen 1988: 26), a passing commentary by Chinua Achebe on the consciousness while dealing with the works of African artists throws a not too surprising light on the situation. Listen to what Chinua Achebe says in that foreword to Cole and Aniakor's *Igbo Arts: Community and Cosmos.* He was reflecting on masking, a peculiarly African dance phenomenon with its own special Igbo gravitas:

> In the past knowing who walked within the mask did not detract from the numinous dramatic presence of a representative of the ancestors on a brief mission to the living. Disbelief was easily suspended! The decline today is merely a symptom of the collapse of a whole eschcatology. But at least in my dreams masquerades have not ceased to represent the panic terror of childhood. (Cole and Aniakor 1984: xii)

And every Igbo will tell you that the incubus induced by the masquerade in dreams is unimaginable in its terror. This quote is a fitting beginning for this article because of those critics of an undomesticated psychoanalysis in African literature who might still miss the pithy point here. A consciousness cannot be defined with any accuracy unless we begin with the ontological, the deep foundry where the ruling images and potent symbols of our lives are designed and forged.

So far much of what we have been doing with the English language while investigating meaning is to either go to the syllabic bases, to phonemes and morphemes, and the extra-cultural and extra-national associations of the language. What we should be doing more often with the language is to pursue the originating base of the translated consciousness to divine the intra-cultural or intra-national associations of expressions. The closest thing to that kind of project or engagement is the sort of instinctive thing we do while trying to understand the onomatopoeic where unfailingly and inevitably, the sound informs on the word. In the project being suggested, cosmological aspects of the expression should inform on the word and its meaning. If one accepts this suggestion, you would begin to see how this affects our understanding of what we ascribe to access or lack of access to the meaning of so many materials in African poetry coming from writers such as Wole Soyinka and Christopher Okigbo. And then instead of cock-eyed theoretical excuses and apologia for certain kinds of work, we would have more systematic and credible and reliable approaches to meaning. So far, what has been going on is that the mis-steps of the critic in a hurry, or the thunder-struck critic, dazed intellectually by the carnivalesque activities of today's fashionable coteries refuses to do the cultural background work required before wading into what is clearly a culturally alien territory. So many critics of African literature, indigenous and foreign, hide today under the works of Foucault, Bakhtin, Derrida, Paul de Man, Lacan and so forth and care little about the philosophical, historical or cultural pedigree of those thinkers. It is a grand masquerade troupe in which the so-called subaltern wearing alien epaulettes pretends to understand the complex African mask but is oblivious of the power of the imperial puppeteer ruling an unsuspecting consciousness. Affiliations and gyrations to such an orchestra affirm only private and fractional and pragmatically driven wisdom. And then the relevance of such exercises, except for the hosting or indeed metropolitan imperial academy, will for ever remain questionable.

The following example from Igbo language and culture was what triggered my present reflections and considerations. Igbo students found themselves helpless when during a sabbatical encounter, I requested a faithful translation of the following from a well-known and powerful Igbo song used for work and war. *Nzogbu nzogbu, enyi mba enyi! Nzogbu, enyi mba enyi!* Translating or transliterating cannot take any one beyond *Trample trample, elephant country, elephant! Trample, elephant country, elephant!* So what would that mean to the non-Igbo or indeed to the Igbo unaware of what is being emoted? If one does not know that the Igbo pride comes from their claim of a big heart in all their endeavours and that that big heart is fully and accurately represented by the massive weight and strength of the elephant, the biggest animal in their jungle, there is really no other way of understanding what is involved in that song, the feeling being emoted! With that cultural blindness before such texts, your guess of meaning would be no better than anybody else's. Meaning would be like reading a root metaphor only by the looks of the symbol rather than through the properties and valency of the symbol.

In the poetry of Christopher Okigbo, you would find these lines in a period of intense poetic excitation in 'Path of Thunder' where the great poet invokes:

the elephant, tetrarch of the jungle
with a wave of the hand
He could pull four trees to the ground

His four mortar legs pounded the ground
Wherever they treaded
The grass was forbidden to be there (Okigbo 1971: 67)

Okigbo's purpose is the same as the Igbo's in the song referred to earlier, invoking the powerful (the elephant/powerful people) and the weak (grass commoners) in unmatched contest. This is perfect trans-emoting understood readily by the two cultures involved, Igbo and English. The same Christopher Okigbo states somewhere that he is not an African poet, he is simply a poet. You may now understand the intent of this other playfully scornful line from another living Igbo poet: '*I am an Igbo poet writing in English!*'[1] What I present here strikes not only at the roots of something deep in the politics of African literary production and interpretation, but also at the rather complicated malaise at the root of how Africans choose the tools with which to probe the problems of gover-nance. There is this chronic diffidence, an underrated and under-examined psychological problem, arising from a colonially induced unwillingness to investigate the numerous ontologically based crises clogging the foundations of the culture. Without this problem, you would see a more aggressive 'home-based' attitude toward the resolution of the multiple crises afflicting Africa.

Here are more examples of what is implied in dealing with what we all flee from in the politics of our cultural engagements or in the cultural engagement of our politics! The Igbo transliteration of 'to sing' is 'to count a melody or a dance', '*i gu egwu*'. Overwhelmed by a singer's perfor-mance, the Igbo would simply say '*o na-agu*'. That returned to English means something like 's/he can count' and not 's/he can sing'. To further complicate this situation, the word 'egwu' in some Igbo dialects could mean dance or song depending on the accompanying verb. Obviously when an Igbo expressing feelings in English settles for 'sing' instead of 'count', a lot of cultural sacrifice goes with that choice. The ramifications become quite interesting for one who accepts that this exercise involves a translation of consciousness. For me, the issue here is that there is a reason why the Igbo think singing is counting melody or counting music or counting dance. All those alternative nouns are there to suggest the possible variations of the same expression in differing Igbo dialects and circumstances. The point remains that such transfers only fractionally emote what the Igbo not just mean but feel about singing or music or melody or dance and so forth. Before you decide to challenge this argument, consider what happens to meaning when the Igbo now define 'to dance' as '*i gba egwu*'. Transliterated that means 'to shoot a song', 'to shoot a melody' or 'to shoot a dance'. Consider what the word 'shoot' does in that circumstance in contra-distinction to a somewhat mellow 'count', and you will again understand further what could be implied and gained by an application of the notion of trans-emoting. Now, Igbo language is full of countless such expressions that are indisputably harnessed to or derived from ontological circumstances. 'The sun is shining' in Igbo, '*anwu na eti*', transliterates into 'the sun is beating' while fire is burning becomes 'fire is shooting', 'fire is dancing' or 'fire is running'. Rain is falling, '*mili na ezo*' probably illustrates best what the ramifications amount to ontologically because it would transliterate into 'rain is drenching'. The clear implication in a comparative reading of the cosmos here makes the cosmos in Igbo elementally active, living, participative, kinesthetic and ultimately sentient. Fire and rain and sun and other such phenomena know what they are doing! Primal forces in virgin activity! Each, you will note, makes absolute sense in terms of that animated kinesthetic or tactile activity. These reflections take me back yet again to Achebe's thoughts on the Igbo cosmos in *Igbo Arts: Community and Cosmos*:

> The Igbo world is an arena for the interplay of forces. It is a dynamic world of movement and of flux. Igbo art, reflecting this world view, is less tranquil than mobile and active, even aggressive. Ike, energy, is the essence of all things human, spiritual, animate and inanimate. Every thing has its own unique energy which must be acknowledged and given its due. (Cole and Aniakor 1984: xiii)

One is tempted to state here that the spirit behind those constructions must also be the same kind of spirit which generated those famed Egyptian heiroglyphs!!! Perhaps it helps to associate the author of *Butterfly Burning* with the same kind of spirit.

Now, bear this in mind while reading Yvonne Vera. Are there reasons why the Igbo read phenomena in those terms? *There must be.* This is why I think the kind of selectivity that comes to play in the creative process of translating a consciousness from an indigenous African language to a colonizer's language is so important in determining the total aesthetic or technical merit of African cultural material. To ignore that would be disrespectful, dishonest, and fraudulent. Granted though that it might pass as ignorance, recklessly commercialized! This is where I think those, like Ngugi wa Thiong'o, who campaign for literature in African languages have a very good point. This campaign, despite its sometimes accompanying melodrama when it is in unguarded and unpragmatic over-drive, needs careful encouragement. Careful in case it becomes like the fine critical program initiated by Chinweizu and his colleagues in *Toward the Decolonization of African Literature*, which foundered on its over-kill. The indigenous languages are bound to preserve and protect the foundations of the so-called vernacular consciousness better than the adopted alien tongue.

How does Yvonne Vera's work fit into all this? Some colleagues have suggested to me that Vera's work is 'very difficult'. More shocking and amusing is the suggestion of a feminist friend and colleague that 'Vera writes like a man'! That of course is a statement, from a woman, with strange political implications for feminism and those feminists who imagine that the feminist vision could be frozen into a one-dimensional interpretive strategy. I have countered by suggesting that Vera's work, especially in *Butterfly Burning* is a worthy new direction in African literature that deserves to be studied very carefully, not lazily. The writing does not suffer from some of the great afflictions of newer African writing, lodestoned by haphazard philosophical posturing, zero circumspection in its righteousness in moral claims, consequently unbearably irritating for its often solipsistic logic, and most importantly the lack of finesse in dealing with that match between language and story that makes the good story unimpugnably real.

Vera's is a new direction in African writing in the sense that it charts a new syncretic and refreshingly complex vista, wins its own special integrity via a completely new way of re-telling a story that indeed has already been told. A new direction must always be a new direction in vision and thought, in aesthetics and craft. A new direction cannot simply be another story. If someone were to challenge me to offer a listed concrete proof for my contention regarding African writing in the 1990s, the following would make my subjective list. Ben Okri's *The Famished Road* (without its redundant sequel(s)), Syl Cheney-Coker's *The Last Harmattan of Alusine Dunbar*, Kojo Laing's *Major Gentl and the Achimota Wars*, Festus Iyayi's *Court Martial*, Isidore Okpewho's *Tides* and Ama Ata Aidoo's *Changes*. The list would also include the works of Chenjerai Hove, Chris Kanengoni, and Paul Tiyambe Zeleza, and also Tsitsi Dangaremgba's *Nervous Conditions* and G.M. Vasanji's *The Gunny Sack*. One or two names have probably escaped my attention, but if questioned further about other names, my contention would be that those are probably powerful stories that have not necessarily constituted a new regime in compelling craftsmanship or craftswomanship ... new directions! New directions must be like sudden and clear and distinctive extraordinary beacons, beyond familiar artistic uniforms, not some vague and artistically polysemous and indeterminate thing merely moving toward a nebulous cultural black hole. New directions must chart different directions from the mass, the beaten path. As a proviso to all this subjectivity, I must hasten to add that the new direction does not mean 'good' or 'bad' in the conventional aesthetic or artistic and crass judgemental sense. I am simply concerned with distinction, with distinction as the trigger for productive agitation and significant change from the status quo, from ordinary creative stasis, the kind of distinction which makes the gramophone give way for the compact disc player despite their uniform activity!

If arriving at a reliable aesthetic measure that would be generally acceptable is our goal, we must bear in mind that sometimes the story writer has the gift of memory and construction which enables recall of event or construction of scenario and circumstance but does not have the language or sense of language. Sometimes the writer has the language but does not have the imagination which enables the necessary inspiriting of the fictive world.

The consequence of such a lack is predictable. What is presumably emoted is not felt. What sails is either a raw crude experience of private joy or pain spuriously advertised by the writer. The product is inchoate and frozen in the private. It is distant from all the transcendencies which move enduring art from personal to public, public to national, and national to the transnational and transcultural.

The successful story always expresses triumphantly the transmutation of the private to the public. And that quickens empathy. If there is anything useful coming out of the much touted and so-called death of the author, it is that fact. It is the thing that establishes that Chinua Achebe is not Okonkwo in *Things Fall Apart* and Flora Nwapa is neither *Efuru* nor *Idu* in those novels of the same titles, and so forth. The triumphant masking traps and sustains our curiosity in an inescapable belief that the fictive world is a genuine new territory worthy of our exploration.

So speaking of new territories adumbrates the novelty of directions. What is new in Yvonne Vera, especially in her novel *Butterfly Burning*? What is new is the author's ostensible conviction that the raw story is not enough. In defining her vision, Vera declares 'I do not write, unless I see it.'[2] That declaration is sharpened in another statement elsewhere: 'The woman writer in Africa is a witness; forgiving the evidence of the eyes, pronouncing her experience with insight, artistry and a fertile dexterity. Her response to theme, event, taboo is vital and pressing.'[3] There is in all that an inescapable alchemy during which the artist's brush engages in a multiple transmutation of various facets of a shapeless raw material. Many debuts in African fiction have passed unnoticed because of a failure to acknowledge that painful creative fact. Many which have remained alive and noticed have remained so from the power of the propaganda or publicity of the publishing house and the fawning habits of some critics.

The novel qualities of Vera's work have the potential to rise to the level of power in the writings of North American women such as Margaret Craven (*I Heard the Owl Call My Name*), Louise Erdich (*Love Medicine*) and of course, Toni Morrison. I have tried to be careful in my choice of league. These are writers who have the right and precise measures in that artistically infallible alchemy of myth, public and private memory, history, and the delicate politics of distributive justice comfortably housed in a credible cosmology.

I have read and re-read Vera's *Butterfly Burning* and cannot help feeling that her aesthetic advances some of the things theorized by great American novelists like Henry James who felt that the poetic facility in fiction is as vital for expressive power as the complex linguistic nuances which we think is exclusive to poetry. For Vera, there are two critical aspects of that process of production. One is language, and the other is the multiple prong of lines of the same story.

Now, the cement of language. Language in Vera's work is not a casual deployment. It is a vehicle within a vehicle. If Vera's work is a dance, the storylines are doing their own dances with the language but the language has agenda which branchiate into cosmic invitation, participation, and integration. The author is not merely interested in telling a beautiful story but also invoking and weaving or stitching other vibrant essences into the storylines. We have in the end things and phenomena waking up into active parts of the cosmos. This notion of essences is very important. To Vera the cosmos in its entirety is sentient and vibrant. All elements share in an animate kinesthesia and tactility. Every thing lives in Vera's writing. And the cosmos is as seamless as it is stitched together. There are no boundaries between phenomena and numina. Think now about my earlier suggestions and examples from Igbo language and culture, and then reflect on the possibilities in the following generous expressions from *Butterfly Burning* to see how teleology stitches or weaves together human action, even vegetation action, and other cosmological activities:

> The movement of their arms is like weaving, as their *arms thread through* each thicket, and withdraw. *This careful motion is patterned like a dance* spreading out, *each sequence rises like hope* enacted and set free. Freed, stroke after stroke, holding briskly, and then a final whisper of release. The grass falls arm and arm of it. It falls near and close to each curled body. *The grass submits* to the feet of workers who step over it to arrive where *the grass is high and stands defiant* ... They cut and level the grass till the sun is a crusty and golden distance away and *throws* cool rays over their worn arms, and the sky dims, and everything is quiet except the *spray of light breaking and darting between the grass* tossing back and forth ... *the grass is swishing hopelessly ... its sound folds* into a faint melody which dims with *the slow dying of the sun*, and *each handful of grass becomes a violent silhouette, a stubborn shadow grasped* ... (*Butterfly Burning* 5)

Think about my earlier suggestions about how things come alive in the Igbo cosmos. Reflect on the diction of the above passage from Vera's work. I have italicized much of it to keep our eyes on the operating and inspiriting and animating and active expressions. Certainly, it is with good reason that I suggest that there is a seamless stitching or weaving together of the cosmos in such a participatory fashion that every cosmic entity plays a role in affirming disparate identity at the same time that collective integrity and oneness is being stressed. Take for example this subtle relationship between the strong woman, Deliwe, and the weak woman, Phephelaphi, intertwined in what I call the musical sub-text of this work. The story of their relationship rises in incremental relays till it comes summarily to a ritualistic, folk-tale like, and incantatory crescendo about two thirds of the way through the novel:

> Deliwe ... shoved Phephelaphi inside the house, sat her down on a stool, and gave her a glass of water. It was the glass that rescued her. A long glass with a blue tint to it which looked lovelier than sunlight and which, as Phephelaphi brought it to her lips, made her senses gather together like needles of incandescent light,

as though her butterfly wings were closing on pollen, just touching, closed till a breeze lifted and touched the pleat. Finally she was able to look up at Deliwe and tell her all her shame. Deliwe listened carefully.

> Deliwe who had been Gertrude's friend
> Deliwe who knew Fumbatha
> Deliwe who had the pride of an eagle
> Deliwe who had the eyes of scorpions (*Butterfly Burning* 104)

From this woman-to-woman relay of role and energy, we head to the other crescendo in the finale of the tale. Phephelaphi, leads us through a series of courageous reflections and decisions into her bonfire of self-immolation, demonstrating that even a delicate-looking butterfly is capable of heroic action to free the human spirit from dross. After reading that would one not safely opine that the consciousness of this writer is one which not only celebrates the oneness of the cosmos but also its beauty, a beauty which comfortably rests on the teleological relationship of all parts? And we may indeed pursue all this further by suggesting that like the German philosopher, Schelling, Vera sees the cosmos as some form of architectural still, ex camera, waiting for life and animation, and she mobilizes and rouses that still with her delicate and peculiar art brushes. Always, all things live, and when they do not, their essences do. Elsewhere in the novel, you will notice how such a penetrating artistic vision, like in poetry, tells us more than we are wont to accept about the environment and the things in the environment. Once we create or release, the things we create or release become alive, become sentient and join us in either affirming, in celebrating or enacting the thing called life. It is in this light that Vera's own peculiar poetry makes sense in the following: 'She is searching the air with her voice...' (14) 'Afterward they see the men rising from the ditches, like rainbows.' (22) 'And night comes like a thief, with a gentleness that caresses the eyes with gleaming broken rays ... and then a sudden downpour of stars.' (23) 'The city has swallowed the river.' (24) 'Kwela music brings a symphony of understanding ... Kwela strips you naked' (7) 'They find new names for the dead ... The men are buried in their mouths.' (12) 'These were girls bright-eyed but soft like sunrise and much calmer than a breeze.' (93) 'The scorpions had risen in her eyes after she fell out of the police van...' (61) 'Fumbatha sees the sky peel off the earth; that is the distance between the land and the sky' (68). The frequency of these neo-hieroglyphs and their strategic placements is astonishing. But such is the character and quality of this new direction! I am tempted to bastardize an old European thought here by suggesting that the world is both will and idea here in good represen-tation, hence the harmony we find in the integration of the formations of the various characters within the stream of time and space and history.

Butterfly Burning is fantasy. It is symbolic action. It is both parabolic and realistic action in lock-step. The novel could simply be the story of a young woman who burns herself to death because she loses the love and trust and care of her man, but there are many story lines. The first story line is that of a nebulous butterfly which waxes invisibly in its transmutation toward an essence that is supernatural and neoplatonic. It is also an evolution of a love story from a woman's surrender to male desire and power to courageous self-immolation and freedom. It is the story of the growth of a girl from childhood to womanhood and its various perils. It is the story of the weak woman and the strong woman. It is the story of men and women fighting to survive in a city in repressive, perplexing and brutal colonial circumstances. It is the story of man and woman in the familiar games and contests for power in volatile political and socio-economic circumstances. It is the story of the conflict between past and present, between Africa and the West, between urban and rural life, and of course the great crisis of the colony under European imperialism. It appears the power of the story repeatedly echoes the story of women under the great insuperable forces of indigenous African patriarchal tradition in league with the complex patriarchy of imperialism bolstered by unsuspicious and innocuous and subtle apparati of governance. If that echo is strong, so is the story of a man (Fumbatha) peering into the past to understand what happened to his father and his people under white rule. And on the stage of all this complex enactment, in the parlance of theater directors, God is full back. And the colonial power too is full back. Both constitute an even more potent power in their absence. And of course power becomes most formidable because ultimately that is why things are the way they are. See how the writer captures this last point in the labour of men at work 'The work is not their own: It is summoned. The time is not theirs: It is seized. The ordeal is their own. They work again and again, and in unguarded moments of hunger and surprise, they mistake their fate for fortune' (5).

But who indeed are the characters in *Butterfly Burning*? Whose interests do they represent? They represent human beings. They do not represent women's voices making statements against men or vice versa. The characters, like other aspects of the cosmos, jointly and collaboratively represent a world with clashing interests and colliding motives, private agenda against private agenda in dreams and desires and plans and action. There are human beings loving and hating and fearing and flinching or marching forward and falling in the process of expressing their various aspirations and so forth. Indeed everybody is guilty of one thing or the other, in choice or in judgement, in one form of calculation or the other. It is not a programmatic and binary man against woman, not even the colonizer against the colonized. Human beings act and make decisions which affect other human beings for good or ill but in this novel, they are mostly for ill. Because of this, the inclination for our sympathies to rest with the disadvantaged becomes understandable because the writer does not teleguide the compelling sentiment. In short, the truculence which mars all battles for social justice with the stamp of a partisan adversarialism is absent. Perhaps authorial judgement is some-where there, but we sympathize with that judgement because there is a curious kind of blame for the victim who submits to being a victim instead of fighting, as much as there is blame for whoever passes for victor.

Terming this work as a holistic feminist vision is to stress that Yvonne Vera's agenda may be a woman's agenda but that agenda is finessed into the reader's thoughts and sympathies in a fashion which makes the agenda everybody's agenda. One of the first reviewers of *Butterfly Burning* misses this point badly. Writing for *African Literature Today*, Fiona Johnson Chalamanda has the following to say:

> For me, the main discomfort is the over-determined sexuality of all the main female characters, implying a male gaze. Indeed, many of the women earn their existence in the township by selling their bodies, for example, where Zandile traces her clients' histories by tracking the scars on their bodies in, for example, 'The girls wait in tattered skirts which waver over their thin thighs, their breasts are flat like the bottle-tops.'[4]

A modernist Western eye and sensibility visits a peculiar African cosmos here, and misses what the writer and her environment *emote*! In the tradi-tional African environment, the body does not carry the lodestone of prurience which it carries in the west. A so-called African modernity notwithstanding, the bodies in the scene above share a cultural comfort in their peculiar space sans any extraordinary fascination. But Chalamanda is squarely back in perspicacious track when she later hones up her obser-vation declaring '*Butterfly Burning* [is] a novel of immense vividness, both in horror and in beauty, leading the reader through a turmoil of emotions. At times these emotions may conflict, as poverty and depriva-tion are represented with empathetic beauty...'[5] Philosophically or ideo-logically speaking, it is the harmlessly conflictual character of the disparate circumstances or situations of the text which constitute Vera's winning strategy.

This winning strategy, because of its all-inclusive character, generates a very tough act to follow for serious African women writers who desire to be listened to in the legitimate project for social justice. In the light of all these, it is appropriate, I think, to affirm that *Butterfly Burning* emotes a cosmos which speaks to numerous complex issues in the equally complex missions of African life and art.

NOTES

1. Chimalum Nwankwo, Preface to *The Womb in the Heart and Other Poems*. San Francisco: African Heritage Press, 2002, p. xii.
2. Culled from remarks by Yvonne Vera during her guest presentation at the Humboldt University's Versions and Subversions Conference, Berlin, May 2002.
3. Yvonne Vera in her Preface to *Anthology of African Women's Writing*, ed. Yvonne Vera.

Oxford: Heinemann Educational Books, 1999.
4. Fiona Johnson Chalamanda, Review of *Butterfly Burning* in *African Literature Today*, (22) 2000, p. 142.
5. The reconsidered observation is made a few lines down the same page.

WORKS CITED

Achebe, Chinua. *Preface.* In Cole, Herbert M. and Chike Aniakor (ed.), *Igbo Arts: Community and Cosmos.* Los Angeles: Museum of Cultural History, University of California, 1984.
Okigbo, Christopher. *Labyrinths.* London: Heinemann Educational Books, 1971.
Soyinka, Wole. 'Ideology and the critic'. In Petersen, Kirsten Holst (eds), *Criticism and Ideology. Second African Writer's Conference*, Stockholm 1986. Uppsala: Scandinavia Institute of African Studies, 1988.
Vera, Yvonne. *Butterfly Burning.* New York: Farrar Straus and Giroux, 2000.

Representations of the Womanist Discourse in the Short Fiction of Akachi Ezeigbo & Chinwe Okechukwu

Ijeoma C. Nwajiaku

> To the womanist, therefore the vital unity of a people evolving a philosophy of life acceptable to both men and women is a better approach to the wo/man palava than a debilitating and devastating political struggle for women's liberation, independence, and equality with men, to prove a feminist point.
>
> Chikwenye Okonjo Ogunyemi[1]

Auspiciously, the enhanced need for self re-definition and self-evaluation has located the African female at a crucial ideological spike. This assertion becomes even more credible when one considers the intensity, complexity and quality of the multifarious literary activities birthed in the last decade of the twentieth century. Indeed no preceding decade had witnessed a similar development.

The women have thus visibly situated themselves at 'various epistemological positions that are relevant' to the task before them. As Kolawole further puts it:

> They are deconstructing imperialistic images of the African, rejecting liminal and negative images of women that are prevalent in African literature by men and they are reacting to mainstream western feminism. Having broken the yoke of voicelessness, these women are speaking out. (1997: 193).

This acclaimed reaction to 'mainstream western feminism' has engendered continuing discourse among African female scholars. They have begun to occupy front seats in the invention of their own reality. In the process, they are consciously expunging 'externally enforced or condescending ideologies' which might impede or negate the evolution and progression of their conceptualized interpretation of African womanhood. We perceive on the African literary scene then, a conglomeration of heterogeneous theories, being propounded to define the consciousness of the African female. Evinced by such concepts as Ogundipe-Leslie's stiwanism (from STIWA: Social Transformation Including Women in Africa), Acholonu's motherism, Hudson-Weems' Africana Womanism as well as African feminism, gynism, gynandrism, African womanism, etc., one realizes that the African female scholar is unarguably articulating her stance.

Perhaps, this redefinition has been necessitated by the earlier situation in which works by the older generation of African women writers have been interpreted within the framework of Western feminism. A situation which not only placed foremost writers including Nwapa, Aidoo, Bâ and Emecheta on the defensive whenever they were accused of being feminists, but also saw them engaged in a series of denials and counter-denials. Possibly in recognition of or even deference to the African male's dislike of Western feminism. A confounding situation it would seem, particularly as the African woman does not perceive of the expression of her femaleness and its attendant struggle for self-articulation, as having originated from the Western world.

The truth of course is that the situation is not at all confounding, when located squarely within the collective consciousness of African reality. And this is actually the whole point. In the African woman's quest for a positive and wholesome definition of womanhood and empowerment, the African male is not excluded. So that despite the diverse perspectives represented by the multiple theories of female consciousness currently making their runs on the African literary scene, one idea remains poignant: the struggle includes the survival of the female as well as the male.

As Kolawole again observes:

> The African woman seeks self-fulfillment within this plural cultural context. The average African woman is not a hater of men; nor does she seek to build a wall around her gender across which she throws ideological missiles. She desires self-respect, an active role, dynamic participation in all areas of social development, and dignity alongside the men (1997: 36).

The above ideas are significantly subsumed by the principles of the womanist ideology, which so far does appear to be the most dominant and acceptable mode of defining the African female's location. Clearly, womanism calls for dialogism and seeks interactive perception while repudiating absolutism and dogmatism. Obviously Obioma Nnaemeka[2] contributes to this argument by claiming that within what is regarded as 'African feminism', power is a 'negotiable and negotiated' item. It is thus evaluated not in absolute but in *relative* terms (her emphasis); very different from Western feminism's focus on 'power grabbing'.

In *Africa Wo/Man Palava* Ogunyemi identifies 'harnessing of talents and opposing oppression, especially (though not exclusively) its manifestation as wo/man wahala or palava' as the central concern of womanism. To this erudite scholar then:

> Womanism, with its myriad manifestation is therefore a renaissance that aims to establish healthy relationships among people, despite ethnic, geographical, educational, gender, ethical, class, religious, military, and political differences. The oppression emanating from these differences has to be addressed to counter further division and hardships. (1996: 123)

Although Chioma Opara[3] attempts to make a distinction between the above definition and an earlier one by the same Ogunyemi,[4] we would rather enjoin that both theoretical assumptions are still very much under-scored by analogous ideological convictions and Ogunyemi does not really distinguish between them. All she does is claim that her own con-jecture should be perceived as different from Alice Walker's earlier womanism, situated as it is within the African-American context, and 'Clenora Hudson-Weems' utopian Africana womanism' (119).

Significantly, Ogunyemi concedes that Walker's definition 'can help to sharpen [her] focus' in certain assumptions, whereas Hudson-Weems' ideology 'tends to romanticize black female relationships, ignoring its myriad dangers for women' (119). She does add however that Hudson Weems' insistence on the right of the black woman to 'name and define herself' is compelling.

Although Hudson-Weems[5] herself is at pain to carve out 'a separate and distinct identity' for her ideology, it is obvious that the distinguishing characteristic features of all these stances are not always clear-cut. Perhaps this is what has prompted Charles Nnolim (1999) to make the following assertion in his paper titled 'African Feminism: the Scandalous Path':

> The trajectory of the more recent movements of African feminism draws an arc that is most disquieting in its implications. (46)

Nnolim goes on to accuse some foremost African female writers of pushing 'the tenets of feminism to scandalous, even criminal and murderous levels'. According to him the 'plethora of feminist theories' are visible on a 'landscape that [is] uneven and zig-gag in a seasaw of con-fusions'. To cap it all Nnolim declares: 'some African feminists are dancing a furious step, and the feminist drums have gone mad' (46).

Coming from Nnolim, these remarks are quite curious, particularly when we understand his favourable disposition towards the women's struggle in Nigeria (Opara, 1999). Yet Nnolim's vexation appears validated when an erudite female African scholar, Theodora Akachi Ezeigbo declares that 'African feminism and African womanism are one and the same; and we do not see any significant difference'(1999: 139). We do believe these unresolved issues are characteristic of evolving ide-ologies and will progressively be clarified.

For this article however, we would locate our discourse within the framework of womanist ideology as expounded in Ogunyemi's *Africa Wo/Man Palava* (1996) and Kolawole's *Womanism and African Con-sciousness* (1997). Incidentally Ezeigbo and Okechukwu whose collec-tions of short stories we are studying are both college professors and critics of African literature, who have more recently joined the ever-increasing number of Nigerian female writers. Ezeigbo's *Echoes in the Mind* (1994), and Okechukwu's *When Rain Beat the Cow in the Eyes* (1999), are certainly collections of short stories which explore the struggle for survival of the male and female alike in a society exacerbated by mutinous socio-cultural and political determinants.

The stories in the first section of Ezeigbo's collection are appropriately titled 'Growth Through Pain'. Ezeigbo takes us on a journey through the 'minds' of her heroines. We listen to the reverberations of their hearts, we witness a deep psychological probe into the complex motivations and impulses which inform the acts of the protagonists. It is their personal bitter experiences that yield enlightenment and maturity.

Ogunyemi observes how Nigerian novels by women inculcate a 'conciliatory spirit, in spite of controversies' (1996: 106). This womanist tradition is realized in Edoro's determined effort to be reconciled to her people, whom she had abandoned in pursuit of love. In the story 'Agarachaa Must Come Home', Edoro the heroine carries through a resolute decision to marry a Nigerian soldier fighting in a war against her people.

Aware of the implication of her choice, as evidenced by 'the stiff and violent opposition she received from her family, especially her father and brothers' (1994: 8), Edoro still leaves in response to the promptings of her heart. Ezeigbo refrains from passing subjective judgements, and aims at realistic portraiture. We realize that Edoro's choice though 'revolutionary' has, as Grace Okafor[6] rightly points out, 'potential for success or failure' (1997: 86). In this instance Edoro's choice fails and in recognition of her mistake, she makes a bold and commendable effort to negotiate peace with her people.

They in turn ruthlessly confront her with:

> You have chosen your way, your life...
> You are dead to us. The day you stubbornly left with that soldier...was the day we pronounced you dead, mourned you and buried you. (1994: 14)

Symbolically, it is her father, assisted by uncles, who inform Edoro about this communal decision to ostracize her permanently. Ezeigbo's indictment of the sometimes harsh Igbo patriarchal structure is evident. Significantly also, only Edoro's mother who is barely allowed to intervene is able to forgive and accept her back. Yet the ultimate verdict lies with the men, so she helplessly looks on as her only daughter, miserable but courageous, steps again into an unknown but promising world, to make yet another attempt at marriage. A true womanist Edoro must choose from the options before her and continue in the struggle for survival. As female writers continue to explore the dilemma of the woman in a patriarchal society, we encounter the tension generated by tradition and modernity in Ezeigbo's tales.

In a study on the female and the political sphere in Nigeria, Dorcas Akande (1999) declares that Nigerian women as well as men are suffering from the downward plunge of the economy and disregard for human rights and the rule of law. This has in turn resulted in a climactic worsening of the human condition. The womanist ideology recognizes the enduring exclusion of women from participatory involvement in politics in African countries and seeks to redress this anomaly. Thus, Fola in 'The Missing Hammer Head' is poised to 'seek nomination as the senatorial candidate for Obanla district' (18). In her opinion, 'at this time when women are coming into politics to seek for elective posts ... every woman should encourage and support them rather than throwing a spanner in the works' (19).

The immediate intervention of the authorial voice through Lovina is crucial. She cautions against a misconception 'of the whole issue' (19), and insists that 'we don't have to support a candidate simply because she is a woman'. Yet the understanding and unity evident in the close relationship of the three women, is a clear call for the women to bond, this being a vital requirement for their progress.

Thus advocacy for women in politics should be based on firm convictions of the 'rightness' of their candidature. Perhaps Fola's reckless and tactless comments reveal a certain amount of immaturity and lack of wisdom, despite her excellent academic and economic achievements. The writer consequently allows her to undergo agonizing psychological and physical torture at the hands of an irate mob, bent on lynching her, for an offence she did not commit. Her near-death escape, and the realization of the negative effects of her hitherto arrogant attitude, engender the transformation necessary for a would-be leader.

Ogunyemi points out that 'although they might not be consciously and concertedly advocating equal rights ... the writers criticize grossly unfair gender arrangements' (1996: 117). This becomes clear when Ezeigbo descends on the yam seller in the same story. We perceive that the man's anger at Fola's attitude is intensified because of her gender:

> [He] hated her superior ways, her confidence and the air of authority she exuded. He could not live down nor forgive the hard words she threw at him which were like barbs tearing his manhood to shreds. She had impaled him with her haughty words ... (1994: 24)

Clearly the combination of 'superior ways', 'confidence' and 'air of authority' so merged, and so flagrantly exhibited and utilized by Fola to the utter humiliation of this man become too much for his male ego. Typically in his Nigerian culture, such natural attributes remain the sole preserve of men. But Fola adapts them to emasculate him and render him effeminate. So he rationalizes as he speaks to an imagined Fola: 'Na woman you be, upon all the money you get. You be common woman' (1994: 25). Propelled by the magnitude of his venom, he plots his revenge and in a swift and dramatic twist, the man publicly accuses her of really stealing his physical male organ. A situation like this opens up complexities entrenched in what amounts to traditional attitudes, biases and prejudices.

By contrast the story titled 'Inspiration Bug', presents a female writer who enjoys the love, support and encouragement of her husband.

Critically reflecting upon the womanist ideology of collaboration and complementarity, we confront a reversal of the hitherto accepted situation of women offering support, understanding and encouragement to their husbands as they pursue mentally involving careers. Searching her mind the heroine Chinny fails to recall any situation in the past where a man had helped his wife to flourish as a writer. Yet she could recall countless 'spouses, companions, mistresses and lovers of past and contemporary writers' (1994: 77), who helped their men to excel as great authors. The message becomes clear, her husband Ralph may well have to blaze the trail for other men to follow.

To drive home the point, Ezeigbo uses hilarious scenes. Chinny is smitten by the great 'inspiration bug' at the most inappropriate times and places, either in the church during an enthralling sermon or right in the middle of a passionate love-making session with her husband. In either case, Chinny the bold and determined modern woman responds first to the bug-bite.

Any look at recent writing by Nigerian women reveals their involved plunge into matters beyond 'the plight of women in a patriarchal' society. Oppression with its myriad presentations, diverse and complicated guises of corruption, political imbroglio, amidst other convoluted societal problematics equally entrap these writers' attention. Thus Ezeigbo's 'The Verdict', 'Who Said Dead Men Can't Bite?' and 'The Blind Man of Ekwulu' each deal with issues of morality, oppression and cultural myths. In 'The Verdict', the profligate 'symbol of oppression and exploitation' Chief Alagbe, defeats Maduka in a court case over a land dispute. Maduka a poor teacher, has further been 'sapped' by SAP, the Structural Adjustment Programme of the country which 'bulldozed its way into the country' working 'jointly with exploitation and oppression to emasculate the poor' (1994: 80).

Representative of ex-government officials in the country, Chief Alagbe, the self-enriched ex-commissioner of police, builds a three-storey edifice in three months on the land, which had previously been sold to Maduka. Left with little option, Maduka flees to his village to present the case before the priest of Ulasi in the shrine. Assured of victory because of the injustice meted out to him, Maduka returns to Lagos convinced that providence will intervene on his behalf. It does, as the great edifice crumbles and Maduka is certain the gods have vindicated him. Beyond this, however, is an exploration of the traditional and mythical convictions of the culture of the people.

Similarly, 'Who Said Dead Men Can't Bite?' focuses on a man's battle with his conscience. Initially meaning to help an accident victim, Dimaku succumbs to an overbearing temptation and steals twenty-five thousand naira from the injured man's bulging pockets. While Dimaku is still uncertain about returning the money to the sick man's family, the man dies.

Dimaku's negative decision unleashes a chain of unexplainable but disastrous events on him and his family. His mind becomes befuddled as he storms through one bizarre experience after another. Asleep and awake, Dimaku is relentlessly pursued and tormented by visions and the voice of Akobundu, the dead man. Finally, he embarks on a trip to Ibadan to seek help for his now uncontrollable situation. Ironically, he is involved in an accident and ends up in exactly the same position as Akobundu, with his legs fastened up to the other end of the bed.

Ezeigbo here employs an Igbo myth, which cautions against tampering with a helpless person's property. The name 'Akobundu' means 'wisdom is life'; this reinforces the Igbo cultural belief concerning acceptable codes of conduct. This idea appears re-echoed in Obioma Nnaemeka's paper which partly 'interrogates the prevailing colonialist and imperialist idea that African traditional cultures in their *entirety always* constitute an impediment to progress' (1996: 252).

The African belief system, as encapsulated within the dynamism of its culture, had ways of dealing with situations as they arose. Thus although no one knows about Dimaku's hideous crime, his conscience does, and would allow him no respite. It is therefore through a 'verbal war' with his inner voice that, we realize Dimaku had as a student stolen a blind boy's pair of sandals. His refusal to bear the shame of confessing his crime and seeking to make amends continues to land him in further trouble.

Of importance also, is his refusal to confide in his wife, even when matters escalate. So, Ezeigbo typically is critical of the situation in which his innocent wife and children receive the full brunt of his fury. By contrast, Chiaku though completely ignorant of his misdemeanour, which is responsible for his near-neurotic state, shows great understanding and willingness to forgive his physical onslaught on her. Thus she says, 'All right. I forgive you. But please, don't ever strike me again' (1994: 111). One perceives this womanist determination to accept, live and work with men, while calling for an end to unfair treatment of women.

In the same story Dimaku is burdened with sole responsibility for providing for his family of ten. He consequently deems them responsible for his business failure. Ezeigbo is obviously being satiric in this instance. Chiaku whose name signifies the 'creator of wealth, or spirit of wealth', sits at home unemployed, but producing babies, while Dimaku the embodiment of 'husband as wealth' is unable to cope with the demands on him. A situation that calls for attention.

A similar theme is explored in 'The Blind Man of Ekwulu'. Ezeigbo's experimental narrative technique in this story is quite interesting. Told in the first person, we encounter three voices from two narrators. Nnenna, the lady who commences the tale, hands over to her father, who retains the first person perspective as he retells the story of Nwokeke. He assumes the voice of the blind man and narrates the story exactly as it had been passed across to him. Again this story seeks to unveil aspects of the author's Igbo culture. The tale of Nwokeke, like Dimaku's, explores the complexities ensconced within the socio-cultural canons that shape the people's consciousness.

For instance, the story reiterates the symbolic importance of name bearing among the Igbo people. Thus Nwokeke believes his name 'Eziafakaego' stands as an insurmountable obstacle between himself and his ambition to become wealthy. His laboriously contrived efforts to succeed are perpetually frustrated. Events however reach a disastrous climax for the young man, when his father-in-law outwits him and defrauds him of his wages. Nwokeke reasons that it would only be fair to retaliate. So 'he came to the decision to burgle Onumba's house and take back the bride wealth' (1994: 135). Luck runs out on him though, as he does not escape. A mysterious knock on the head renders him disoriented, his wife is taken away by her people and he becomes blind.

While leaving the reader to decide on the complicity of fate and destiny on Ezeokeke's life, we recognize the overt condemnation of crime. As the old man himself declares, 'Robbery was a serious crime in Ekwulu and had its punishment' (1994: 139). He is renamed 'Onye-Mee-Onweye' by the community, an indication that he is solely responsible for his gross misfortune.

Another misfortune in the story should have been Nnenna's. As our first narrator, she reveals that she has three daughters and no son. Clearly a serious problem for any woman within this culture. Yet Nnenna merely regards her beloved husband and father as the men in her life, and her marriage appears unperturbed by her 'sonlessness'. As she puts it:

> My heart brimmed over with love for both of them the men in my life. I had three children, all of them girls. Father and Arinze unabashed spoilt them (1994: 119).

That Nnenna has been happily married to Arinze for twenty years is significant. Similar to her creation of the husband in 'Inspiration Bug', who understands and supports his writer wife, we have here also Arinze who loves his wife and appreciates and dotes on his three daughters. Ezeigbo is thus creating the man who will complement the new African woman.

Because womanism is communally oriented, it seeks to address the destiny of distressed peoples. It also hopes to dialogue about such weighty matters as Ogunyemi says 'in a meaningful context to avert disaster' (1996: 119). This becomes the obvious subject of the story titled 'Degrees of Civilization' in Ezeigbo's collection. The young Oma as an African student in London comes face to face with undisguised racism. Incidentally, and quite ironically, Oma's heart had been filled with compassion for the old white woman whom she felt was too old for the jobs she had to do. Later, however Oma discovers 'that the woman was mean and biased against her blackness' (1994: 93). Things come to a head when the old lady deliberately ignores Oma's request for beef, rather than the pork that she shoves at Oma without asking her preference.

Clearly the issue of racism has continued to plague the minds of African female writers. They realize that overtly or otherwise, discrimination based on race does manifest itself at various levels and should neither be ignored nor glossed over. Thus while Emecheta's older and newer works incorporate this idea, other writers continue to confront the matter, as is evident in Ezeigbo's tale. One recognizes also that the need for a formulation of African women's reality along separate lines was not unconnected with the inability of Western feminism to adequately apprehend the black woman's situation, interlaced as it is with racial prejudice.

Similar to Ezeigbo's work Chinwe Okechukwu's *When Rain Beat the Cow in the Eyes*, is also a collection of eight short stories. Yet it is markedly different, when we realize the latter's specific focus on the Nigerian (Biafran) civil war, fought in the late sixties in the eastern part of Nigeria. One cannot but notice an amplification of interest in the social and political history of that era, as reflected in the recent works of Nigerian female writers, particularly those of Eastern origin. Thus besides Flora Nwapa and Buchi Emecheta, Phanuel Egejuru, Adaure Njoku, Ezeigbo (discussed here), Uche Nwabunike, and Okechukwu have all dealt with dimensions of the war theme in their works.

Okechukwu presents her stories from the secessionist viewpoint and like most other writers dealing with this theme, her voice is laden with often-uncontrollable emotion. She exhibits appreciable preoccupation with the plight of women and children in a warfare situation. Perhaps this explains why the story titled 'Home coming' is told in the first person narrative by the persona, who is a ten-year-old girl. The utter confusion and bewilderment, which assail her young mind at the unusual chain of events, invokes sympathy in the reader.

Kolawole rightly makes the following observation about the position of the family in Africa:

> The centrality of the family is important to Africans, male and female. Women in particular see the family as the nucleus of social development, growth, moral sustenance as well as cultural continuity (1997: 32).

It is possibly against the backdrop of this ideological stance, which is ostensibly shared by womanism theory that we can locate Okechukwu's exasperated denigration of the war. In 'Home coming' Mama Ifeyinwa sobs almost all through the story. Unable to locate her two sons, she is forced to flee to her region for safety saddled with her severely wounded husband and daughter. Similar to her case, are innumerable other cases of women and children who are cut off from other members of their families.

The horrors of the war are graphically recaptured in Okechukwu's depiction of vivid scenes of death, which young Ifeyinwa is not spared the trauma and agony of witnessing. To worsen the situation the now truncated family finally arrives at their destination and discover they have no home to settle into. Ifeyinwa's Uncle had squandered the money remitted for the purpose.

What Okechukwu does with Mama Alafi is to underscore the African female writers' desire to nurture the peaceful co-habitation of the diverse ethnic groups within our communities. She therefore goes to great lengths to describe the hitherto pleasant and cordial atmosphere that had characterized the relationship between the Kafa and Ogboji people. Kafa here representing Northerners, and Ogboji the Easterners. They had witnessed inter-ethnic marriages and the Kafa residents in Ogboji had come to regard the land as their home.

Indeed Mama Alafi though Kafa by birth, 'was born and raised in Otanchara', so 'she had never been to Alafi and did not know what Alafi looked like' (1999: 12). Unperturbed when she hears about the impending war, all she believes is:

> If there is going to be a fight, the politicians are the ones going to fight among themselves ... Yes, the politicians are spoiling things. (1999: 12)

Unfortunately the war is not fought by the politicians among themselves. It includes everyone and as is repeatedly said, the women and children who know nothing about it ironically receive the worst of it. Right before their view, Mama Alafi and other Kafa women together with their children watch the brutal annihilation of their men folk by aggrieved Ogboji men.

We see in the above passage too Okechukwu's subtle indictment of male leaders. Since the women are grossly excluded from political affairs and governance, it is not surprising that we are told: 'The women did not understand why whoever was killed was killed or what that had to do with them' (1999: 19). This re-echoes Adaure Njoku's claim in *Withstand the Storm* (1986) that her husband, a military officer who was involved in governance shortly before the civil war, hardly ever told her details of the sensitive matters that led to the war at that time. Yet the suffering of the women in a crisis situation is often pathetic. Bent on raising emotion, Okechukwu's use of language here includes

> The women and the children stood still in shock ... The women then started screaming. Their children joined them ... men lay dismembered before their mothers, wives and children. The children kept screaming and calling on their fathers. The women huddled together, wailing. (1999: 20)

Okechukwu like most other female writers is particularly concerned with the plight of women in society and not just in a war situation. We therefore note her indictment of Papa Nga's treatment of his wife. She 'was beaten mercilessly every night' by him. Mama Nga has only female children, but would not allow her husband to marry another wife. So he beat her until 'she ran back to her family' and 'Papa Nga married another wife'. Humorously Okechukwu adds that 'that wife continued to have female children'. The author proceeds to make Papa Nga an object of ridicule in the community: 'Otanchara talked. "Papa Nga is a woman. He can't give women male children"' (1999: 11).

We note here the different ways in which Ezeigbo and Okechukwu handle the same issue. Ezeigbo merely presents an enlightened couple who accept their fate and continue to live normal happy lives, while Okechukwu derides the absurdity of blaming women for such situations. As Gloria Chukukere observes, a childless woman 'is considered a failure in her primary duty and often suffers considerably as a result' (1995: 2). This is probably the reason this matter has continued to engage the attention of African female writers, despite the disparaging remarks it has earned them from male critics of African literature.

We recognize in addition that negative myths circulated about women in African societies have grossly affected her image. As Kolawole states,

> Myths recommend, prescribe or validate the society's norms, values, code of conduct, social roles, gender socialisation and a society's sense of identity and collective acceptance. (1998: 7)

This implies that myths clearly affect societal attitudes and values, in fact, significantly shape the culture. This accounts for Ezem's bigoted impression of his female colleagues on the campus. He felt they could not 'have the time to adorn their bodies, especially their faces', and then still cope admirably with their studies. Unveiling his chauvinistic attitudes Okechukwu mocks, 'Ezem never believed that any lady was brilliant enough to score higher than he did in class, his grades being below the average notwithstanding'. So deeply rooted are his warped convictions that he seeks to find a solution to the ability of the female students to give brilliant answers in class. He 'was sure that the lecturers prepared them ahead of time' (1999: 31).

One task before the female writers has been, as Grace Okafor's work shows, the dismantling of negative and stereotypic images of the woman in our society. They have in this respect been striving to rewrite prevalent myths of female subordination. This is evident in Ezeigbo's depiction of the character of Fola in 'The Missing Hammer Head'. We are told 'she was the best student in her class. She took it as a challenge to beat all the men in the class. In the end she took a first class degree. In business she has been no less aggressive' (1994: 23).

Okechukwu on her part makes an effort to grapple with the politics of deception, acts of vandalism, terrorism, corruption, and manipulation that attend modern warfare. This is a validation of the assertion that contemporary African female writers are currently exploring issues beyond the plight of women. Thus 'Ike and Pitakwa Ladies', focuses on the excesses of a young civil servant whose promotion was misguided, being as it was an aftermath of the massive destruction fomented by the war. The innumerable deaths substantially affect the number of well-qualified men, so the civil service must make do with whatever is left. Adopting the myth which labels most Pitakwa girls 'ghosts', Okechukwu sets about making a caricature of Ike as he goes about bent on gratifying 'his appetite for these legendary girls'(65).

Within the nation's civil service corruption is so rife that an engineer 'was rumored to have put down on his list of expenses an item which he called 'Man no be wood' (1999: 66). Thus Okechukwu stylistically resorts to ironic humour, to satirize what she considers absurd or ludicrous developments in the society.

Similar to Ezeigbo's war story we detect a condemnation of Afulenu's immoral tendencies in 'Happy Survival'. Her boyfriend Maaka worked with 'Caritas, an organization that brought relief popularly known as Kwashiorkor food' (1999: 60). Out of desperation for self-preservation and survival, Afulenu obtains from her lover some of the free food meant for the starving masses, this she cooks, to sell to the public. As if this is not deplorable enough, she allows herself to be blackmailed into sleeping with Dr. Oli, who demands sex in return for helping her to terminate an unplanned pregnancy. Oli's concupiscence here parallels Ndubisi Ohaeri's in Ezeigbo's 'The War's Untold Story'. Both writers clearly condemn such excesses, the offending war situation notwithstanding.

'Ndende' and 'Ifeguluonye or Whatever Pleases One' further afford avenues through which Okechukwu probes more deeply into the female experience in a war situation. Typically, as in the other stories, we are regaled with distressing images of the pogrom in Obigbo. The story of Ndende reminds one of Achebe's 'The Madman'. Also called Ndende, the protagonist is a harmless but demented woman who considers herself sane, since her activities do not differ from those of the so-called sane ones in the society. Paradoxically, it is the sane ones who engage in a war forcing Ndende to sing a grief-stricken song in plea for an end to the war.

The irrationality of the senseless war is again pronounced when Ndende too, like the pregnant woman, her new born twins and countless other people become victim of a situation they neither wished for nor understood.

It has been our aim in this paper to locate the texts in focus within the dialogic framework of the now well acclaimed womanist ideology. That African womanism strives to maintain a balance between the inner female reality and the sociological determinants has clearly been underscored by our texts. In depicting the female, we recognize that like the earlier African female writers, the newer ones still feel the need to re-visit issues of the position of, and the so-called powerlessness of the women.

We see for instance that in virtually every war story by a Nigerian female, the absence of the man always necessitates the enthronement of the woman. Okechukwu's graphic rendition in 'Ifeguluonye' comes to mind here. True, the actions of the protagonist by the end of the story suggest degrees of abnormality, yet she displays an aptness in taking over the chores of a man. Womanism strongly makes the point that women in Africa certainly are not as incapable as some men would have us believe.

That the concept of womanism is accommodating, far embracing and not separatist is equally obvious. This validates Kolawole's 1997 assertion that 'its cultural and geographical relativism is wholesome'. Our study also authenticates its culture-based claim of seeking the survival and progress of whole peoples irrespective of gender.

Ezeigbo, in particular, attempts to dismantle stereotypes which confine women within positions of reliance or submergence. Consciously, therefore, her texts reveal the quest for more veracious representation of the female who would transcend these diverse but nonetheless adverse limitations. Okechukwu's approach signifies the adoption of a maternal role. Boldly stepping into the acclaimed image of the African female as 'Mother', she becomes the ventriloquist. In re-enacting stories of the war about three decades after it was fought, she aims to warn her crisis-laden nation about the dangers of fighting yet another war.

It is clear, therefore, that Ezeigbo and Okechukwu as up-and-coming writers on the Nigerian literary scene are bent on making their voices heard. They prove through their works that the African female writer is not always (as Kolawole asserts) 'preoccupied with woman-centered epistemology to the exclusion of other considerations' (1997:87). That is to say that they are propitiously involved in the challenges of societal reformation.

NOTES

1. See Chikwenye Okonjo Ogunyemi's *Africa Wo/Man Palava*. Chicago: The University of Chicago Press, p. 121.
2. Obioma Nnaemeka raises this point in her introduction to *Sisterhood, Feminisms and Power: From Africa to the Diaspora*, ed. Obioma Nnaemeka. Trenton: N.J.: Africa World Press, 1998, p. 11.
3. See Chioma Opara's 'Making Hay on Sunny Grounds', which is her introduction to *Beyond the Marginal Land: Gender Perspectives in African Writing*, ed. Chioma Opara. Port-Harcourt: Beltop (Nig). Co., 1999.
4. In the same introduction Opara makes reference to Ogunyemi's earlier paper on Womanism and attempts to make distinctions.
5. Article by Clenora Hudson-Weems in *Sisterhood, Feminisms and Power: From Africa to the Diaspora*, ed. Obioma Nnaemeka, (ibid).
6. Grace Okafor in 'Rewriting Popular Myths of Female Subordination: Selected Stories by Theodora Akachi Ezeigbo and May Ifeoma Nwoye' in *Writing African Women: Gender, Popular Culture and Literatures in West Africa*, ed. Stephanie Newell. London: Zed Books Ltd., 1997, p. 81–94.

WORKS CITED

Adebayo, Aduke (ed.) *Feminism and Black Women's Creative Writing*. Ibadan: AMD Publishers, 1996.

Adimora-Ezeigbo, Akachi. *Echoes in the Mind*. Lagos: Vista Books (1994) 1999 Rpt.

Akande, Dorcas Mofoluwake. 'The Socio-Political and Intellectual Milieu of the Female in Nigeria'. *Journal of Cultural Studies*. Vol.1, No.1 (1999).

Chukukere, Gloria. *Gender Voices and Choices: Redefining Women in Contemporary African Fiction*. Enugu: Fourth Dimension Publishing Co. Ltd, 1995.

Davies, Carole Boyce and Anne Adams Graves (eds) *Ngambika: Studies of Women in African Literature*. Trenton, NJ: Africa World Press, 1986.

Egejuru, A. Phanuel and Ketu H. Katrak (eds) *Nwanyibu: Womanbeing and African Literature*. Trenton, NJ: Africa World Press, 1997.

Ezeigbo, Theodora Akachi 'Gender Conflict in Flora Nwapa's Novels'. In Stephanie Newell (ed.) *Writing African Women: Gender, Popular Culture and Literature in West Africa*. London: Zed Books Ltd, 1997.

Gwamma, O. Okechukwu, Chinwe. 'When Rain Beat the Cow in the Eyes', 1999. Review in *Jenda: A Journal of Culture and African Women Studies*, 2001.

Kolawole, Mary E. Modupe. *Womanism and African Consciousness*. Trenton, N.J: Africa World Press, 1997.

—— (ed.) *Gender Perceptions and Development in Africa: A Socio-Cultural Approach*. Lagos: Arrabon Academic Publishers, 1998.

—— 'Self-Representation and the Dynamics of Culture and Power in African Women's Writing', in *Journal of Cultural Studies*. Vol.1, No.1 (1999).

Newell, Stephanie (ed.) *Writing African Women: Gender, Popular Culture and Literatures in West Africa*. London: Zed Books Ltd, 1997.

Njoku, Adaure. *Withstand the Storm*. Ibadan, Heinemann, 1986.

Nnaemeka, Obioma. 'Development, Cultural Forces, and Women's Achievements in Africa'. *Law and Policy*, Vol. 18, Nos 3&4, July/October (1996).

—— (ed.) *Sisterhood, Feminisms and Power: From Africa to the Diaspora*. Trenton, NJ: Africa World Press, 1998.

Nnolim, Charles E. 'African Feminism: The Scandalous Path'. In Chioma Opara (ed.) *Beyond The Marginal Land: Gender Perspectives in African Writing*. Port-Harcourt: Belpot (Nig.) Co. 1999.

Ogunyemi, Okonjo Chikwenye. *Africa Wo/Man Palava*. Chicago: The University of Chicago Press, 1996.

Okafor, Grace. 'Rewriting Popular Myths of Female Subordination: Selected Stories by Theodora Akachi Ezeigbo and May Ifeoma Nwoye'. In *Writing African Women: Gender, Popular Culture and Literatures in Africa* Stephanie Newell (ed.) London: Zed Books Ltd, 1997 pp. 81–94.

Okechukwu, Chinwe. *When Rain Beat the Cow in the Eyes*. Rockville, Maryland: Eagle and Palm, 1999.

Opara, Chioma (ed.) *Beyond the Marginal Land: Gender Perspectives in African Writing*. Port-Harcourt: Belpot (Nig.) Co., 1999.

Calixthe Beyala Rebels Against Female Oppression

Tunde Fatunde

One of the salient features of francophone African literature towards the end of the twentieth century was the emergence of female writers. The period between 1988 and 1995 witnessed the proliferation of creative writing by women whose major preoccupation was to highlight the plight of women. It also saw their various attempts to create a new and non-oppressive enabling environment in which they could resolve their problems.

Calixthe Beyala, a Cameroonian, is prominent among these emerging francophone female writers. Her works have attracted a lot of attention within academic circles and women's organisations especially in francophone communities in Africa, Europe and Canada. Amongst her colleagues, she remains one of the most prolific. She publishes a novel almost every year: *C'est le soleil qui m'a brûlée*, 1987; *Tu t'appeleras Tanga*, 1988; *Seul le diable le savait*, 1990; *Le petit prince de Belleville*, 1992; *Maman a un amant* 1993; *Assèze l'Africaine*, 1994; *Lettre d'une Africaine à ses soeurs occidentales*, 1995; *Les honneurs perdus*, 1996; *La petite fille du réverbère* 1998; *Amours sauvages*, 1999; *Lettre d'une Afro-française à ses compatriotes (vous aves dit racistes?)*, 2000; and *Comment cuisiner son mari à l'africaine*, 2000. The first three novels focus essentially on the plight of women in her country, Cameroon. Subsequent novels describe African women living in Belleville, a suburb of Paris, where poor African migrant families reside. In all her novels, the clash of cultures experienced by the main characters is a recurrent theme.

There are a number of reasons for the campaign against female oppression in the writings of Beyala and her francophone colleagues. Professor Aduke Adebayo, a leading critic of female francophone writers is of the opinion that,

> whether she lived in the bush or in the city, however, the African woman was and is still doubly oppressed. Firstly, she is oppressed by colonialism and neo-colonism like her male counterpart and, secondly, she is oppressed by the patriarchal arrangement whereby the women and the children belong to the minority group in the sense that they are denied some privileges and freedom,

which society normally allows for the dominant group. In this case, the dominant group is the male. It is this destiny of the subaltern, of the minority group, which becomes the focus of many francophone women's writings. (Adebayo, 2000: 281)

Without mincing words, Beyala further justifies her literary commitment towards defence of womanhood. In her words:

The African woman faces three types of battle. First, she has to struggle because she is a woman. Next, she has to assert herself as a black woman. Finally, she has to struggle for social integration. She is without doubt, the human being in the world with the greatest problems. And at the same time, she carries a lot of burden ... (*Amina*,1996: 11, my translation).

A true reflection of her determination to defend the female cause is manifest in her choice of characters. The major protagonists of her novels are young girls and women who do not belong to either middle or upper class society. Most of them would form an integral part of the poor in an urban setting in Africa or reside in a migrant workers' community such as Belleville. Some of her female characters are unemployable, uneducated, and abandoned. They are forced by social circumstances to make a living through prostitution. Ateba, nineteen years old, was abandoned by her mother, a prostitute, and left to fend for herself in an African ghetto, where the future was bleak. She was overwhelmed by poverty, the suffocating heat and sun (*Cest le soleil qui m'a brûlée* (*CMB*): 93). Through Ateba, one is informed about two other young girls, Irene and Ekassi, who have to make a living by selling their bodies to any man who comes their way (ibid.: 170).

An identical situation of teenage girls condemned to prostitution features prominently in Beyala's novel, *Tu t'appeleras Tanga* (*TTT*). Tanga was raped by her father when she was twelve years old. She was later abandoned by her mother and eventually plunged into prostitution. According to Tanga, 'I have slept on several beds, day after day, with men from several countries, of all colours, these men who pounded me were in search of their desired dream' (*TTT*: 160, my translation). Security agents raided the slum where she lived as a prostitute and almost raped her before she was sent to prison. Tanga eventually died in prison and her corpse was picked up by her mother.

The phenomenon of poverty-stricken female characters is also the theme in Beyala's *Seul le diable le savait* (*SDS*). Megrita, the main character, was born to a prostitute. Her mother, who married at the age of fifteen, was deserted by her father. According to Megrita: 'It was always necessary to make use of my body in order to survive ... all my life I have been a slave to fear.' (*SDS*: 122, my translation). Abandoned by her mother, Megrita who was earlier told by her mother that her father was either a white man by the name Alexandro Gomez or an African man, made up her mind to go in search of her father(s). During her quest, which took her from the African countryside to Paris, France, Megrita made a living as a sex worker. At one point, she gets married to a man known simply as a 'stranger', the marriage was shortlived, however, as her mother-in-law made sure it was scuttled.

Subsequent novels written as from 1992 till date still focus essentially on the lot of female African migrants living in Belleville. Eve-Marie, alias Mademoiselle Bonne Surprise, is an African and the main protagonist in Beyala's *Amours sauvages* (*AS*). Frustrated in Africa and dreaming of a better future, she smuggles herself into Belleville where she makes a living as a prostitute in a brothel owned by a Frenchman called Monsieur Trente Pour Cent (Mr 30 per cent). In the brothel, she meets a client, Plethore Gerbaud, who finally decides to marry her because of her 'sexual prowess'. Eve-Marie sends for her mother who lives in Cameroon. She finally arrives in France by passing through 'Mali via Niger and Nigeria, then through Morocco in a big truck and Spain by hiding under canvas covers' (*AS*: 25, my translation). With the arrival of her mother, Eve-Marie opens an African restaurant in Belleville where both herself and her husband jointly operate a new brothel.

In *Maman a un amant* (MAA), a married African woman, Madame Traore goes on summer holidays in the south of France with her husband, an immigrant worker living in Belleville. During the holidays, she falls in love with a Frenchman, Tichit, who is also on holiday. Traore reports the disappearance, of his wife to the police. She was eventually caught making love with Tichit. One of the policemen is not surprised about female infidelity. In his words: 'Oh yes my friend, one should say that you are lucky. As for me, I have never succeeded in catching my Juliet in the act and she ran away with her boyfriend and she demands from me a monthly feeding allowance of three thousand francs. Oh the bitches. And they are doing this thing right under your nose! What is the world turning into?' (*MAA*: 137, my translation).

Still on African female migrants, Beyala, in another novel *Comment cuisiner son mari à l'Africaine*, gives a graphic description of Miss Aissatou, who leaves Africa in search of an Eldorado in Belleville. She meets and falls in love with a Frenchman, Mr Bolobolo. Apart from sexual seduction, Aissatou goes the extra mile to straighten her hair and bleach her skin, all in the name of pleasing her breadwinner, Mr Bolobolo. In *Les honneurs perdus*, Beyala presents a group of African girls led by Saïda Bénérafa, who clandestinely arrive in France in search of greener pastures. These young girls have no other qualification than their bodies. And they end up as commercial sex workers.

Not all the female characters in Beyala's novels who are forced into prostitution accept their predicament passively. Many angrily reject prostitution. They attack, without hesitation, the patriarchal system, whose by-product is female subjugation. Despite the male control and obvious supervision of the oppressive patriarchal system, these female characters boldly point out that there are also women accomplices in the perpetration of female prostitution. Consequently, these characters equally condemn male and female executors of patriarchy, whose other by-products are polygamy and monogamy. Ateba, the heroine in *C'est le soleil qui m'a brûlée* points out to an important male character, Jean Zepp, her client, that the root of her problems is male oppression: 'For me you represent everything I hate about men, a mixture of arrogance, absurd vanity, serious and chaotic inanity – all these I hate' (*CMB*: 109, my translation). Beyala also suggests a complete dismantling of polygamy. Hear her:

> Polygamy must be banished entirely. No matter how intelligent a man may be, he should not have many wives. In my opinion, one is already too much. We should ask for the pill. Then free abortion. Men should not force us to make babies. Our bodies belong to us. (Translated by Adebayo: 289)

Western type monogamy is not, according to Beyala, any better than African polygamy. Bertha, a female character in *Seul le diable le savait* rejects monogamy which she likens to the permanent enslavement of the woman. 'You sign a pact of slavery. Carry water. Do the cooking. Do the ironing. Open your body to the male. Give your belly to maternity.' (Translated by Adebayo: 290). Beyala equally holds women responsible for female enslavement within the patriarchal system. Tanga who was forced into prostitution mainly because she was abandoned by her irresponsible mother, does not see why she should respect motherhood if it supports female exploitation. According to Tanga:

> I *destructure* my mother. It is an accident of birth. Madness to believe that blood links are indestructible. Stupid to think that belonging to a clan is a trademark. Like time, like the oracle, I am immobile despite my old mother's desire to guide my way in order to devour me better. (Translated by Adebayo: 289)

Beyala's solution to battered African womanhood lies in the absolute autonomy of the woman vis-a-vis the man. She is in favour of Simone de Beauvoir's theory of the complete independence of women as the most viable alternative to their oppression. Most of Beyala's characters desire freedom, happiness and prosperity outside all forms of marital arrangement with men. Her characters permanently distrust men. Even where there seems to be a successful matrimonial home, death comes in to destroy such an arrangement. Consequently, female separatism becomes the only viable option and remedy to female oppression. This is one of the cardinal principles of European feminism to which Beyala adheres. Beyala's brand of extreme European feminism is defined by Coquery-Vidrovitch, in the following terms: 'For the European feminist, it is the woman's right to demand her autonomy, her independence; to decide for herself, in her mind and conscience, in her capacity as a full-fledged individual; to exercise control over her body, her desires and aspirations' (Adebayo: 292). Here, one is tempted to declare that Beyala's preference for the extremist brand of European feminism is informed by the fact that she had been living, studying and writing in France since the age of seventeen. Although she claims to be a Cameroonian, her thought processes and her ideological perceptions of relationships between a man and a woman have largely been informed by Western feminism. One should quickly add here that it is her inalienable right to choose her ideological and philosophical options. However, extreme European feminism as a solution to female oppression in Africa has been rejected by the majority of African female writers and critics. Instead, they opt for what Chikwenye Ogunyemi calls *womanism*. 'Womanism is black-centred. It is accommodationist. It wants a meaningful union between black women and men and children, and will see to it that men will change from their sexist stand' (Nnolim 1999: 46).

In tackling the various dilemmas confronting women, Beyala proposes diverse and eclectic solutions. The latter comprises the individual-survivalist option and pseudo-metaphysical strategies. Nowhere in her writing do women come together and engage in collective action with a view to putting pressure on decision-makers for some reforms aimed at improving the lot of women. The metaphysical and individualist option is elaborated in her novel, *Assèze l'Africaine (AA)*. Two principal female characters in *AA* are cousins: Sorraya and Assèze. The latter had no father and was brought up by her mother and grandmother in the hinterland of Cameroon, a typical scenario in most of Beyala's novels. Awono, a civil servant who later becomes the boyfriend of Assèze's mother, takes over parental responsibilities for Assèze. Sorraya, Awono's biological daughter, does not like Assèze. Twice, Assèze and Sorraya fought over the same men: Ocean and Alexandre. All these incidents happened in Paris, where these characters emigrated in search for a better life. Neither of them succeeded in getting the attention of Ocean. And the love–hate affair continues between Assèze and Sorraya. The next boyfriend, Alexandre decides to marry Sorraya. Sorraya eventually dies from acute mental depression. And a few weeks later, Assèze marries Alexandre! This sets the stage for anguish and trauma for Assèze. She gets into an identical state of depression. To resolve her psychosis, she quickly embraces Christianity in a half-hearted manner. However, Assèze has a confused notion of God. In her words: 'This God is neither white not black nor African. He is like the birds, the trees, even the insects and lays claim to universal magnificence' (Debeaux 1996: 80, my translation). Assèze was not sure if she could get adequate assistance and eventual salvation through the Christian God. She does not perceive God as capable of solving human problems collectively. Her own salvation and not others is paramount to her. In another novel by Beyala, *La petite fille du réverbère* which is acclaimed by critics as an autobiographical piece, the same individualist and survival options, to the collective dilemma of woman, pervade the novel.

Two of Beyala's writings are epistolary in nature. They are: *Lettre d'une Afro-française à ses compatriotes* (letter from an African Frenchwoman to her compatriots) and *Lettre d'une Africaine à ses soeurs occidentales* (letter from an African woman to her European sisters). The epistolary genre 'is the principal source of information and facts about everyday lives of women and their own perceptions about themselves and their lives: in other words it is a source of both objective and subjective information just like the autobiography to which it serves as a complement.' (Adebayo: 280).

Beyala explores the epistolary mode of writing to express her personal views on issues related to both African and European women. She urges African women to be wary of those Europeans who openly claim that they are not racist. These Europeans would claim that they have liberal views on religion and proclaim their love for African culture and even go to the extent of wearing African attire. Beyala is of the opinion that some of these people in fact harbour racist tendencies. In a letter to her European colleagues, Beyala who has constantly advanced the idea that all men discriminate against women, warns the women not to put all men in the same basket. She is now convinced that some exceptional men indeed believe that women are their equal. However, she cautions the women to be on their guard because several centuries of discrimination against women cannot be wiped out overnight. Beyala calls upon the European women to assist in fighting for the liberation of African women from oppression in all its ramifications.

It is obvious that Beyala's major preoccupation in her writings is the graphic description and condemnation of female oppression in Africa and within African migrant communities in France. However, the socio-political situation of Africa does not escape her attention. Her characters freely comment upon the problems of the continent. A strong dose of Afro-pessimism is a common denominator in the comments made by these characters. For them, there is no solution on the horizon to the legion of problems confronting Africa. The state of mind of these characters is perhaps not surprising in the sense that none of them have envisaged collective social action to resolve their own individual problems. They criticize and lament Africa's neo-colonial situation, but they do not proffer any collective solution. In *Les honneurs perdus* (*HP*) the main protagonist, Saida Bénérafa could not hide her Afro-pessimism. In her words:

> In the tropics, thoughts melt quicker in the sun than a piece of chocolate. They disappear as fast as the twilight. The more one wants to think about the past the less one succeeds. The heat, the exigencies of existence like eating, sleeping without disturbance from colonies of mosquitoes or eating vegetables devoid of parasites – these are the problems! (*HP*: 68, my translation)

Assèze, a neurotic female character, in *Assèze l'Africaine* laments her lot as an African:

> I represent Africa whose survival is highly compromised. I was born in a developing environment. I live in a disappearing environment. I am not neurotic. No

psychological problem. My anguish is elsewhere, towards Africa undergoing rapid decadence and she sees herself only through the shades of her own ruins. (Debeaux, 1996: 80, my translation)

Afro-pessimism, expressed by some of Beyala's characters could, to some extent, be justified. Forty years ago, a Cameroonian writer, Ferdinand Oyono wrote a popular novel, *Chemin d'Europe*, in which the main character looked towards Europe as a model of development from which the African continent could derive positive inspiration. Forty years later another Cameroonian, Calixthe Beyala depicted the same Africa where her citizens are doing everything possible to escape from the continent with a view to settling in Europe as a more viable alternative!

A close study and analysis of Beyala's feminist discourse reveals that it is broadly provocative, raw and 'pornographic'. Most of her novels are filled with erotic scenes in which the male and female reproductive organs are described in crude and uncouth language. Beyala describes how Ekassi, a prostitute in *C'est le soleil qui m'a brûlée*, submits herself to men who derive pleasure from sexual intercourse, 'The belly offered itself, welcomed their stupid manhood; then poured out their useless sperm into the empty space where she retired. She submitted herself to all desires but held her belly in absence' (Translated by Adebayo: 290–91). An identical pornographic discourse was present in the feelings of Tanga, the prostitute in *Tu t'appeleras Tanga*. 'I brought my body to the bed under his muscles. He was snoring, the man continues to snore. I was not feeling anything. Unknown to me, my body tranformed itself into a body made of stone' (*TTT*: 30–31, my translation).

Magri, a sex worker, depicts in *Seul le diable le savait* (*SDS*) how one of her clients, Jean-Pierre, makes love to her: 'He fucks me like a cock or like a guinea fowl. Small fast and dry strokes ... once he pours out his desire, he gratifies me with only one kiss on my lips, he rolls away and sleeps off, satisfied that he made love. And what about my own pleasure?' (*SDS*, pp. 9–10, my translation). Assèze describes men as carrying their sex organ in their brain. And she exclaims 'All women are prostitutes of men' (*AA*: 126, my translation). Justifying her use of obscene language to describe sexual intercourse between a man and a woman, Beyala strongly believes, in absolute terms, that, 'anywhere a woman associates with a man, she is always enslaved' (*Amina* 1996: 16, my translation). Pornographic realism?

Born in Douala, Cameroon, in 1961, Calixthe Beyala is the sixth in a family of twelve children and is mother of two children. Some of her novels have won prestigious prizes. *Assèze l'Africaine* won two prizes: Prix François Mauriac de l'Academie Française and Prix Tropiques. *Maman a un amant* won the Grand Prix Littéraire de l'Afrique noire. *La petite fille du réverbère* obtained the Grand Prix de l'UNICEF and *Les honneurs perdus* the Grand Prix du Roman de l'Academie Française.

In spite of her enormous success, Beyala has been enmeshed in controversial 'scandals'. A high court in Paris found her guilty of plagiarism. She was accused of lifting several passages from a novel, *La vie devant soi*, written by Romain Gary and she incorporated these passages into her novel, *Le petit prince de Belleville*. The second case of plagiarism was raised by Paule Constant, the author of *White Spirit* who also accused Beyala of copying several passages from his book and integrating them into *Assèze l'Africaine* which won two prestigious prizes. Another prize-winning novel by Beyala, *Les honneurs perdus*, came under attack. The French publishers of *La route de la faim* (*The Famished Road*) written by Nigeria's Ben Okri accused Calixthe of incorporating 'verbatim', passages from Okri's novel into *Les honneurs perdus*. She has consistently denied these charges.

On the social front, Calixthe has been involved in the defence of women's rights and those of African immigrants residing in France. At the first international conference of Francophone Women which took place in Luxembourg on 4–5 February 2000 she campaigned vigorously for international support for women who are victims of AIDS. And the secretary-general of Francophonie, Egyptian Boutros-Ghali, threw his weight behind Calixthe's campaign. She is the current president of a pressure group based in Paris and made up of African artistes and intellectuals. The group, known as *Collectif Egalité*, has been in the forefront, amongst other things, of the campaign for an increase in the number of Africans presenting news and current affairs on French television.

WORKS CITED

Adebayo, Aduke. 'Feminism in francophone African literature: from liberalism to militancy'. In Olusola Oke and Sam Ade Ojo (eds) *Introduction to Francophone African Literature* Ibadan: Spectrum Books, 2000.
Beyala, Calixthe. *C'est le soleil qui m'a brûlée*. Paris: Stock, 1987.
—— *Tu t'appeleras Tanga*. Paris: Stock, 1988.
—— *Seul le diable le savait*. Paris: Le Pré aux Clercs, 1990.
—— *Maman a un amant*. Paris: Albin Michel, 1993
—— *Assèze l'Africaine*. Paris: Albin Michel, 1994
—— *Lettre d'une Africaine à ses soeurs occidentales*. Paris: Spengler, 1995.
—— *Les honneurs perdus*. Paris: Albin Michel, 1996.
—— *La petite fille du réverbère*. Paris: Albin Michel, 1998.
—— *Amours sauvages*. Paris: Albin Michel, 1999.
—— *Lettre d'une Afro-française à ses compatriotes (vous avez dit racistes?)*. Paris: Mango, 2000.
—— *Comment cuisiner son mari à l'Africaine*. Paris: Albin Michel, 2000
Debeaux, Genevieve. Cinq ans de littératures 1991–1995. *Notre Librairie*. 125 (Janvier–Mars 1996): 90.
Nnolim, Charles. 'African feminism: The scandalous path'. In Chioma Opara (ed.) *Beyond the Marginal Land. Gender Perspective in African Writing*. Port Harcourt: Belpot, 1999.

MAGAZINE CITED

Amina (11 Rue de Téhéran, Paris), August 1996.

Ken Bugul's
Le Baobab fou:
A Female Story About a Female Body

Ada Uzoamaka Azodo

> There can be no clear-cut separation between sexuality, history, economics, and politics in texts that are written about women's lives in a postcolonial context, where some flexible gender ideologies have been replaced by less flexible ones, and where power relations have shifted drastically and have put women in more disadvantaged conditions. An important point is that these texts are not 'duplicating,' 'reflecting,' or 'writing back' to radical feminist critiques on sexuality. They are creating a space for themselves by questioning a combination of oppressive conditions that are both traditional and specific to their colonial heritage and postcolonial context, a context that posits their protest beyond the limits of radical feminism.
>
> (Juliana Makuchi Nfah-Abbenyi 1997: 30)

Many African traditional societies permit a non-distinctive, genderless subject pronoun, which in turn 'allows a more flexible semantic system, in which it is possible for men and women to share attributes. This system of few linguistic distinctions between male and female gender also make it possible for men and women to play some social roles, which in some other cultures, especially those of the Western world, carry rigid sex and gender association' (Amadiume 1995 (1987): 28). Amadiume was speaking specifically about Igbo matriarchy in Nigeria in *African Matriarchal Traditions: The Case of Igbo Societies*, but we believe the same can be extended to many African cultures, including the ethnic groups of Senegal, one of which, Wolof, forms the subject of this article. In an earlier, well-known text, *Male Daughters and Female Husbands* (1987),[1] Amadiume asserts that gender relations and sexuality are not given phenomena, out of reach of human agency, nor are they *a priori* drives uninfluenced by social conventions. They are not part of our nature, that is to say, naturalistic. Rather, posits Amadiume, gender and sexuality belong to the constantly shifting world of social practices and cultural meanings as individuals alter their sexual practices and mental constructions of erotic desire to suit the moment. Women can play roles normally played by men in Igbo cultures (Amadiume 1995 (1987): 29). Gender and sexuality, therefore, demand serious attention in the postmodern contemporary and global era as humanity marches forward in attempts to mainstream its minorities. As Roger N. Lancaster and Micaela di Leonardo put it: 'Metamorphosis in sexual and gender relations has always been inseparably linked to political, economic, and cultural changes' (1997: 1).

Ken Bugul's masterpiece, *The Abandoned Baobab*, the first of her three-part autobiographical trilogy, which includes *Ashes and Embers*, and *Riwan ou le chemin de sable*, provides an appropriate focus for examining and articulating gender and sexuality in written African literature.

Earlier, Florence Stratton, in *Contemporary African Literature and the Politics of Gender* (1994), articulated the effects of patriarchy and gender on the development of African literature. Speaking from the perspective of a woman writer, Stratton outlined at great length 'the features of an emerging female tradition of feminist discourse in African fiction', including leading traditionalist writers such as Ama Ata Aidoo, Grace Ogot, Flora Nwapa, and Buchi Emecheta. At the same time, Stratton challenged canonical males like Chinua Achebe, Ngugi wa Thiong'o and Wole Soyinka, whose gender biases had not been recognized. Stratton thus produced the first truly balanced picture of female/male literary tradition in African literature through the lens of gender and politics.

It is, however, in Juliana Makuchi Nfah-Abbenyi's *Gender in African Women's Writing: Identity, Sexuality, and Difference* (1997), an admixture of Western feminist and postcolonial theories, that we see gender treated as a category of analysis under colonialist tradition, with women as subjects and authors in literary texts. Both female characters and authors are radically brutalized by history, giving rise to individuals of multiple identities. That is what Trinh T. Minh-ha has referred to elsewhere as 'infinite layers' of identities, meaning women at once insiders and outsiders (1989: 94).[2] According to Nfah-Abbenyi, the politics of identity and gender-as-difference or as otherness thus becomes a struggle that involves the colonizer and the colonized, the dominator and the dominated, the actor and the victim, the First and the Third World (1997: 32), and the list continues.

It is through this lens that we hope to do the present study. We shall argue that Ken Bugul constructs gender and sexuality as two terms in flux in the context of other identities and other situations and circumstances in a postcolonial (read neo-colonial) era. The goal is to contest the reduction of all the complexities of the postcolonial or postmodern African (read human) sexual destinies and practices to what Judith Butler has termed normative and regulatory 'performativity' (Jackson and Jones 1998: 137–40). We ask the following pertinent questions: Does femininity equate simply as attractiveness to men? Does sexual conquest of women confirm femininity? Is sexual difference essential to sexual desire? Is heterosexuality, what Tamsin Wilton refers to as 'heteropolarity', normal and homosexuality abnormal? Is sexuality a pre-given drive or essence that is 'repressed' or controlled by social forces? If sexuality is a pre-given drive, how then do we account for cultural and historical variations in sexuality, like bisexual, lesbian, and gay sexualities?[3] It is by seeking answers to these questions that we shall explore Ken Bugul's search for her fragmented Self and the Other in *The Abandoned Baobab*.

•••

How do we explore gender and sexuality in *The Abandoned Baobab* without first finding our way through the tremendous variations of feminist theories on the topic in the postmodern period? We have no choice but to go with those thinkers whose ideas and thoughts are anti-essentialist. They are also those whose thinking is akin to Amadiume's presentation of gender and sexuality in traditional (read pre-colonial) Africa.

According to essentialists, specifically erstwhile biologist, Ann Oakely, and Gayle Rubin, who later became a student of the psychologist Michel Foucault – gender and sexuality are variables existing *a priori*. We mean to say that gender and sexuality are not fixed by nature. They are not in the social and cultural structures, discourses and practices that give rise to the term. On the other hand, femininity and masculinity vary according to historical and cultural variables. (Jackson and Jones 1998: 133). For example, the term 'woman' means different things to different people at different times and cuts across differences of class and race.[4]

By way of digression and illustration, among the traditional Igbo, whom we have cited earlier in reference to Amadiume's phenomenal work, a man who has not achieved as expected is seen as an *agbala*, that means 'a woman' (Achebe 1958).

The materialist feminist view on gender and sexuality is akin to Oakely and Rubin's revised views; it sees a hierarchical structure that emphasizes inequality, exploitation, and class (patriarchy) in a way that recalls Marxist views. Accordingly, the existence of the bourgeoisie gives rise to the working class or the proletariat. For materialist Monique Witting, 'there are no slaves without masters' (1992: 15). Every society arranges males and females for heterosexual purposes and for marriage and kinship. A French *avant garde* grouped around the Questions Féministes (QF) in 1970, including other materialists, such as Christine Delphy, Colette Guillaumin and Nicole-Claude Mathieu (see Adkins and Leonard 1996), hold a radical view and refuse any notion of 'woman' that is not related to social context. They see sex as a social construction, just as gender is a social construction (Delphy 1984: 144). In 1993, Delphy concludes that 'woman' is also a social construction.

These feminists, although radical in their outlook, take an anti-essentialist view of gender and sexuality, arguing that the terms 'woman' and 'man' are not there *a priori*. On the other hand, they believe, 'man' and 'woman' are social categories in relationship with one another that have no pre-social biological basis or essence. It is in their anti-essentialist view of gender and sexuality that materialists are similar to postmodernist feminist thinkers and are particularly useful for our project.

Postmodernist feminists, led by Judith Butler, therefore take an anti-essentialist view of gender and sexuality. But, rather than emphasize structural relations like the materialists, they focus on cultural explanations, which discursively construct categories of 'men' and 'women'. The same kind of questioning of the gender divide as in Delphy can also be seen in Judith Butler, who questions the binary of two genders. If gender does not follow from sex, then how do we arrive at only two genders for the multitude of human beings on earth, asks Butler in *Gender Trouble* (1990: 6).

> The presumption of a binary gender system implicitly retains the belief in a mimetic relation of gender to sex whereby gender mimics sex or is otherwise restricted by it. (Butler 1990: 6)

Butler deconstructs sex, saying that sex is culturally constructed, just as gender. She analyses the 'heterosexual notions' that tie sex and gender into normative heterosexuality. This idea had found its variant in Queer Studies, where gay political and theoretical priorities deem the binary division of humanity into male and female genders as oppressive to gays and lesbians and women (Butler 1990: 113; Jackson 1998: 141). Gender, argues Butler, is 'regulatory fiction,' constructed through discursive and non-discursive practices, meaning that the body is not pre-given to any sex. On the other hand, bodies are rendered intelligible through gender. (Butler 1990: 8) Gender is not a part of our inner essence. Rather, gender is 'performative'. 'To be feminine,' says Butler 'is to perform femininity... A drag Queen only performs at being feminine. Nothing is in his essence, for the Drag de-naturalizes gender, takes apart its performative elements and displays the functionality of their coherence and reveals the imitative structure of gender itself' (Butler 1990: 137).

What Butler means here is the practice of 'naming', 'pronouncing' or 'citing' past practices, referring to existing conventions, reiterating known norms (Jackson and Jones 1998: 137), as we have seen with the Igbo societies that Amadiume studied. Butler's perspective is postmodern, seeing 'woman' as a construct, with no reality or unity prior to discourse. What can we say about Igbo societies? Are they traditional and post-modern at the same time? One thing is clear; Butler's view is similar to the traditional African notion of gender as a fluid construct, a phenomenon in a flux that changes meaning according to circumstance.

Another postmodernist feminist, Denise Riley, also sees women as 'erratic, inconstant, but also as a fluctuating identity' and a 'volatile collectivity' (1988: 1–2). This category of 'women' is exclusionary; but, at the same time, it also destabilizes other identities such as 'black', 'lesbian', etc. Some feminists (Fuss 1991; Spivak and Rooney 1994) resist the so-called postmodern 'risk' of essentialism, in the sense that treating women as disembodied sets of cultural categories tends to dilute and do away with the reality of women's experiences (Brodribb 1992).

In this study of gender and sexuality in Ken Bugul's *Abandoned Baobab* we find that there is no risk of losing sight of women's experiences. Indeed, feminism and postmodernism cross each other's paths, for they have a common denominator; the exploration of new ways of narrating subjectivity. The protagonist, Ken Bugul, is a hybrid on the margin, neither quite African nor European, but at the border of both, hence her difference, adherence to multiple cultures, languages and backgrounds or origins. With her area of influence blurred and her perceived nationality not clearly defined – thinking she was French and white, having been taught by French colonialists back in Senegal that her ancestors were the Gauls and still in denial as to her identity with the abhorrent Toto that she read so much about in the elementary school readers – Ken Bugul's writing becomes 'hybrid writing'. Lidia Curtis, who earlier used this term, explains:

> Hybrid selves are translated into hybrid writing, moving on the border between memory and fantasy, fable and history, tradition and innovation: standing between essay and fiction, poetry and prose. (Curtis 1998: xi)

In exploring Ken Bugul's search for self-identity in her seminal autobiographical work, *The Abandoned Baobab*, we shall at the same time examine notions of gender and sexuality in the novel.

•••

Ken Bugul could be said to have a somewhat national identity, for after all she is Senegalese. But, her 'French-Senegalese' hyphenated nationality is peculiar. Ken was always aware of that, for she leaves home in Senegal to journey to Europe, her other home, in search of the Golden Fleece and a better understanding of herself and her destiny. In Europe, she discovers that her so-called 'ancestors, the Gauls' do not recognize her, nor does she find a cultural identity with the white Belgians in whose country she has a scholarship to pursue secretarial studies. When she leaves 'home' in Senegal, Africa, and journeys to Belgium to start a new life, in what she thinks will be 'home' away from home, we already have the makings of a botched adventure in a postcolonial era. She has imbibed the ways of a Western culture that holds her in contempt. At the same time, she is distanced from her traditional culture that she despises or holds in turn in contempt.

Thanks to problems of race, class and gender, the author-narrator feels dislocated from herself and her roots. As far as her writing goes, we have a mutual reflection of the narrator's body and writing on each other, what Lidia Curtis calls 'a journey of diegetic transgressions – genre, gender, style, languages' (1998: xii).

The Abandoned Baobab is thus a mixture of a mythical tale or an epic.

It is a tale, but a different kind of narrative that is the autobiographical story. The book begins with a preamble, a fabulous tale about the 'Pre-History of Ken,' in which African civilization from the pre-colonial to colonial times is related. A pacific period gives way to a violent period caused by a destructive fire that consumes all, except the baobab tree in the middle of the village. Thanks to the arrival of a stranger, the lost civilization is renewed around the baobab tree. Traces of modernity in the form of railway tracks and factory products, such as shoes, conveyed by trains are evident everywhere. The 'History of Ken,' again a mythical-cum-romanticized tale of beginnings in Africa, links the heroine to a mysterious old man, the only one who survived the conflagration. He is an ageless and immortal man described as mad, *'fou'* from whom Ken is descended. This old man gave the book its title, according to the author's explanation to this writer in a recent interview. Thereafter, the author-narrator narrates her journey to Europe aboard an Air France jet and her subsequent experiences as a village girl from Louga, Senegal, in a strange culture abroad. The rest of the plot of the autobiographical text qualifies the book to be called a novel.

When Ken Bugul arrives in Brussels, observes Walker, it is her exotic body that Western culture wants for consumption (1999: 173). In the brothels, men relate to the black girl, 24–25 years old, only in terms of her sex and gender, as a commodity fit for consumption. Notice the effect of 'naming', for the moment Ken Bugul was named 'black' and 'exotic' she begins to 'perform' (Butler 1993) the role put on her. She becomes a tropical exotic fruit fit for consumption. White people, surprised at her haughty attitude at the beginning, would quickly remind her that she was black and young, adding that with those two attributes she could do nothing else but sell her body. Was she in Brussels to study? No one cared.

In *'New' Exoticisms: Changing Patterns in the Construction of Otherness*, edited by Isabel Santaolalla (2000: 82), Satendra Nandan explores the notion of paradise and examines the exotic and erotic moment when this notion of paradise becomes embedded in the psyche of the colonial masters and their peoples. Citing the example of the South Pacific Fiji islanders, Nandan posits that the so-called paradise was hell for those natives, whereas for their European colonialists and their peoples back home a non-existent was romanticized. The lands of the 'foreign' and 'strange' people were violated and appropriated.[5]

Similarly, Ken Bugul, the protagonist of *The Abandoned Baobab*, is violently uprooted from her African base, and becomes a drifting, lost body, bearing the scars of her history. Her only companions are alienation and exile, as she searches in vain for a place to anchor her emotions, a home away from home. She turns into a 'ware' for men, and would latch onto just any man who showed the least understanding towards her. In short, her sex and gender become objects of exploitation in Western society.

Dislocation soon leads to melancholia, and the narrator-author undergoes a kind of schizophrenia. As Keith Walker put it:

> It is, in fact, Ken's need to share affection that entangles her in social/commer-
> cial/sexual relations of all varieties: modeling, nude photography, 'playing
> hostess' in night clubs and saunas, *ménage à trois*, heterosexuality, bisexuality,
> and a lesbian relationship. (1999: 201)

Ken Bugul, the narrator is, however, unwaveringly lucid about her
ambiguity. She goes through a crisis of identity and a feeling of alienation,
pain and loss that push her over into drugs, debauchery, melancholy and
feelings of worthlessness and even contemplation of suicide. She engages
both in hetero- and homosexual expressions of her erotic desires, not
knowing for sure her identity. Was she a human being? Was she an animal?
Was she human and animalistic at one and the same time? She did not know.
No one cared to know. Ken Bugul was eternally searching for answers.

According to Sigmund Freud in *Three Essays on the Theory of
Sexuality* (1905: 145n) 'Psychoanalytic research has found that all human
beings are capable of making a homosexual object-choice and have in fact
made one in their unconscious' (Dean and Lane 2001: 93). Dean and Lane
rejoin that Freud has 'universalizing' rather than 'minoritizing' ideas
about homosexuality, since he believed that homosexuality was everywhere and in the psyche of the most 'normal and presentable individuals'
(ibid).[6] Taking Freud's statements as a springboard, Tim Dean and
Christopher Lane then argue today in this manner:

> If we accept that everybody has made a homosexual object-choice in his or her
> unconscious, then it is homophobia, the irrational fear of same-sex desire –
> including one's *own* same-sex desire – that generates internal strife and thus
> neurosis. (2001: 4)

One could say that Ken Bugul has a problem, if one sees heterosexuality
as a normal behavior, where homosexuality is seen as abnormal. But how
justifiable would such a viewpoint be, in view of the foregoing assertions
by Freud, Dean and Lane?

In New York, a group of gay and lesbian physicians in *Disorienting
Sexuality: Psychoanalytic Reappraisals of Sexual Identities* joined forces
to challenge the normalizing impulses in contemporary clinical theory
and practice with a goal to demystifying negative attitudes towards same-
sex desire. They argue that perhaps it is heterosexuality that constitutes a
deviancy, since all human beings have their 'anima' and 'animus' sides
(Domenici and Lesser 1995).

In literary circles, Ken Bugul, the author, has been hailed as a rising
star, for becoming the voice of a new generation of women who speak up
about their views, including their views on gender and sexuality. In
Okapi, a magazine edited by Billy Elliot a twelve-year old bourgeois
child, Jean-Yves Dana adopts the author Ken Bugul as his model of a
famous person (*Special Issue*, January 2000: 3), citing her statement on

her life's travails as his motivation: '*J'ai fait de ma vie un roman*' ('I turned my life into a novel'). To him, Ken Bugul had amply demonstrated that it was all right to be different from the majority. A little further down the page, he expatiates on his views, citing Ken Bugul's life passion as '*se battre contre les idées reçues sur la femme africaine*' ('to combat fixed ideas about African women'). And Ken Bugul speaks up against all facets of oppression against women.

In *The Abandoned Baobab*, dreams of self-destruction plague Ken Bugul in Europe, partly because of racism, and partly because of her ambiguous sexuality. And, dreams of self-destruction should always be taken seriously. Ken's particular suicidal feelings arise from patriarchal abuse and the abuse of 'a black girl' in Europe in the 1970s. She feels lost and throws herself at all and everyone that comes her way. We have already said this. Ken's progress or degeneration, from assimilation, alienation and dilemma, is similar to what Aimé Césaire has called 'dementia praecox', an early insanity that announces schizophrenia (Walker 1999: 200). The situation gets worse in Brussels as Ken undergoes psychological self-analysis. She states, reinforcing what we have said earlier, namely that sexuality is subject to shifting history, economics, politics and cultures:

> And it suited me. The despair of living led everywhere. Why hadn't they foreseen the Black Woman's reaction to neo-colonialism?
> One must absorb the muteness of the drives that partly ensure equilibrium, the blossoming of the defined self. (*Baobab*: 96–7).[7]

> *Et cela m'arrangeait. Le désespoir de vivre menait à tout. Pourquoi n'avoir pas prévu la réaction de la femme noire au néocolonialisme?*
> *Contenir la soudeur des pulsions qui assurent en partie l'équilibre, l'épanouissement du soi défini.* (113)

Disadvantaged and feeling worthless, thanks to her black skin and loneliness, Ken resorts to one-night stands that do nothing to bring her comfort. She sells her body, since experimenting with all the various kinds of sexualities have no effect on her symptoms.

It is at that point in time that Ken emerges as a maternal figure for bisexual lover, Jean Wermer. She nurses him as he is ill with contagious hepatitis B. She kisses him and sleeps with him, even when his own family would visit and not approach him for fear of contracting the disease. It is during all her travails in Europe that Ken arrives at the magnificent insight that historical and cultural events also shape sexuality: She states that sexuality is culture and atmosphere:

> In every exodus there is a change in the sets of values. (51)
> *Dans tout exode, il y a altération de l'échelle des valeurs.* (65)

Ken Bugul develops a penchant for the suffering soul, bourgeois or commoner. The more 'abandoned' people appear, like her, the more she is drawn towards them. The lost souls of the 1970s count among them the hippies, beatniks, not to mention women of Africa whose problems she has first-hand knowledge of from personal experience working in prisons, brothels, family planning clinics and other non-governmental organizations.

Psychoanalysis is thus an inevitable part of the exploration of the story of wandering among postcolonial subjects, especially those who journey from Africa to Europe. Ken's journey from her hometown in Louga, Senegal, to Brussels can be seen as a journey into otherness, into solitude, madness and death. Julia Kristeva's exploitation of depression, hysteria and women's melancholic sexuality in *Black Sun* (1989) is very pertinent here.

In Europe, Ken dies to her self and to her original culture, because she is separated from it and ill-adapted to the new culture. Death in this instance is certainly not clinical death, but rather a kind of rite of passage. As the author explained to this writer in the interview referred to earlier, there are always women in Africa, who are not able to escape their worries, and so fake madness as an escape mechanism, like Mon Dioum a fatalistic character in her fourth novel, *La Folie et la Mort*. Death could also be contrived to be lassitude, this obsessive desire to return to the mother's womb and be reborn. The author explained that Mon Dioum's obsession for rebirth is also Ken Bugul's obsession, seen in the autobiographical trilogy, less so in the fourth political novel.[8] The obsessional wish to die and be reborn is a surrealist desire to reenact the 'Phoenix act': die and rise from one's own ashes. Even suicide, from this angle of vision, can be an elevating phenomenon that is not final, that constitutes an escape to a new beginning. As Ken Bugul put it at the height of her depression:

> I had reached the final stage where only suicide was left, pure and simple. Without any analysis. (155–6)

> J'étais à l'ultime étape où il n'y avait plus que le suicide pur et simple. Sans analyse. (178)

A little later again, she adds:

> My consciousness of everything that had happened to me so far away from the village where I was born made me pray to God to let me be born again as if almost a quarter of a century hadn't happened. (157)

> La conscience de tout ce qui m'était arrivé si loin du village où je suis née, me faisait prier Dieu de me faire renaître, comme si presque un quart de siècle de tourment n'avait jamais été. (180)

Ken's predicament or 'madness' could be interpreted as a case of cultural schizophrenia, arising from confused notions of her identity, race, gender and sexuality. As she progressively lost hope of redemption, she blamed her fate or destiny for her ordeal, and so she contemplated death as an escape to rebirth. Her hope for her self and for Africa is the only thing that stops her taking her life. As it turns out, her 'return' to 'her native land' (Aimé Césaire) performed the magic. She was cured as she rediscovered what she had abandoned, namely her true identity as an African and, for that matter, as a Senegalese. For as Jean Wermer tells her:

> You know, I think you ought to go home, back to your country, get some distance. You're young, intelligent, and profoundly African, you'll be all right, but time goes on. You should do something about it very soon. (158)

> Tu sais, je pense que tu devrais aller dans ton pays, prendre du recul; tu es jeune, intelligente, profondément Africaine, tu t'en sortiras, mais le temps passe. Il faut que tu fasse rapidement quelque chose. (180)

As the assimilationist self, 'a lost childhood that had flown away one afternoon, the first time I (Ken) ever saw a white man' (158), eventually finds again the lost nativist self, which 'had made a date with the baobab tree' and had not shown up and did not alert it, hence causing it to die. Ken Bugul regains her equilibrium back in Senegal (Walker 1999).

•••

We have attempted to think critically about gender and sexuality as primary categories of human identity, especially as told in Ken Bugul's *The Abandoned Baobab*. If we understand the 'abandoned baobab' as the author-narrator, one of the newer voices in the second wave of African feminism – Calixthe Beyala is another one in the same vein – we see at once how in a postmodern era of shifting boundaries and transnational navigation of subjects, both terms make meaning only in the context of shifting and evolving histories and cultural and social practices. Evidently, writers and theorists continue to challenge and reinforce ideas about the differences and similarities between men and women.

We have explored the contributions of Ifi Amadiume, Monique Witting, and Judith Butler among others. An enduring question in Africa, however, is whether men and women think differently about gender. A second enduring question is whether literary representations of class, race, gender, sexuality and nationality are different from the everyday world. A third enduring question is whether homosexuality is a psychiatric disorder, a rebellion, and by extension, whether heterosexuality is normal? Do they not both represent shades of normal human sexuality? As Sigmund Freud put it, again in *Three Essays on Sexuality*, 'the conclusion now presents itself to us that there is indeed something innate lying behind the perversions, but that it is something innate in *everyone*' (Freud 1905: 171; original emphasis). By arguing that human sexuality is a drive that is separate and distinct from natural functions, Freud defines it as unnatural, *contra naturem*, posit Dean and Lane. In effect, Freud 'queers' all sexuality, maintain the two illustrious authors (Dean and Lane 2001: 5).

In the end, the question is no more resolved than when we started. But, that is a positive sign, namely that human beings will continue to make progress through dialogue. The idea is certainly not to come to a resolution, but rather to prolong the questioning, the assertions, and the interrogations, in order that the subject of discussion becomes clearer and clearer. A facet of Mikhail Bakhtin's dialogic asserts that dialogue continues only when one answer gives rise to a new question. It aptly illustrates Chinua Achebe's view, taken from the Igbo world view, which states that when one thing stands, it is beneficial to stand another thing beside it. Third and lastly, according to John Stuart Mill:

> The only way in which a human being can make some approach to knowing the whole of a subject is by hearing what can be said about it by persons of every variety of opinion and studying all modes in which it can be looked at by every character of mind. No wise man (and woman!) ever acquired his (her!) wisdom in any mode but this (qtd. in Williams, 1999: 9, and Egendorf 2000: 9).

Ken Bugul's *The Abandoned Baobab* certainly provides a new alternative voice on issues of race, gender and sexuality in African literature.

NOTES

1. Amadiume states:
   'Two examples of situations in which women played roles ideally or normally occupied by men, that is, what I have called male roles, in indigenous Nnobi society, for example, were 'male daughters', daughters who have been accorded the status of sons to enable them to continue their father's line of descent, and 'female husbands', women who married other women. In either role, women acted as family heads. The Igbo word for family head is the genderless expression *di-bu-no*. The genderless *di* is a prefix word, which means specialist in or expert at or master of something. Therefore, *dibuno* means one in a master relationship to a household and those who live in the house. As this word is genderless, a woman in this position is referred to as *dibuno* in the same term as a man in this position would be called. A husband was simply *di*, that is, one in a master relationship to others, whereas in English, because of rigid gender construction, a female head would be referred to as mistress and a male head as a master. In indigenous Nnobi society and culture, there was one head or master of a household at a time, and 'male daughters' and 'female husbands' were called by the same term, whose English translation would be master. Some women were therefore masters to other people, who included men and women' (1995 (1987: 29).

2. Trinh T. Minh-ha, *Woman, Native, Other: Writing Postcoloniality and Feminism*. Bloomington: Indiana University Press, 1989, p. 94. See also Trinh T. Minh-ha, 'Not You/ Like You: Postcolonial Women and the Interlocking Questions of Identity and Difference,' in Anne Mcclintock, Aamir Mufti, and Ella Shohat (eds) *Dangerous Liaisons: Gender, Nation & Postcolonial Perspectives*. Minneapolis and London: University of Minnesota Press, 1998, pp. 415–19.

3. Stevi Jackson, 'Theorising Gender and Sexuality', in Stevi Jackson and Jackie Jones (eds) *Contemporary Feminist Theories*, 1998, pp. 141–3.

4. According to biologists, Ann Oakley and Gayle Rubin, the binary of masculinity and femininity that presently constructs the world's contemporary societies are heterosexist and male-dominated (Jackson and Jones 1998: 133). Contemporary feminist ideology combats this biologist thinking, striving to keep sex, gender, and sexuality apart. In 'The Traffic in Women: Notes on the Political Economy of Sex' (1975: 165), Rubin takes up the baton from Oakley, relating gender to reproductive sexuality. Later in 1984 (179), however, Rubin revised her sex/gender system by stating that 'gender is socially imposed division of the

sexes' and a 'product of the social relations of sexuality' (1975: 179).

5. Nandan, states in Isabel Santaolalla's *'New' Exoticisms: Changing Patterns in the Construction of Otherness*, 2000: 82:

> These [reconstructions of European classical illusions in foreign lands] symbolized the very fate of modern man: shipwrecked and stranded, yet dreaming of a rescue by a fair maiden, or at least with her on an island... But the encounter was erotic as well as exotic...

6. Tim Dean and Christopher Lane, 'Homosexuality and Psychoanalysis: An Introduction,' p. 4. See also Sigmund Freud, *Three Essays on the Theory of Sexuality. Standard*, 7: 123–243, 1905.

7. In a later novel, *La Folie et la Mort* (Madness and Death), Ken Bugul talks about female characters, like Mon Dioum, who are traded for sex to men by a male pornographer. In brothels, women are made to appear and disappear like mirages to entice men. Later, accused of having killed Mori, who has in fact been killed by the agents of the father of the nation, Timoni, Mon Dioum chooses to feign madness, in order to escape social injustice.

8. It is also noteworthy that in *La Folie et la Mort*, the fourth novel, all the female characters become crazy, are violated by men, including religious men, and are eventually killed, in what seems like a politically orchestrated elimination of women. It is clear how sex, gender, and sexuality issues can easily have enormous social and political repercussions.

WORKS CITED

Achebe, Chinua. *Things Fall Apart*. London: Heinemann, 1958.

Adkins, Lisa and Diana Leonard (eds). *Sex in Question: French Materialist Feminism*. London: Taylor and Francis, 1996.

Amadiume, Ifi. *Male Daughters, Female Husbands: Gender and Sex in an African Society*. London: Zed Books, 1987.

—— *African Matriarchal Traditions: The Case of Igbo Societies*, Trenton, NJ: Red Sea Press, 1995 (London: Karnak House,1987).

Appiah, Anthony Kwame. 'Is the Post- in Postcolonial the Post- in Postmodern?' In Anne McClintock, Aamir Mufti and Ella Shohat (eds) *Dangerous Liaisons: Gender, Nation and Postcolonial Perspectives*. Minneapolis and London, The University of Minnesota Press, 1998.

Bâ, Mariama. *Une si longue lettre*. Dakar: Les Nouvelles Éditions de Dakar, (NEA), 1980.

—— *So Long a Letter*, translated from the French by Modupé Bodé-Thomas. Portsmouth, N.H.: Heinemann, 1989.

Beyala, Calixthe. *The Sun Hath Looked Upon Me*. Paris: Éditions Stocks, 1987.

—— *Your Name Shall Be Tanga*. Paris: Éditions Stocks, 1998.

—— *Loukoum, the Small Prince of Belleville*. Paris: Éditions Stocks, 1992.

Brodribb, Somer. *Nothing Mat(t)ers: A Feminist Critique of Postmodernism*. Melbourne: Spinifex, 1992.

Bugul, Ken. *Le Baobab fou*. Dakar: Les Nouvelles Éditions Africaines, 1983.

—— *The Abandoned Baobab*, translated from the French by Marjolijn de Jager. Chicago: Lawrence Hill Books, 1991.

—— *Cendres et Braises*. Paris: L'Harmattan, 1994.

—— *Riwan, ou le chemin de sable* (Grand Prix littéraire de l'Afrique Noire 1999, ex aequo de l'ADELF, Association des Écrivains de Langue Française), Paris: Présence Africaine, 1999.

—— *La Folie et la Mort*. Paris: Présence Africaine, 2000.

—— Interview, 'J'ai fait de ma vie un roman'. *Okapi*, Special Issue, January 2000.

Butler, Judith. *Gender Trouble: Feminism and the Subversion of Identity*. New York: Routledge, 1990.

—— *Bodies that Matter*. New York, Routledge, 1993.

—— 'Against Proper Objects'. *Differences*, 6 (2/3) 1994: 1–26.

Curtis, Lidia. *Female Stories, Female Bodies: Narrative, Identity and Representation*. New York: New York University Press, 1998.

Dean, Tim and Christopher, Lane (eds). *Homosexuality: Psychoanalysis*. Chicago and London: The University of Chicago Press, 2001.

Delphy, Christiane. *Close to Home: A Materialist Analysis of Women's Oppression*. London:

Hutchinson, 1984.

—— Delphy, Christiane and Diana Leonard. *Familiar Exploitation: A New Analysis of Marriage in Western Societies*. Oxford: Polity, 1992.

—— 'Rethinking Sex and Gender'. *Women's Studies International Forum*, 16, (1) 1993: 1–9.

—— 'The Invention of French Feminism: an essential move'. *Yale French Studies*, 87, 1995: 190–221.

Domenici, Thomas and Ronnie C. Lesser (eds). *Disorienting Sexuality: Psychoanalytic Reappraisals of Sexual* Identities. New York: Routledge, 1995.

Egendorf, Laura K. (ed.) *Male/Female Roles* (Opposing Viewpoints). San Diego: Greenhaven Press, 2000.

Foucault, Michel. *The History of Sexuality: Volume One*. Harmondsworth: Penguin, 1981.

Freud, Sigmund. *Three Essays on the Theory of Sexuality, Standard* 7 1905: 123–243.

Fuss, Dana (ed.) *Inside/Out Lesbian Theories, Gay Theories*. New York: Routledge, 1991.

Gagnon, John and William Simon. *Sexual Conduct*. London: Hutchinson, 1974.

Hayes, Jarrod. *Queer Nations: Marginal Sexualities in the Maghreb*. Chicago and London: The University of Chicago Press, 2000.

Jackson, Stevi. 'Gender and Heterosexuality: a materialist feminist analysis'. In M. Maynard and J. Purvis (eds) *(Hetero) Sexual Politics*. London: Taylor and Francis, 1985.

—— *Christine Delphy*. London: Sage, 1996.

—— *Concerning Heterosexuality*. London: Sage, 1998.

—— 'The amazing deconstructing woman: the perils of postmodern feminism'. *Trouble and Strife*, 25 1992: 25–311.

Jackson, Stevi. 'Theorizing Gender and Sexuality'. In Stevi Jackson, and Jackie Jones (eds) *Contemporary Feminist Theories*. New York: New York University Press, 1998.

Jackson, Stevi, and Jackie Jones (eds). *Contemporary Feminist Theories*. New York: New York University Press, 1998.

Kristeva, Julia. *Black Sun – Depression and Melancholia*, translated from the French by Leon S. Roudiez. New York: Columbia University Press, 1989.

Lancaster, Roger N. and Micaela di Leonardo (eds). *The Gender Sexuality Reader: Culture, History, Political Economy*. New York and London: Routledge, 1997.

Nfah-Abbenyi, Juliana Makuchi. *Gender in African Women's Writing: Identity, Sexuality, and Difference*. Bloomington and Indianapolis: Indiana University Press, 1997.

Nnaemeka, Obioma. 'Contre la clôture: espace et architecture de la liberté chez Mariama Bâ'. In Ada Uzoamaka Azodo (ed.) *Emerging Perspectives on Mariama Bâ*. Trenton, N.J.: Africa World Press, 2003 (forthcoming).

McClintock, Anne, Aamir Mufti and Ella Shohat (eds). *Dangerous Liaisons: Gender, Nation, and Postcolonial Perspectives*. Minneapolis and London: University of Minnesota Press, 1997.

Oakley, Ann. *Sex, Gender and Society*. Oxford: Martin Robertson (reprinted in 1984 by Blackwell), 1972.

Price, Janet and Maigrit Shildrick. *Feminist Theory and the Body: A Reader*. New York: Routledge, 1999.

Questions Féministes Collective, 'Variations on a common theme'. In E. Marks and I. de Courtivron (eds), *New French Feminisms*. Brighton: Harvester Wheatsheaf, 1981.

Riley, Denise. *'Am I That Name'? Feminism and the Category of 'Women' in History*. London: Macmillan, 1988.

Rubin, Gayle. 'The Traffic in Women'. In R. Reiter (ed.) *Toward an Anthropology of Women*. New York: Monthly Review Press, 1975.

—— 'Thinking Sex: notes for a radical theory of the politics of sexuality'. In C. Vance (ed.) *Pleasure and Danger*. London, Routledge, 1984.

—— 'Sexual Traffic' (Interview with Judith Butler). *Differences*, 6 (2/3), 1994: 62–99.

Santaolalla, Isabel (ed.) *'New' Exoticisms: Changing Patterns in the Construction of Otherness*. Amsterdam, Atlanta: Rodopi, 2000.

Shildrick, Margrit and Price, Janet. *Feminist Theory and the Body: A Reader*. Edinburgh: Edinburgh University Press, 1999.

Spivak Gayatri, Chakravorty and Ellen Rooney. 'In a Word', interview in N. Schar and E. Weed (eds), *The Essential Difference*. Bloomington: Indiana University Press, 1994.

Stratton, Florence. *Contemporary African Literature and the Politics of Gender*. London and New York: Routledge, 1994.

Trinh T.-Min-ha. 'Not You/Like You: Postcolonial Women and the Interlocking Questions of Identity and Difference'. In Anne McClintock, Aamir Mufti and Ella Shohat (eds),

Dangerous Liaisons: Gender, Nation, and Postcolonial Perspectives. Minneapolis and London: University of Minnesota Press, 1997, 415–19.

—— *Woman, Native, Other: Writing Postcoloniality and Feminism.* Bloomington: Indiana University Press, 1989.

Walker, Keith L. *Countermodernism and Francophone Literary Culture: A Game of Slipshot.* Durham and London: Duke University Press, 1999.

Wiegman, Robyn, and Elena Glasberg. *Literature and Gender.* New York: Longman, 1999.

Williams, Mary E. (ed.) *Homosexuality* (Opposing Viewpoints). San Diego: Greenhaven Press, 1999.

Wilton, Tamsin. 'Which one's the man? The Heterosexualisation of Lesbian Sex'. In Diane Richardson (ed.) *Theorizing Heterosexuality: Telling it Straight.* Buckingham: Open University Press, 1996.

Witting, Monique. *The Straight Mind and Other Essays.* Hemel Hempstead: Harvester Wheatsheaf, 1992.

┌───┐
│ From Liminality to Centrality   │
│ Kekelwa Nyanya's *Hearthstones*:   │
│ A Case in Point   │
└───┘

Monica Bungaro

Feminists in Africa and in the rest of the world generally agree that the market in women's fiction is currently experiencing a boom. They strongly disagree, however, about the political value and significance of this boom and this touches the concerns of African women writers too. Should the publishing of novels by women writers be regarded positively as helping to promulgate and popularise feminist attitudes? Or does it represent, on the contrary, an example of the publishing industry cashing in on feminism and, in certain cases, conning readers into accepting 'feminist' novels which, in actual fact, are not? The boom is even more evident when one looks at the scenario of world literature written in English, which of course includes African literature, and which is nowadays registering an amazing blossoming of literary works by women. In spite of the fact that the growing demand among publishers for culturally diverse life (hi)stories indicates a recognition of plural realities and experiences as well as a diversification of inherited Eurocentric canons, often this demand takes the form of the search for more 'exotic' and 'different' stories in which individual women write as truth-tellers and authenticate their oppression.

In other words, the proliferation of Third World women's texts in the West at least, owes as much to the relations of the marketplace as to the conviction to 'testify' or 'bear witness'. Thus the existence of African women's narratives is not in itself evidence of decentring hegemonic histories and subjectivities and the recent upsurge of Third World women's writings should not to necessarily be read as a revival of feminist tendencies. One must first work out whether the message these works promote is feminist at all. It is the way in which these works are read, understood and located institutionally which is of paramount importance. After all, the point is not just to record one's history of struggle, or consciousness, but how it is recorded. The way we read, receive, and disseminate such imaginative records is also immensely significant.

Having said this, if the awards to African women writers[1] are a sign of the way things are at the turn of the century, then one can claim that there

91

is an ongoing battle for voice and that some men (publishers, critics, writers) are listening and responding to women.

Until very recently, African literature by women has been identified with a few authors who have succeeded in gaining recognition abroad, namely Nadine Gordimer, Ama Ata Aidoo, Buchi Emecheta and, to a lesser extent, Bessie Head and Flora Nwapa. These authors have received much attention inside and especially outside the continent, becoming the representatives of the female aesthetic and the cultural experiences from which they derive their inspiration. It is also true that, with the exception of Nadine Gordimer, not until the mid to late 1990s did extensive or book-length critical studies of a single African woman author appear on the literary scene.

Yet, much has still to been done, especially with regard to recent trends in literature and emerging new authors. From here, the necessity to explore texts from little-known or almost ignored women writers who have also been constructing a new, assertive image of woman, one which, by offering alternative female behavioural models, contributes to the ongoing debate about African womanhood.

Pioneering African women writers have questioned and attacked the neglect of their work through the ongoing exercise of the act of writing. They have slowly but surely used their writings as weapons to throw out their voices, to occupy spaces that have been male-dominated for too long. By so doing, they have made tangible gains along the way. African women, marginalised by gender and race (other differentials are also important such as class, ethnicity, religion, etc) from literary production have therefore battled against multiple forms of oppression in economically and politically unstable, male-oriented societies, where language, access to literary resources, literary standards and available publishing outlets have been Western, white and male-dominated. They have demanded their place at the pulpit and have given the spectrum of contemporary African writing a wider dimension.

This is a most welcome phenomenon primarily because it has filled the gender gap between male and female characterisation and shown the other side of the coin. Writing, in this sense, acts as a non-violent but effective weapon in counteracting the dominance of male mythologies; it is an act engaged not only in formulating alternatives but also in accurately recording what is, in fact, already there. The African woman writer is not only involved in making herself heard, in changing the architecture of male-centred ideologies and languages but in discovering new forms and languages to express her experience.

At the time when pioneering female writers were writing their novels it was necessary for them to reassess and rebalance wo/men's position in a society founded upon role expectations and social taboos. Since these writers were placed in the unique position of responding to the images of women created by men, they were highly concerned with faithful portrayals of their visions. Often departing from male fantasies and mono-lithic stereotypes, they have exploded myths about women through their realistic and in-depth exploration of their heroines' fictive lives.

Most novels by today's African women writers demonstrate an attitude which not only confirms the tendency established by their predecessors, as they are heirs to previous forms and concepts, but also a more radical way of tackling thorny issues. In the recent development of African women's literature symbolised by a new, younger generation of writers, feminine speech has become more aggressive, more insistent within an auto-representative mode that has become more and more complex. This is probably the result of women ascending the social ladder and strug-gling for their rights. The provocative appeal of today's female narratives from Africa is also more evident than ever before because, in the general atmosphere of open discussion and debate about delicate and controver-sial issues which characterises most African societies nowadays, women writers feel readier to expose themselves to both local and international readers in their determination to reveal painful truths, to name the disease, as a first step towards curing it. Rather than idealise womanhood in order to exonerate it, their narratives fascinate with their inherent con-tradictions as they reveal strength and weakness, beauty and ugliness, ambiguity and clarity, in unfolding the politics of oppression.

Like their predecessors, younger women writers, are bringing not only their points of view but lived experiences as women to their writing. Their lives still bear testimony to the glaring inequality between men and women that easier access to education, to qualified jobs, and the discovery of alternative ways of being, such as single mother, divorced or career woman, have not yet corrected.

While the first generation of writers was engaged in talking back to its male counterpart as a result of its late arrival on the scene and the perceived urgency to correct inappropriate and stereotypical images of women as created by male authors, the younger generation today seem to have moved beyond that stage and underline other priorities.

Stages in the development of female writing can be recognised which trace a movement from self-discovery and self-awareness to experimenta-tion on both thematic and narrative levels. Over the last decade in fact, there has been the appearance of more complex writings that not only explore in explicit language cultural, social, political and sexual zones that until recently have been taboos (divorce, career, abortion) but also search for bold alternatives with no sign of regret or fear of societal punishment.

On the thematic level, the novels of the 1990s are not limited to pointing an accusing finger at the aftermath of colonialism or simply at patriarchy in all its subtle or overt manifestations. Recent African women's novels often preserve traces of the engagement that has long been a force in African literature. Their works are still novels of protest and contestation but their authors' voices seem more openly rebellious, directly engaged and markedly visible in both themes and expression. Up to the early 1980s, the female protagonist had spoken in a biographical or semi-autobiographical mode: speech bore witness to her difficulties, particularly the suffering she experienced as part of a couple, part of a polygamous social structure and confronted with the issue of sterility.

Today, the process of rebellion has been infused within a larger systematic provocation, which is itself articulated on two levels: language and/or theme. As far as language is concerned, in the general climate of relativity that characterises African societies, emerging African women writers are experimenting, in a number of intriguing ways, with notions of provisionality and with a heterogeneity of narrative techniques. The thematic level is in turn articulated in two movements: first, through the choice of female protagonists who are marginal in relation to their societies, through addressing and problematising socio-cultural-sexual areas which are of paramount importance today (abortion, infanticide, career, high-level education, man-woman cooperation, mother-daughter relations); second, through reflection on the hidden mechanisms that explain the increasing instabilities of contemporary Africa, through a search for alternatives to socio-political and economic questions about a stagnant postcolonial Africa.

The other recognisable stage is the shift in focus from the concern with the image of women in African literature to women's self-representation through formal innovations and other strategies aimed at expressing the intersection of gender, racial, class, cultural, economic and political oppression.

'New' African voices all share the common trait of confirming both African woman's self-appropriation of speech and writing and the new visibility of the feminine African novel and its determination in treating urgent social questions. The emphasis on personal and emotional relationships and the questioning of the masculinist legacy of their societies are accompanied by the exposure of the socio-economic and political malaise which characterises most African societies today.

Being an African woman writer today means being fully involved in both the struggle for the freedom and fulfilment of African people in the face of racism, neo-colonialism and oppression and the struggle by women against social, cultural and political marginalisation. This double-sided battle reflects African women writers' attempt to venture beyond the conventionally established confines ascribed to women's literature (romance, love, drama) and emblematises the way in which the categories of public and private break down in African women's discourse.

Although the reclamation of suffering is still the beginning of women's literature, the new generation of African women writers is going beyond reclaiming suffering to its re-investment. These female writers who, like their predecessors, are struggling to articulate a personal vision and to

verbalise other areas of feminine experience that have remained unex-
pressed, if not repressed, for long, are engaged in an attempt to excavate
those elements of the female self which have been buried under the
cultural and patriarchal myth of selfhood. Women's marginal position
often becomes a space of strength within and between which they
fluctuate, as the act of dissecting reality makes them no longer just
'outsiders within', but also 'insiders-within'. This is often clearly seen, for
instance, when their fiction is informed by historical and socio-economic
actuality. The very simultaneity of being both the subject (the known)
and the object (the knowledge) of women's studies means that everything
is personal as well as political, that it is not possible to dissociate oneself
from what one encounters. Social and private life are seen as integrally
related: the exploration of history and character, of external and internal
worlds becomes entirely indivisible.

Kekelwa Nyanya's *Hearthstones* (1995) is an illustration of the fact that
areas of life such as sexual relations, marriage, childcare and domestic
violence, previously regarded as purely personal in import, have increasingly come to be examined for the larger meaning in the culture's
treatment of women. By taking a microcosmic unit of society and using it
as a spy-hole into a wide network of social, cultural and political structures, she demonstrates the political import of private spheres of being
and, by transcending the limitations of subjectivism, she shows that the
answers to big questions about life cannot only come from women as individuals but also from a whole people. In other words, she realises,
together with other African women writers, that the personal is always
located within heterogeneous discursive processes. It is never a given
intact identity, but always polarised along interconnected lines.

Nyanya is an emerging writer from Zambia, currently living in Jordan
with her family. Like a great deal of contemporary material, written and
published locally, her work is almost unknown to critics outside the
country of production. *Hearthstones,* her first and only novel, touches on
a number of issues which other writers before her had already examined:
female bonding, education, gender relations, racism. In reality, as Nyanya
is fruitfully engaged in the description and unveiling of the problematic
nature of female experience in a changing world, the vision of life incorporated in the text has broader horizons. The text in fact intersects with
several other needs and contexts, that is, with the more intimate realities
of women as women and with larger historical facts of existence in a
world mediated by other worlds.

Nyanya's interweaving of three life stories is thus further complicated
by the exploration of the dilemmas of Africans in contact with Europeans
in their own countries, (but also elsewhere), of poverty, economic and
political instability and ignorance, of living in Africa after the euphoria of
independence and of the difficulty in finding a path out of the quagmire
of neo-colonialism and imperialism. All these perspectives cohabit in the

narrative with the three protagonists' telling of their personal experiences, providing the novel not only with a historical context and background, but also with a fresh insight into the various facets of heightened tensions which have characterised Africa in the decades before and after independence, up to today.

If this interdependency of the local and the global, the private and the public, marks the first departure from more common tales of woman-centred experience based on the psychological evolution of the character in an alien/oppressive environment, the second break-point from more traditional ways of telling is reached through dialogical writing, that is, through the integration of multiple heterogeneous voices. *Hearthstones* therefore does not give in to the monological temptation. There is no omniscient narrator with its fictional authority used to impose a single reading with only one meaning. The narrative eschews a fictionalised third person protagonist, opting instead for first person narrators, each telling their stories in turn and each inserting that same story into the wider context of the societies they live in. In this sense, they are both internal narrators and protagonists of the stories they tell.

The novel covers a large span of time in the lives of Chifuya, Tengani and Likande, from the days of their childhood to maturity and adulthood. These are meticulously recollected and reconstructed by the protagonists in an effort to look into their own past and see how far they have gone. The recollection and rebuilding of memories and episodes is therefore an intentional act aimed at revisioning one's own life and experience in the light of a newly acquired sense of the self and of the community. Self-reflection in the form of memories functions to clarify the past and bring about a new understanding, a self-awareness. What is even more peculiar in the novel is the fact that the flow of memories is not simply artificially constructed, (as it is in most women's works) as simply a narrative device to go backwards in time to events which have to be necessarily regained little by little in order to give sense to the story itself. The self-reflection strategy here is an exigency that the three protagonists share and on which they totally agree. It is 'an agreement' they have consciously made with one another while sitting in the 'large and screened verandah of Chifuya's ranch',[2] ten long years after their last reunion. The novel starts from this point, in time, that is the present: Chifuya is a doctor at the University Teaching Hospital in Lusaka, she is married to a lawyer and has two sons; Tengani is a politician engaged in the battle for women's liberation and Likande is a happy wife and mother of a girl.

From now on, each chapter is focused on the protagonists' reconstruction of past events and bears the name of the female character whose story is about to be told. Chifuya is the one who starts off her trip into storytelling by going back to her family history. The reader learns from the start that Chifuya's father, a miner, believes in the power of education to climb up the social ladder, whereas her mother cannot understand this obsession with education. Like many African women, Chifuya's mother wants her daughter to go through the same rituals of puberty she has experienced in her village. Her expectations of her daughter do not go beyond her duties as a would-be wife and mother. Conversely, her father is the one who encourages Chifuya to pursue her dream of becoming a doctor and with this thought in mind he sends her away to Chipembi Girls' missionary school. It is here that Chifuya meets and makes friends with Tengani and Likande. Paradoxically, Nyanya shows that the main enemies to women's self-realisation are sometimes women themselves for they function as accomplices to the very structure other women are trying to deconstruct in order to emerge from the margins and give sense to their lives. A role reversal is operating here with Chifuya's father supporting her struggle for education and her mother putting up obstacles to her social and cultural advancement.

Tengani, defined by her friends as a trouble-maker, tells her family history of pain and sorrow, love and death: her mother was killed by white mounted policemen fighting the production of illegal home brew; her mother's cousin, Mandarena, now her stepmother, mistreats her; her brother, a freedom fighter, with whom she lives for a while, ends up in prison; her caring father enrols her in Chipembi girls' boarding school. From the very start, Tengani shows a deep interest in the cause of national freedom and liberation from the British rulers and more generally, in the battle against political and economic exploitation.

It is in the descriptive passages about Tengani that the authorial voice of the writer takes hold of the narrative and reveals itself, even though it pretends it is the voice of Tengani, the one we hear. No shift in voice (still first-person narration) and focalisation (still internal) is in fact signalled. Nyanya's reflections and considerations on the state of things in her country soon after independence start flowing through the narrative. Her act of detecting and digging out problems and consequently, their causes and long-term effects, responds to her eagerness to bring the reader to see what African reality is and what needs to be done to better it. Nyanya's preoccupations revolve around both the salvation of women and the salvation of her whole people. She highlights that though gender is still a stigmatising marker in African societies, poverty, lack of job opportunities, political instability and class divisions all contribute to affect women's lives. Her nationalism and feminism are inscribed as two sides of the same coin, as Tengani's remark clearly demonstrates: 'After all, it was said that to educate a man is to educate an individual, but to educate a woman is to educate a whole nation. I was therefore at the centre of making history' (106). Nyanya thus desires to bring opposites such as the domestic and the social, the public and the private, the individual and the collective, together where the survival of the nation is conditional on the survival of the woman and the community. The personal and the communal thus converge through politics. From this angle of vision,

Nyanya joins the rank of other colleagues of hers, like Ama Ata Aidoo, and many South African female writers, who are generally considered more overtly political in their commitment, and of some male writers as well, who have, at one time or another, stated that there can be no liberation of Africa without the liberation of women and who hold that the tyranny of gender roles hampers women's political, social and economic contributions in Africa. Nyanya's articulation of feminism is shaped by the awareness that the committed writer is concerned not only with promoting the cause of women on the continent, but also with building the nation, the continent.

During school times, Likande was fascinated by her defiant friend Tengani, her fascination with her deriving not only from Tengani's external do-not-care attitude, under which, according to Likande, 'there was a soft and vulnerable spot' (46), but from her friend's commitment to a cause, a mission in life. If her peers see Likande as a role model for her leadership qualities and her dedication to her studies, she instead sees herself insecure and anxious about her future. Tengani's project of improving women's, and more generally a whole people's, predicament is seen by Likande as a way of combining both personal and communal fulfilment. The nature of Tengani's 'revolutionary' mission also gives her the psychological freedom to transcend parental expectations and cultural constraints as her militant attitude is seen by everybody as the only possible reaction to the status quo. Likande, on the other hand, is torn between her parents' expectations and desires and her own idea of self-fulfilment as a social worker. Initially meeting the expectations of her parents, she goes to university until one day she is offered the opportunity to go to college in Florida. After taking her degree in history, Likande comes back home and, against her mother's will, takes up teaching in Lusaka. Her mother wants her to apply for a teaching job in their hometown where her father could help her but Likande instead wants to find her own job somewhere else and live her own life, because she says: 'I needed space to work things out for myself' (157). She then starts working as a senior buyer for an industrial company and meets Musa to whom she gets engaged. It is at this point that another clash between mother and daughter is represented in the novel. Likande's mother wants her daughter to follow tradition, that is, Musa has to meet the family and make arrangements for bride-price. Likande's reaction to her mother's attachment to traditional rules and conventions calls attention to the generation gap informing their relationship, as the daughter's defiant words clearly demonstrate: 'Bride-price? I couldn't believe it! I wrote an angry letter to my mother telling her that I was not for sale and that there would be no bride-price for me. Her response was, either we did as tradition demanded or we could go ahead and get married in your own way. But do not expect to see us at the wedding. She added a postscript to the letter in which she said "just because I had been to America didn't mean that I should forsake our traditions"' (168).

Likande's questioning of those situations that potentially construct and position women as objects of exchange with no status as subjects casts light on the realisation that gender discrimination is only one dimension of the struggle for identity and self-definition, the others existing alongside gender, may be called women's self-colonisation. Western education has indeed made it possible for Likande to conceive of marriage, and generally of her life, in very individualistic terms. It has taught her the ability to effectively cut herself off and dissociate from the traditional practices which still inform her community. However, the re-entry into her mother's world cannot but affect her personal decisions if she wants to keep any ties with her family. Musa's final bending to custom and tradition is an obligatory act to keep Likande's family quiet but it also functions here as an act of reconciliation with not only his would-be wife's family but also with the community at large, whose approval still has its significance for the educated individual. Musa proves a loving and considerate husband, especially when Likande starts getting involved in voluntary work before she becomes pregnant. Unlike Chifuya's husband, Musa accepts Likande's triple role as wife, mother and career woman and helps her out by cooperating in the house-running and the child-caring. Nyanya here cleverly rejects 'male-bashing' as a form of compensation or self-reward for female marginalisation. Rather, she highlights that gender conflicts in African societies cannot be solved by simply inverting the binary logic which informs gender roles in an effort to move men into the margins and place women at the 'centre'. This is why she is unwilling to confine both men and women into frozen, pre-packaged behavioural codes which would lead to further conflicts and misconceptions. If 'bad men' seem to be the norm against which women must fight, 'good men', like Musa, and Likande's father, also exist and do represent a growth in gender awareness.

Gender-lined divisions are also clearly represented in the way girls at a very early age are confronted with masculine and feminine notions of identity. Chifuya wants to take up Latin and leave French out as Latin is more useful for studying medicine but her teacher ridicules her for wanting to become a doctor as that profession is not considered a female activity: 'If I were you, I would stop dreaming about the impossible and plan to be either a teacher or a secretary. Those are the kinds of jobs available for African girls these days. Who knows, things might change.' (56)

Despite her teacher's forecasts, Chifuya succeeds in becoming a doctor. However, she immediately finds out how difficult it is to be a female medical doctor, as 'not only were my male colleagues sceptical and con-descending toward me, but patients felt they had 'a really good doctor' only if it was a man. A Zambian female doctor was a rare commodity, and at first many patients called me 'nurse' or 'sister' (59). Nyanya points out here that myths about masculine traits and privileges are still in operation in African societies and tend to be an entitlement to social areas which are considered male preserves, with the consequent exclusion of women. The passages about Chifuya's work at the hospital are beautifully written and like many other passages in the novel reveal the author's intention to construct female characters who, by being forceful and articulate, excel in roles other than the ones conventionally ascribed to them, (such as that of daughter, wife, mother, mistress) and can therefore be appreciated as individuals and not as types. Furthermore, these passages highlight her insights into the problematic of gender in African societies, where the urgency to solve political, economic and cultural instabilities may contribute to the erasure of gender differences in the name of a communal struggle, of both men and women, against any form of exploitation and oppression.

If the workplace is shown to be a terrain of male–female confrontation, marriage is represented as by far the primary battlefront between the sexes. Zelani, Chifuya's husband, is despotic and chauvinistic in his insistence on his wife leaving her job to take care of the house and their new-born child. Furious battles between husband and wife start taking place, but Chifuya defends her position fully convinced of her right to juggle her career and her duties as wife and mother. Chifuya succeeds in a career which was previously a male preserve and does not fall into the trap of predetermined gender/role hierarchies that aim at constructing and positioning women at the bottom of power structures. She in fact refuses to give up her job to meet the expectations of her husband and tries to work out individual solutions to juggle her life. Chifuya's capacity to think about issues centred on her career and marriage and her ability to make choices for herself represent her strength.

Nyanya here explicitly attacks and subverts entrenched hegemonies within African society and by focusing on the educated woman she grounds and problematises the materiality of women's construction of subjecthood and agency in fast-changing contexts. Resented by his wife's independent spirit and resistance, Zelani starts sleeping around and being abusive and domineering at home. The cultural norms operating within Chifuya's society nearly force her to endorse the inhumanity of the gender ideology as a biologically and culturally inescapable fact. She starts thinking about leaving her job and tries to be more committed to her marriage for her baby's sake. Though psychologically conditioned by the popular concepts of 'true femininity', Zelani's attempt at shaping her identity and womanhood through motherhood and in the shadow of his manhood, wealth and power, fails miserably before Chifuya's refusal to be victimised.

The double quarrel about which Nyanya speaks is clearly delineated through the dichotomies – gender on the one hand and society on the other – that her representation of women brings across. Western education has, on the surface, put these three women in advantageous social and class positions, but they are still plagued by their gender and socially constructed gender roles. Nyanya points out that it is only through the acquisition of hyphenated selves and bifurcated consciousnesses that female characters might be able to navigate between their professional selves and their gender roles and responsibilities. She shows how Chifuya, Tengani and Likande re-think this double quarrel and make themselves an intrinsic part of such inquiry, especially through subjecting themselves to self-analysing practice.

It is this act of self-reflection and self-analysis which brings Chifuya to finally divorce her husband and fight him for the custody of their daughter. She therefore proves militant if one considers the power of her self-awareness and the challenge to patriarchy posed by the very act of rebelling against stifling and oppressive constructions of African womanhood in her society. Her militancy is even more evident when one considers that she initiates legal divorce, despite the stigma attached to divorced women in many African societies, thereby indicating that she values herself as a human being and not as an object for the gratification of the male ego. In *Hearthstones*, the woman who finds the courage to rebel against multiple forms of oppression is likely to be rewarded in the end. Chifuya's reward eventually comes when she marries her lawyer, who proves to be a patient and trustworthy man.

As for Tengani, she joins the Women's Brigade, a group involved in organising and mobilising African women. A year after independence (1964), Tengani moves to Lusaka, because it was 'the centre of things, where all the action was' (105). From that moment on, Tengani starts making speeches around the continent until she finally wins the election for the Women's Committee with a resounding victory. Her gender concerns however never take over more general, and just as important issues, like 'preventing the widening gap between the haves and have-nots and creating a truly equal society based on the principle of humanism' (106). Tengani's radical and rebellious attitude towards any form of discrimination and oppression against women becomes evident when she realises that the women actually speaking in the conferences she attends, are, like her, the educated and wealthy. She starts feeling inadequate in their presence for, as she puts it: 'it was a question of us and them, or the haves and have-nots'. In the realisation of her privileged position as 'elite woman' and her intention to help other less fortunate women to speak for themselves lies her credible commitment to the cause of women's liberation. Though Tengani's vision of things may sound utopian at times, she nonetheless demands attention as a character as she asks questions about women's position in society and their socially assigned roles, bearing testimony to the cost of the struggle to change fundamental gender-relationships and socio-economic inequalities.

Like Chifuya's love story, Tengani's relationship with Sifanu is subjected to cultural and moral sources of man's authority. Falling back on myths of femininity and womanhood which construct the African woman as subservient or docile, Sifanu cannot cope with what he considers a 'too independent, too emancipated, too intimidating' woman (115). The educated, autonomous, self-reliant woman is thus shown to be a threat to men, as within or outside marriage she seems to challenge the cultural ideal of submissive womanhood.

Nyanya seems to imply here that even if society is undergoing drastic changes, there will always be some men who will act as if nothing has changed. She also infers that the requirement of a change in mentality lies both on the shoulders of men and women.

Through the portrayals of Tengani, Chifuya and Likande, Nyanya seems to point out that if one's commitment has been maturing over the years, then of course, one is not going to continue to write about the tragedies of life, but to try and see, even while the tragedies are still happening, whether there are some rays of hope.

By engaging in quests of self-exploration and by struggling their way through a world in transition with tenacity and endurance, Likande, Tengani and Chifuya come alive as speaking subjects and agents for change. Moreover, their individual gains along the way to self-actualisation and self-fulfilment are not only represented as personal victories but also, on a larger scale, as valid contributions to the progress of their people, especially women. Their victories, in fact, set an example for the present and coming generation of women who are called to pick up the challenge against oppression engendered by patriarchy, colonisation, imperialism. In this sense, the more personal the work appears the more indeed it calls back to the more public basis of the fiction.

Likande, Tengani and Chifuya are proof that educated, career-oriented, married women can juggle the contradictions they encounter in their daily lives with their husbands, children and families, and still be able to live fulfilling family and love lives. Nyanya records the social and cultural upheavals, the continuities, the aspirations as well as the traditions and in so doing she informs the present and the future with the past.

She also shows that her female characters' strength lies in accepting both gains and losses on their way to self-attainment, thanks to the support and help they also give to one another. The truly loving relationship, a different love story behind the many love stories told in the novel, might be seen to be the warm, mutually supportive friendship between the three women. The stress of the novel is on the nature of friendship as an even more fulfilling choice and perhaps the most constant relationship between individuals. Nyanya's belief in the power of female bonding draws on the realisation that, in an African context, women should stick with each other to challenge manifestations of patriarchal power and colonisation. Likande, Tengani and Chifuya are each yearning for change and their coming together is an essential step towards emancipation.

Together they can conflate the personal and the political, a major achievement in African feminist consciousness.

Nyanya deals not so much with the milieu of contemporary feminism as with charting the experience of women's oppression without separating one form of oppression from another: sexism over racism, or sexuality/the erotic over material experiences, the sexual division of labour over poverty and economic exploitation, etc.

In so doing, she promotes a decentring of discourse and experience and focuses upon the fact that feminism in Africa, as Catherine Acholonu states, 'must define its priorities and resist the ideology of gender warfare that has been imposed upon it by Eurocentrics.'[3]

African women writers today attempt to redefine the contradictions inherent in gender relations by appropriating feminist theories of gender while concurrently offering updated insights into controversial issues. Their texts are not just giving voice, nor are they just reformulating the question of African woman's identity; they are forcing readers, critics and, more generally, men to reflect on the issues that they have conveniently brushed aside.

Like writers from the first generation, emerging female authors seem willing to employ any vehicle, creative, theoretical or otherwise in order to claim the legitimacy of their voices. In a more conscious and explicit way than their predecessors, they theorise via their creative texts, using a character or characters to engage in theoretical discourse as pertinent to the plot. Creative and theoretical texts in this case cannot always be separated but they are merged into one text. The creative text, in this sense, serves as not only a literary work, telling a story, but a work which puts forth and attempts to grapple with the same issues that recognised theorists observe and discuss.

NOTES

1. The most recent award, The Caine Prize 2000 for African Literature in English has been awarded to a young Sudanese female writer, Leila Aboulela for her short story entitled *The Museum*.
2. Kekelwa Nyanya, *Hearthstones*, East African Educational Publishers, Nairobi, 1995, p. 1. All references to the book will refer to this edition and will be given in the text by page numbers only.
3. Catherine Acholonu, *Motherism: The Afrocentric Alternative to Feminism*, Owerri, Afa Publications, 1995, p. 167.

'Submit or Kill Yourself … Your Two Choices'
Options for Wives
in African Women's Fiction

Helen Cousins

Grace Ogot wrote in her 1966 novel, *The Promised Land*, that 'marriage [is] a form of imprisonment'.[1] The forms and meaning of marriage have changed in most African societies through colonialism and the shift to a capitalist economy, yet it seems that contemporary women novelists in Africa are still using their writing to interrogate the institution of marriage and to explore what marriage means for African women today.

In *Getting Rid of It* (1997), Lindsey Collen draws a direct parallel between the institutions of marriage and of slavery. Like slaves, women are voiceless, without agency or freedom, particularly in patrilineal systems. In these, a woman can be passed from the authority of her natal male relatives to ownership by her husband's family without ever acquiring autonomy. Thus, Jumila in *Getting Rid of It*, is forced into an arranged marriage by her brother who assumes a right to arrange her marriage to a man of his choice despite her preference for a different man. The issue of her consent within such a structure is irrelevant. There are no allowable forms of speech through which Jumila can refuse or argue: 'She was silent. By silence she meant no. But [her brother] knew that you can make a girl's silence mean assent'.[2] Both Jumila and another character, Rita, suffer physical constraint; Jumila is tied to her husband's bed and Rita is refused permission to leave the house at all. Confinement is not always physical, however.

Constraints can be more psychological but are still powerful in keeping the women paralysed in their place. Jumila's widowed sister has sunk in to a depression in marriage that persists after the husband's death. Collen's explanation is that 'the lies' she had been living as a wife have been so internalised that even widowhood cannot free her from wifehood.

The impulse to 'submit or kill yourself' (*GR* 192) is labelled in the novel as a 'slavethought' and, like slaves, women are conditioned to be submissive, to repress any resentment over their condition and escape it only through suicide when compliance becomes impossible. Through this fictional mode, Collen sets out to show the price women pay by submitting and why suicide is often the only perceived escape from the suffering caused by submission to wifely social norms. Furthermore, she explores other options for women than to submit to a wifehood defined entirely by the patriarchal ideology of their societies.

The notion of what wifehood might mean to African women is also a concern of the two other novelists being considered here. It is not only formal marriages that come under scrutiny but marital-like relationships where women still find themselves viewed as possessions. In Yvonne Vera's novel *Butterfly Burning* (1998), Fumbatha says of Phephelaphi: 'He could never free her ... He would hold her. Fumbatha wanted her like the land beneath his feet'.[3] He becomes preoccupied with how to 'keep her close. Somehow. All the time. He must make her belong' (*BB* 59).

For Ama Ata Aidoo, the main issue is the impossibility of fulfilling the multiplicity of tasks required from a wife. When a man marries he gets:

a sexual aid;
a wet-nurse and nursemaid for [his] children;
a cook-steward and general housekeeper;
a listening post;
an economic and general consultant;
field-hand and,
if [he is] that way inclined,
a punch-ball.[4]

In her novel *Changes: A Love Story* (1991), Aidoo shows the impossibility of fulfilling all these roles through a comparison of two female characters. Opokuya is labelled a traditional woman who puts caring for her family first, fitting her career round this; Esi kicks against 'tradition', blatantly prioritising her career over traditional wifely duties. Yet neither woman finds her position satisfactory. Whilst Esi admires Opokuya's 'full life', Opokuya is jealous of 'Esi's freedom of movement'.[5]

In trying to develop her identity as a career woman, Esi rejects marriage but as an unmarried woman is socially ostracised as a pariah. The disintegration of Esi's second marriage (which appeared at first to allow her to combine career and wifehood) exposes the difficulty of operating outside of 'normal' marital structures. However, Aidoo uses Opokuya to suggest the problems of operating within them. Opokuya is always tired, always over-worked and has no time for herself.

Through these various characters and situations, the authors explore the effects on women of submission to such marital ideology and what happens when the option of submission becomes closed. Aidoo reminds us though that 'submission' itself is not a simple issue. Opokuya is not servile, abused or without love in her marriage, only tired of having to put everyone else's needs above her own. Aidoo also makes the point that through structures of deference, women can manipulate the men of their families. When Mma Danjuma wants to persuade her brother to leave his child with her to be educated, she kneels and praises him before making her request (which is granted). This episode clearly shows that, for Aidoo, women can create space within this paradigm of submission to take some control within their marriages. A 'submitted' wife is not automatically equivalent to an abused wife.

Much more could be written about the strategies through which women across the African continent manage marriages where they are publicly considered minors, dependants and property. However, I want to focus on marriage in fiction where the more common representation is of wives who find that they cannot remain in marriages without equality and autonomy. For these characters, the space that might make submission possible has been closed down through abuse or through a realisation that submission perpetuates women's private and public subservience.

First, I want to consider how the authors expose the potentially destructive effects for women of a culture of submission; second, to explore how suicide is constructed as the almost inevitable alternative to marriage; and third, to discuss the alternative scenarios to accepting conventional marriage or suicide put forward by these writers.

Marriage is often represented in African women's fiction as a way of structuring men's authority over women, not necessarily legally in modern Africa but through social and cultural attitudes. In both Collen and Aidoo's novels this authority is made explicit through incidents where male authority is translated into violence against wives. In *Changes*, Oko rapes Esi partly to assert his authority over her. In his terms, this is an attempt to save the marriage by restoring the male–female power balance that should pertain and which Esi refuses to recognise. It has been noted above that Jumila in *Getting Rid of It* is tied to her husband's bed after her arranged marriage. This is to allow her husband to rape her in order to consummate their marriage and consequently to impregnate Jumila. In the same novel, Rita's imprisonment is reinforced by veiled threats from her husband: 'He told me I was lucky he wasn't a drunk and that he didn't beat me ... up every night' (*GR* 121). This is not an assurance that he won't beat her, only that he chooses not to as long as she conforms. The instant she dares to step outside the home, he beats her viciously and ties her up. Thus, his authority is reinforced by physical force.

It appears that beating wives and forced sex in marriage is a socially acceptable expression of male authority in marriage in several African cultures. Recent sociological research in Ghana found 'a high level of acceptance for beating women ... as a way of training and bringing them to order'.[6] This research and evidence from the novels suggest that such marital violence is often condoned by the social group. Because of this, physical abuse (unless it is severe enough to endanger the woman's life) is not usually seen as a reason to end a marriage. In fact, it is more likely to be viewed as a vital mechanism for sustaining marriage because it teaches women to conform to behaviour patterns that are acceptable to their husbands.

The authors being considered here widen their definition of abuse to include the psychological. In *Getting Rid of It,* Liz (usually referred to as the historian's wife which is significant in itself) has not been physically abused but subject to years of psychological abuse from her husband because he feels she is not good enough for him: 'all this despising I've had from him, it's nothing. Husbands often do it' (*GR* 94). At an individual character level, all these female characters are shown to resent the violence to which they are subjected but for Collen there are greater social implications. Collen develops Liz's attitudes from feeling that she is 'courageous' to put up with derision to a realisation of the wider impact of her private acceptance of her husband's judgement. Through Liz, Collen reveals 'the meaning for other people, for people who come after [Liz], of [her] having accepted, having bowed down' (*GR* 94). Her submission is a public collusion, signalling to other people (particularly her son and daughter) that it is permissible, in this example, to despise people because of their differences.

Aidoo's portrayal of Mma Danjuma, in *Changes*, manipulating men through apparent submission, could be open to the same charge of collusion. Her behaviour bestows only temporary control and, in fact, reinforces the idea that any important power (such as decisions about children) does reside with men because they have to be manipulated into approval. In this situation, Mma Danjuma is successful partly because she is not petitioning on her own behalf but for a child's welfare; something that the whole family would wish to ensure. Crisis is engendered when the wife and husband begin to have different expectations of married life making it unlikely that the husband will accept covert manipulation. The texts make it clear that the fictional relationships are eroded more by differing needs than by any violence – although an episode of violence can provide a turning point for the wife.

Oko and Esi's marriage in *Changes* disintegrates over Oko's expectations that Esi will fulfil a domestic role and Esi's determination not to compromise her career. The rape is a symptom of these tensions but only serves to crystallise the marital difficulties for Esi. It is these problems as a whole, and not the rape *per se* which make her leave Oko.

Similar tensions arise in *Butterfly Burning* between Fumbatha and Phephelaphi. He assumes that Phephelaphi will be content with a domestic and reproductive role. For him it is simple: 'We are happy together. I work. I take care of you. It is not necessary for you to find something else' (*BB* 59). Phephelaphi cannot make her relationship 'the beginning or end of all her yearning' (*BB* 64). Her future includes training to be a nurse which at the time the novel is set (1943) is incompatible with marriage and motherhood. Thus, tension is introduced into the relationship and into the narrative.

Having discussed the way that these authors problematise a marital mode which requires women's submission, I want to explore why suicide is so often presented as the only way out of unacceptable marriages in African women's fiction.

Once the submission is questioned and can no longer be sustained, women's response is to remove themselves from the situation. Although I will limit my examples to the three novels I have chosen, it can be seen over a range of novels by African women that suicide is frequently offered as a resolution to women's dilemmas. Common scenarios include young women getting pregnant in a marital-type relationship who are abandoned by the man, and wives finding marriages untenable. In the texts under consideration here, Rita, Sara, Liz and Jumila's sister all take this option in *Getting Rid of It* as does Phephelaphi in *Butterfly Burning*. The question to ask is: why is suicide so often presented as a solution?

One answer could be that it is viewed as defiance and not capitulation. In her discussion of gender violence in Africa, December Green suggests that suicide can be a strategy of resistance for women as part of what she calls 'disengagement'.[7] In *Butterfly Burning*, Vera implies that Phephelaphi has achieved a type of freedom through her action. Doused in kerosene she 'waits, ready to be harmed, to be freed' (*BB* 129). Certainly, she has agency here and her death resolves the impasse in which she finds herself. Equally, through the reaction of the husbands, Collen points out to her readers in *Getting Rid of It* that suicide is a powerful act capable of creating fear. However, for Green, attempted suicide is an effective strategy only within particular cultural parameters where the threat of suicide is taken seriously. A successful suicide is clearly pragmatically problematic as a resistance strategy on an individual level.

Collen has reservations over suicide being positive at all. She certainly suggests that it creates fear for men in the novel but this is not to the benefit of other women. The fear only engenders more violence against women to counteract what they perceive as an aggressive act against them: 'Murder of husbands. And would they be next? It could happen to me too. Twelve men killed their wives in three months. Preemptive strikes. Got to teach them a lesson, other men whispered' (*GR* 151). So, suicide not only destroys the individual woman who reacts in this way but puts other women in danger. A consideration of certain cultural factors begins to explain why suicide is often the only realistic way for women to escape dysfunctional marriages.

Collen suggests that some of her characters have considered leaving their marriages but mainly this confirms its impossibility. Sara says: I should have just upped and offed a few years back. Now it's too late' (*GR* 104) and Liz can only imagine leaving the marriage as something done to her: 'I think I would be better kicked out. But of course he would never do me that favour' (*GR* 89). Leaving is not always a viable option as marriages in most African communities are considered unions between families rather than individuals. Green notes that divorce is not always possible for several reasons: the woman's family may have to repay the bride price;

the women herself risks the possible loss of her children to her husband's family; she may face alienation from her own community and family if they disapprove of the divorce.[8]

African feminists have identified several strategies used by African wives to signal their displeasure at the way they are being treated. These include refusing to cook food, refusing sex, and shaming the man publicly often with the help of their age mates. These strategies are not widely represented in contemporary African fiction which does not imply that they are ineffective. However, these strategies were directed at preserving marriages, retaining those gender roles whereby women are responsible for domestic duties. Perhaps their non-representation in current fiction suggests that modern African women are more interested in redefining marriage on more equal lines. It also hints at the risk to women inherent in these strategies. Where men are expected to discipline their wives physically and are assumed to have sexual rights over their wives, women's refusal to fulfil their duties can expose them to more violence.

Another reason that suicide might present a more satisfactory solution than divorce is the pressure on women to be wives. Aidoo highlights this in *Changes*. A conversation between Opokuya and Esi confirms that it is still not acceptable for women to remain single in contemporary Ghana, even though there have always been women who find themselves single:

> 'Our societies do not admit that single women exist. Yet...'
> 'Single women have always existed here too...'
> 'Oh yes, all over the continent...'
> 'Women who never managed to marry early enough.'
> 'Or at all. Widows, divorcees.'
> ...
> 'I'm sure that as usual, they were branded as witches', Esi said laughing.
> (*Ch* 46–7)

Women are only socially acceptable if they are under the jurisdiction of a man; their father, brother or husband.

Aidoo shows that even a strong, independent and well-educated woman, such as she has created in Esi, cannot remain single in Ghanaian society. She unwillingly remarries and finds herself in another (differently) difficult situation. Collen corroborates the pressure women face to be wives. In *Getting Rid of It*, pressure is brought to bear on Jumila to return to her husband through isolating her from the community and her family; no one is 'allowed' to help her so that she will have no other choice but to return. Thus, in leaving one marriage women are more than likely to find themselves socially forced into another relationship where the same problems of equality will pertain.

So far, I have only considered the female point of view regarding marriage. Nevertheless, the authors are aware that the strong social pressures which sustain marriage constrain male behaviour as well as that of women. Husbands' actions stem primarily from those ideas of masculinity which insist that to be a 'real man' includes the dominating and controlling of wives.

Aidoo makes it clear in *Changes* that Oko acts as he does partly in response to social expectations of male behaviour. Oko sincerely believes that raping Esi is an expression of his frustrated love. His claim that this was 'part of his decision to give the relationship another chance' (*Ch* 36) is genuine. What he does not express explicitly is how far his actions are rooted in cultural expectations of masculine behaviour. He knows that he is a figure of fun to his friends because he has not forced Esi to conform to wifely stereotypes but it is Aidoo who links this with the rape by placing this complaint just before he attacks. After the rape Oko wants to tell Esi he is sorry but 'he was convinced he mustn't' (*Ch* 10). Again, whilst Oko does not articulate why, Aidoo shows that this feeling is a product of cultural attitudes which warn men '[i]t's not safe to show a woman you love her' (*Ch* 7) as a woman will dominate any man who shows deference to her.

A similar dilemma is presented by Collen through the description of Jumila's first marriage. She notes that it is 'expected of him' (*GR* 35) to consummate the marriage and impregnate his wife, insists that it is not 'his fault', that he feels justified in attaining this through rape. The community expects him to fulfil his masculine role and does not condemn his actions. Men who are reluctant to act in accordance with masculinity threaten the social order based on a doctrine of male domination. From the way Collen writes about the husbands' reaction to their wives' suicide in *Getting Rid of It*, it is clear that she is aware of men's consciousness that their position of power is precarious. Vera implies this too; Fumbatha 'forbids' Phephelaphi to apply for the nurse training but he 'wonders if she will apply. Phephelaphi wonders if he can stop her' (*BB* 61). The authors suggest that men might act violently to prevent their power being eroded.

This is not to suggest that the male characters are demonised. In *Butterfly Burning*, Fumbatha's need to own Phephelaphi is an expression of his love for her, not a malicious impulse to possess. He expresses this love through a discourse of possession because this is the way he understands male–female relationships. Yet, Vera also suggests that by conceptualising his relationship in this way, he is socially 'normal'. His negative reaction to Phephelaphi's abortion (which defies his right to progeny) positions Fumbatha firmly within the social group whilst isolating Phephelaphi in a reversal of their previous social positions. Love that was less mediated through social expectation of relationships might have allowed dialogue and understanding between the characters.

I am not suggesting that the novelists have no choice but to show male characters working out their social fate. There is an element of choice involved as Collen shows by depicting other male characters who do not conceptualise their relationships in terms of ownership and paternalism.

Aidoo, Collen and Vera are sympathetic to the pressures that encourage choices that are culturally acceptable but are critical that men choose to follow social norms at their wives' expense.

In reflecting the cultures from which they write, it can be seen how the authors construct suicide as the easiest escape from marriage. However, the novelists also appear to have an agenda to challenge social norms. Whilst Vera suggests suicide is at least a way women can grasp their own destiny, Aidoo and Collen explore the way female solidarity can enable women to leave their marriages.

One of the most important points that these authors make is that it is easier for women who are not isolated to leave unsatisfactory relationships and to contract partnerships on their own terms. Phephelaphi's main problem in *Butterfly Burning* is that she is increasingly isolated from those women she thought were her friends. In *Getting Rid of It*, it is harder for the three wealthy women to walk out of their marriages than for Jumila. This is partly due to the public nature of their lives, the narcoleptic effect of their material comfort, and the difficulty of giving up position and wealth, all of which could be argued as impediments not privileges in these circumstances. Jumila's poverty forces her into closer physical proximity to her peers than the women of the wealthy suburbs. This engenders a feeling of community as her problems are more public.

The notion of solidarity is strong in Aidoo's novel as well as Collen's but Aidoo presents quite a complex position. It is primarily Esi's financial independence which permits her to end her marriage. She retains the support structure made up of her female relatives (mother and grandmother) and friend Opokuya, but they are doubtful whether she will or even should remain single. Aidoo makes the point that women can work collectively to preserve the *status quo* which preserves male privilege, not through collusion but in the belief that it is better for women if they conform. Thus, Fusena is persuaded by the older women in her family to accept her husband's second marriage (to Esi) rather than risk her own relationship.

Women's associations which promote women's 'common economic, political, and social interests'[9] are part of the social structuring of many groups in Africa. Although the associations based on age groups have been eroded by colonialism, emigration and urbanisation, women still form mutually supportive groups often based on profession. It does appear that the primary role of such groups in the past was to prevent women's status being eroded whereas the present focus is more on gaining rights for women to develop gender equality. In the novels there appear to be two ways this solidarity is manifest: one which I will call 'sisterhood' – the co-operation between women on a personal basis; the other 'collective action' which brings women (and sometimes men) together in a group which has specific political objectives.

Collective action is represented in *Getting Rid of It* by the 'Party' and the 'House Movement'. Here are ways of 'making things change with their own hands' rather than just 'getting on with it' (*GR* 195). However, these are more class- than gender-based. Other types of solidarity in Collen's novel are predicated on female friendship: for example, the friendship of Goldilox Soo, Sadna and Jumila. This is a form of sisterhood which effectively eases the burden of femaleness within this patriarchy. When Jumila has a miscarriage, the problem of disposing of the foetus becomes a mutual one: 'call it *ours* now ... we're dealing with it together now' (*GR* 24).

Sisterhood can imply a somewhat romanticised notion of women's ability to form close bonds with each other. This is not a natural phenomenon as Green's suggests:

> Women's solidarity is conditional. Unity must be constructed; it is never given. Even when unity exists, it is always conditional and tends to collapse under the pressure of acute class conflict. It is also threatened by differences of race, ethnicity and nationality.[10]

Novels are a way to construct such solidarities so it is acceptable if they seem to offer somewhat romanticised versions of friendship and unity. Importantly, *Getting Rid of It* also imagines sisterhood operating across the class divide (in the friendships between Goldilox Soo and Sara, Jumila and Liz, Sadna and Rita), making it predominantly a strategy to challenge gender inequality.

However, whilst sisterhood is supportive, it is only a managing strategy not one which will engender change. Sadna, Goldilox Soo and Jumila presenting themselves at the barracks with the miscarried foetus, challenge the police to arrest them for abortion. They rationalise that 'if someone had gone to Line Barracks long ago, maybe we would not be sneaking around like criminals today' (*GR* 100). But pragmatically they only have the choice of trying to discreetly get rid of it without officialdom finding out. They question: 'how could they take on the State?' (*GR* 101). If they are jailed who will take responsibility for their children?

Aidoo also insists that individually women may try to change their lives but this remains impossible to sustain if social structures remain the same. Esi's defiantly single stance is quickly undermined by the strong social expectation that she will remarry. Within a realistic setting, Aidoo cannot offer a paradigm for women to operate outside of marriage, yet, neither can she depict a way for men and women to operate happily within it. Her text ends on a question: 'what fashion of loving was [Esi] ever going to consider adequate?' (*Ch* 166) which remains hanging.

Collen is more successful at reinventing ways in which men and women can relate sexually other than through marriage which encodes gendered hierarchy. Although the setting of and events in *Getting Rid of It* are recognisable, her text is placed just outside realism by the use of myth and fairytale. This makes it more possible for Collen to present alternative relationships which are sexual and equal. Describing Jumila and Rahim's sexual encounter after she has left her marriage, Collen reverses the usual sexual imagery of male aggression. His nakedness is 'Exposed. Tender. Vulnerable' and Jumila is not penetrated but '[draws] him into her' (*GR* 42–3). Significantly, they are described standing breast to breast. This image is repeated in the sexual encounter between Goldilox Soo and Sara. Depicting a lesbian relationship is controversial as for many African women the notion of lesbianism is at worst repugnant and at best claimed to be irrelevant.[11] However, in an exploration of equal sexual relationships for women, lesbianism cannot be ignored. The concession Collen makes is not to attempt to sustain this relationship throughout the narrative but it is clear that she is supportive of explorations of sexual identities for women that are not also potentially reproductive.

A heterosexual and homosexual relationship might be assumed to be at opposite ends of the spectrum of sexual relationships, but Collen emphasises their similarity. Unlike the other marriages in the novel, both of these are marked by choice and a lack of possessiveness. This is not a claim that Collen advocates 'free love' but a way of radically reconceptualising monogamous relationships. Marriage is predicated on the assumption that if one partner (usually the women) is not constrained they will be unfaithful. As marriage partly arose from a need for men to be assured of paternity, infidelity is more than just an issue of sexual jealousy although this aspect cannot be discounted. Collen suggests a model based on choice and trust. In this way what marriage means in a society begins to change, allowing it to encode equality (even if individual relationships are still 'flawed') rather than gendered inequality.

This re-imagination of a social institution is a powerful way that writers can alter their societies. As Françoise Lionnet notes:

> Women writers are often especially aware of their task as producers of images that both participate in the dominant representations of their culture and simultaneously undermine and subvert these images by offering a re-vision of familiar scripts.[12]

Not all commentators would agree with this; for example, Ruth Meena notes that fictional images cannot 'automatically change the subordinate position of women in society.'[13] Of course, she is right that literature does not have an automatic or immediate effect on people's lives but surely it does affect gradual culture practice because, as Lionnet puts it, literature is a discursive practice which 'encodes and transmits as well as creates ideology.'[14] Thus, these novels not only expose the social practices which trap women but offer the reader imagined alternatives, and with this vision, the possibility of change.

NOTES

1. Grace Ogot, *The Promised Land*. Nairobi: Heinemann Kenya, 1996: 46.
2. Lindsey Collen, *Getting Rid of It*. London: Granta Books, 1997: 34. All other references are in the text as *GR*.
3. Yvonne Vera, *Butterfly Burning*. Harare: Baobab Books, 1998: 23. All other references are in the text as *BB*.
4. Ama Ata Aidoo, 'To Be a Woman' in ed. Robin Morgan, *Sisterhood is Global: The International Women's Movement Anthology*. Harmondsworth, Middlesex: Penguin Books, 1985: 261–8: 262.
5. Ama Ata Aidoo, *Changes: A Love Story*. London: The Women's Press, 1991: 56. All further references are in the text as *Ch.*
6. Dorcas Coker-Appiah and Kathy Cusack eds. *Breaking the Silence and Challenging the Myths of Violence Against Women and Children in Ghana: Report of a National Study on Violence*. Accra: Gender Studies and Human Rights Documentation Centre, 1999: 15.
7. December Green, *Gender Violence in Africa: African Women's Responses*. Basingstoke and London: Macmillan, 1999: Chapter 5.
8. Green: 38.
9. Audrey Wipper, 'Women's voluntary associations' in eds. Margaret Hay and Sharon Stichter *African Women South of the Sahara*. Harlow, Essex: Longman. First edition, 1984: 69–86: 69.
10. Green: 202.
11. See for example Olabisi Aina, 'African Women at the Grassroots: The Silent Partners of the Women's Movement' in ed. Obioma Nnaemeka, *Sisterhood, Feminisms and Power: From Africa to the Diaspora*, Trenton, NJ: Africa World Press, 1998: 65–88: 72.
12. Françoise Lionnet, 'Geographies of Pain: Captive bodies and violent acts in the fictions of Gayl Jones, Bessie Head, and Myriam Warner-Vieyra' in ed. Obioma Nnaemeka *The Politics of M(O)thering: Womanhood, identity, and resistance in African literature*. London and New York: Routledge, 1997: 205–227: 205.
13. Ruth Meena ed. *Gender in Southern Africa: Conceptual and Theoretical Issues*. Harare: SAPES Books, 1992: 1–30: 12.
14. Lionnet: 205.

Exile & Identity in Buchi Emecheta's *The New Tribe*

Clement Abiaziem Okafor

> By the rivers of Babylon, there we sat down, yea,
> We wept when we remembered Zion
>
> We hanged our harps upon the willows in the midst thereof.
>
> For there they that carried us away captive required of us a song;
> and they that wasted us required of us mirth, saying,
> Sing us one of the songs of Zion
>
> How shall we sing the Lord's song in a strange land? (Psalm 137)[1]

The anguish that is expressed in the psalm above indicates that exile, the physical separation from one's homeland, is a cruel form of punishment. As happened in the case of the Jews and many others, an entire nation can be punished in this manner. In Sophocles's *Oedipus the King*,[2] Oedipus decrees exile as the appropriate punishment for any citizen found guilty of regicide. This shows that banishment was used as punishment for individuals during the ancient Greek period, too. The banishment of Napoleon Bonaparte of France, the Asantehene of the Asante, the Oba of Benin and King Jaja of Opobo in Nigeria also prove that exile is still considered appropriate punishment for individuals, even in more recent times.

Exile, however, is not just a form of punishment inflicted on people by others. It may sometimes be self-inflicted as a remedy for catastrophic situations in one's homeland. Here, the biblical story of Joseph and how his entire nation came to dwell in Egypt readily comes to mind. Again, in more recent times, the exodus of people from the impoverished areas of the world and their migration to the wealthier nations shows quite clearly that people readily embrace exile in foreign lands when they are confronted with calamitous conditions in their homeland.

All the same, sequestration from one's homeland usually exacts a terrible price from all that have been separated from their communities and network of support groups. Principal among these penalties is the issue of how to maintain one's self-identity as an island surrounded by a sea of strangers, whose way of life is the dominant culture. This is the primary concern in Buchi Emecheta's *The New Tribe*.[3]

115

Set in the small seaside town of St Simon in England, the novel portrays Chester Arlington's quest to discover his identity. Born of a Nigerian single mother, Catherine Mba, who herself has been living in exile in England since her youth, Chester is adopted and raised by a white English couple – the vicar Arthur and his wife Ginny Arlington.

Catherine has chosen the vicar and his wife to adopt Chester, her eighteen-month-old son, because of the Arlingtons' earlier celebrated success in adopting and raising a newly born baby girl, Julia, abandoned in a Tesco supermarket bag in a telephone booth. Julia initially does not have much of an identity crisis, since she is white and can be mistaken by strangers as the real daughter of the Arlingtons. For Chester, however, such a mistake is not possible on account of his race and color. As the only black person in the entire small town, Chester realizes quite early in his life that he does not belong to that community:

> Chester could not remember the exact moment when he knew he was adopted. It was like learning to feed yourself. You knew you must have been taught while you were in the cradle, but you could not pinpoint the exact minute or particular hour. It began as a glimmer and gradually became a solid awareness, established, but somehow imprisoned inside him. However, even at the age of four or five, he felt a sense of unbelonging. (p. 9)

Chester's feeling of alienation from the community of St Simon goes back to his first encounter with the outside world: his first day at school. At lunchtime he is tired and cries on realizing that he cannot go home before the end of the school day. Then, the teacher, Miss Slattery, invites Julia to pacify him. In her innocence, young Julia tells both Miss Slattery and the headmaster that Chester is different; hence, their mother asked her earlier to take special care of him in school. The next incident that draws attention to Chester's difference from the rest of the community occurs during the preparation for the school nativity play. As the children rehearse for the Christmas nativity play, the teacher assigns Chester the role of leader of the three wise men from the East; in her view, these kings must have looked like Chester.

Perplexed that the neighbors address him as 'Chester king of the Orient', he asks his adoptive mother for clarification. Prior to this moment, he imagined that the Arlingtons were his parents:

> 'What's the East? He pursued. Ginny was silent for a moment, then she said, 'Africa's in the East. Where your people came from.'
> In bed that night he thought about her words. 'Your people.' He thought the Arlingtons were his parents. The sense of unbelonging strengthened. (p.12)

This information produces the unintended result of deepening the young boy's sense of alienation. However, the defining moment of Chester's life occurs when the vicar later informs him of the circumstances of his adoption. Up till that time, other people have defined Chester's identity. The teacher defines him as being like one of the Magi and the good-natured neighbors concur by calling him 'Chester king of the Orient'.

Some malicious ones, though, refer to him as 'the king of the devils'. However, after that moment of truth, the youngster is driven by the consuming passion to discover and appropriate his own identity. One's identity depends to a great extent on identification with one's parents. Now imagine how traumatic it must be for someone to discover that his parents are not really his parents. That means that his parents are not the people he thought they were, which means that he is also not the person he thought he was. All this confusion creates a tremendous psychological loss and creates a deep lacuna in the person's self image and knowledge. For the person concerned, this raises the questions: 'Who are my ancestors? What is their medical history?' This, in turn, creates a deep sense of insecurity and vulnerability as the person wonders constantly: 'Who is there for me?' Chester's trauma is compounded by the fact that he does not know much about his cultural heritage either. So, in addition to the burden of not knowing his biological parents, he also lacks a sense of his cultural affinity. Consequently, he sets out on a quest to discover his cultural identity.

The quest

The object of the quest is embodied in a dream of Africa that his adoptive mother has implanted in his subconscious mind: an idyllic image of a rustic African village. The village comprises a central dwelling that is surrounded by a number of round and small thatched houses. In addition, handsome young men wearing armlets and brightly colored pleated skirts sweep the compound. Some of the women inhabiting this compound carry pots of food, while others carry pitchers of water on their heads amidst the happy noise of young girls heard everywhere. This village is located within a city whose entrances are guarded by gate men, who collect tribute from farmers returning to the city from their farms beyond the city boundaries. As time passes, Chester internalizes the features of both the compound and the city and appropriates them to himself. Furthermore, he begins to believe that both the compound and the city exist in reality and are his to inherit some day. More importantly, they are later transformed into the Holy Grail of his quest and he believes that he is the lost prince of this kingdom. In the end, the youngster uses this dream vision as the mental refuge into which he retreats whenever he is faced by any unpleasant situation.

For the other adolescents at St Simon, leaving home is a rite of passage that marks their transition into adulthood. Many of these young people leave their rural community and go the cities in search of their fortune and often return to display their newly acquired resources. Chester would have loved to do that, too. However, he has a more pressing pursuit: the quest for his identity and the search for a community with which he shares bonds of kinship – one that will not regard him as an outsider.

Because other people have defined Chester on the basis of his race and color, he instinctively begins the search for his identity within the Black community; this is a community with which he has racial affinity. The absence of a Black community in St Simon makes it imperative for Chester to travel to wherever he can locate one. Since the only Black family he knows is resident in Liverpool, he sets out uninvited for the home of the Ugwus whom he had met during his earlier temporary employment at the Clinton Chalets in St Simon. At the holiday resort he had developed an immediate rapport with Enoch and his sons.

Chester's quest, which takes the form of a journey, begins appropriately during the period of Advent, which is the time Christians expect the birth of the Savior. This journey in search of a community to which he can belong later becomes a quest for cultural self-identity. Thus, while the Christians await the birth of their Redeemer, Chester looks forward to the birth of his cultural self-identity. As is often the case with such quests, Chester's entails a journey into both a physical and geographical domain as well as the psychological and spiritual terrain. Chester's journey into the geographical space comprises two segments, namely, the journey within England and the one to Africa. Taken as a whole, however, the quest may be considered as a three-phased journey. The first phase is terrestrial, the second aquatic, while the third is aerial. Again, the terrestrial phase is made up of two journeys. The first terrestrial journey is the trip to Liverpool, while the second is the round trip from Lagos to Benin.

The first terrestrial phase

The journey within England begins in the rural, white community of St Simon and terminates in the Black urban community in Liverpool. This journey by train was precipitated by Julia's disappearance and the apparent theft of the sum of two thousand pounds from the vicarage. Chester feels instinctively that he is a suspect for no other reason than the fact that he is a Black person. Hence, he leaves before anyone accuses him of a crime he has not committed. This journey to Liverpool is merely a preparation for the longer and more complex and tasking second leg – the journey to Africa: the ancestral home of the Black Diaspora.

The physical and geographical journey to Liverpool has a metaphysical and psychological parallel too. When Chester lives in St Simon, he knows very little about Black people and their way of life. His sojourn with the Ugwus for three years is, therefore, a period of initiation into Black culture. Here, he acquires the rudiments of Black culture and Nigerian cuisine. With time, this familiarity begins to deepen as he acquires certain elements of the Black ethos by participating in the family life of his host. For instance, he learns that Africans share their first fruits with their kinsmen. Consequently, when he receives his first salary from his workplace – the leisure centre – he uses part of it to buy presents for the new family he lives with. Thus, he purchases caps for the young boys and a brown woollen head warmer for Enoch, their father. In addition, he procures cigars and a bottle of whisky, with which Enoch offers a libation on his behalf. Furthermore, he learns that the contents of the glass of whisky that has been offered as libation is swallowed in one gulp. More importantly, Enoch convinces him that he is not merely an African, but that he is indeed a Nigerian. Hence, he accepts the new African name that is given to him by Enoch: *Iloefuna* – 'Your community will not be extinct.' Although this period of acculturation lasts three years, it is merely a period of psychological and spiritual conditioning for Chester's total immersion into African culture when he visits Nigeria later.

As has been mentioned, the point of departure for Chester's quest for self-identity is the landscape of the dream vision that his adoptive mother has earlier implanted in his subconscious mind. Chester does not know, however, that this vision is based on an ancient legend of the Lost Prince of Idu, which is built on a paradox. In this narrative, the preferred wives of the King of Benin have not been able to bear him a son and heir. Since the monarch is desperate for a son, he engages the services of a powerful herbalist to prepare a special fertility potion for his wives. To this end, the herbalist cooks a special meal in which he conceals a male seed. Paradoxically, none of the king's favorite wives finds the seed. In the end, only Mkpulasi the hated wife who is not even expected to taste the meal, receives the seed and becomes pregnant, as a result. Fearing for the life of Mkpulasi and her unborn son, the herbalist spirits her away to the white missionaries. After the birth of her son, Mkpulasi begs the missionaries to take the child to their country in the hope that when he grows up he would return to reclaim his kingdom.

This ancient Benin legend portrays the injustice and sexual inequity that are practiced in many real life African polygamous families. In such situations, the patriarch – who has married many wives – may hate one of his wives for one reason or the other. As a result, he victimizes the hated wife (Mkpulasi) in every conceivable way. Whenever he purchases new and expensive clothing for his favorites, he buys an inferior one for her. Hence, on special occasions when his other wives are decked out in attractive attire, the hated spouse appears like a poor relative of her co-wives. This unfair and unequal treatment of the wives creates a binary opposition within such polygamous households, with the favoured wives on one side and the victimized one on the other. Worse still, the hatred is often passed on to the offspring of the hated wife, also.

Thus, the irony in this ancient Benin legend is that the victimized and despised wife of the king gives birth to the heir to the throne, rather than the favorite ones. However, since the hatred of the mother is passed on to her son, the new baby is in mortal danger. Consequently, he is spirited away from the hostile environment of his home and given to the foreign missionaries, who offer him refuge in their distant homeland in Europe. According to the legend, he will return from exile some day to reclaim his kingdom.

The aquatic phase

The aquatic phase of Chester's journey begins in Liverpool after the youngster has been acculturated into the African way of life for three years under the tutelage of Enoch Ugwu. As a result, he begins to long for a trip to Africa in furtherance of his quest. This time he comes under the influence of Jimoh omo Garuba, a Nigerian economic migrant. Jimoh is representative of a new breed of African diaspora that is made up of people in short-term exile. His wife and two children are in Nigeria, and he has come to England for the sole purpose of acquiring the material resources that will enable him to return to Nigeria and give his family a better life.

This indomitable survivor has gained Chester's confidence and in a short while convinces him that his dream vision is indeed the prompting of his *chi* (guardian spirit) that is steering him towards the destiny. As this investigator has shown in an earlier work,[4] in Igbo cosmology, a person chooses his or her destiny before his incarnation. In addition, the person's *chi* witnesses the choice made. Consequently, although the individual suffers amnesia at birth, his *chi* always remembers and directs the person to the destined end. In effect, Jimoh is suggesting that Chester will attain his destiny by following his dream to Nigeria.

To this end, Jimoh proposes a scheme that will ostensibly benefit both of them. By swapping passports, he will have the means to procure a better paying job that will enable him to accumulate money faster. In turn, Chester will have the wherewithal to travel to Nigeria:

> 'I get idea,' Jimoh said excitedly, biting off another piece of kola as if it were chocolate while Chester struggled to swallow his.
> 'You for get a job on a ship going to Nigeria. My wife go come met you for Lagos, then you can stay in Benin area for as long as you like. You go see that your kingdom.' (p. 110)

Eventually, Chester is convinced that Jimoh is really a messenger who has been sent by divine providence to help him, the lost prince, find the kingdom which is the main object of his quest.

The sea voyage begins in Liverpool on board *Sisi Eko*, a Nigerian cargo ship. Freetown, Sierra Leone is the first African port of call, with Takoradi, Ghana, as the second. Chester experiences a major culture shock in these two ports; he is stunned that there are Black people everywhere. For the first time in his life he lives in a city where Black people constitute the majority of the population.

Chester's debarkation at Lagos Marina in Nigeria terminates the sea voyage. It is also the beginning of a series of culture shocks that the young man experiences during his quest. He experiences the first shock when he notices that women carry heavy loads on behalf of men, unlike in England. As a result, Chester is the more embarrassed when Jimoh's wife, Mowunmi, insists on carrying his luggage from the wharf. The next disconcerting experience is the humid heat of Lagos, which overpowers the young sojourner; it makes him so dizzy that he has an out-of-body sensation. However, by far the most frightful culture shock that the youngster experiences on his arrival in Nigeria is the chaotic driving culture of Lagos. In this city, there seem to be virtually no traffic rules and cars overtake one another at extremely high speed, regardless of the road conditions. Often, the drivers are so impatient that they climb onto pavements, rather than wait in queues. The resulting chaos makes Chester begin to wonder if his dream can be realized within such a disorganized society.

The second terrestrial phase

The second terrestrial phase of Chester's quest begins in the Lagos suburb, Festac, which is one of the best neighbourhoods of the big city. After a night of well-deserved rest and recuperation, Chester and his guides set out for Benin, their ultimate destination. This journey by road exposes Chester to other culture shocks. First, he is scared to death by Karimu's reckless speeding on the dangerous highway. Second, he experiences first hand the culture of corruption nurtured by the Nigerian police. He is stunned by the number of checkpoints mounted by the police and the fifty-Naira notes in the envelopes with which the driver buys their passage to yet another checkpoint. On a happier note, however, he marvels as Mowunmi unabashedly breast-feeds her child in his presence and wonders whether he ever bonded with his own mother in the way this mother relates to her baby.

When the sojourner from England finally arrives in Benin, he is disappointed by the shabbiness of the ancient city. The houses in the outskirts of the city are constructed with scraps and have rusty roofs. Although Chester is pleasantly surprised that Benin has a university, he is disappointed by the general disorderliness everywhere. Most of the houses are painted orange – the colour of the unpaved mud roads – and the home of his host is even worse. It is an uncompleted house that had unfinished floors and neither doors nor windows. Besides, it has an outside shack as bathroom. Worse still, it has an open drain in front of it, and the stench emanating from the drain makes Chester sick. Furthermore, the room assigned to Chester is congested with all kinds of household goods and has just enough room for the mattress that Karimu squeezes into the room and on which he sleeps on the floor.

Chester is amazed that in spite of the obvious inadequacies of the house, his hosts consider it a charmed dwelling. They consider it a charmed house because Jimoh began his career as an evangelist here and made enough money to buy the land where he has built his church. Still, Chester is unimpressed by these signs of negligence and poverty; hence, he begins to wonder, once again, if his dream could indeed be realized in such a dreadful environment. However, he does not despair. On the contrary, he perseveres, spurred on by the amazing generosity of his hosts, who – despite their privations – do everything to make him feel at home. As Karimu says to him:

> Make you no worry, this na your home. Every black person, whether he dey for America or for England, he must visit Nigeria before he die. Because when he enter heaven, God fit ask him say, 'Did you go to Africa?' And if the person shake his head, God fit send him back to be a fowl or a goat in his next life. (p. 118)

The rest of Chester's sojourn in Benin is a period of deep immersion into African culture and it enables him to experience the stark reality of Nigerian life. For instance, he learns to enjoy the new cuisine of corn porridge and akara (deep-fried bean cake) as well as the ever-present garden eggs. All the same, he is alarmed that he is charged for the taxi fare from Lagos to Benin more money than what Jimoh had earlier told him would last him an entire week. He also has first-hand experience of the difficulty of procuring genuine drugs in a country that is flooded with fake ones. Finally, when Chester realizes that Jimoh has not made the arrangements he promised he would to enable him see the Oba (King) of Benin, it suddenly dawns on him that Jimoh might also renege on his pledge to return his British passport. Consequently, Chester feels that he is trapped in this unfamiliar terrain and has a panic attack.

Even the main object of Chester's quest – the visit to the Oba's palace – almost ends disastrously. As it turns out, the decrepit road sign leading to the palace is indeed ominous of terrible future events. Unfortunately, Chester does not interpret it accurately. Rather, he is carried away by the affinity between the red walls of the palace to the African compound of his dream vision. Nevertheless, reality soon dawns on him when he meets the old gatekeeper, who is asleep on his duty post. This cynical old man is unimpressed by Chester's story about being the lost prince, who has returned to reclaim his kingdom. He has heard the story innumerable times before in the folktales of his people and does not believe that the young man in front of him is the incarnation of the legendary prince. His skepticism is embodied in the question he puts to Chester: 'In England, is it the custom that any passer-by can have an audience with the Queen?' Thus, it is clear that he regards the young man as no more than an ordinary tourist. It is only after Chester has presented him with the gift of a bottle of schnapps that he cooperates with him and thereafter leads him and Karimu, his guide, into the adjoining courtyard of the old section of the palace.

Here, Chester encounters one of the Oba's wives: a young woman draped with a cloth from her chest to her ankles. Everything about her – the small hut she enters as well as her coiffure – is a replica of his dream vision. However, Chester does not realize that men like him risk having their eyes gouged out for daring to look at the Oba's queens. Even so, this is a minor transgression when compared to the ultimate abomination that Chester commits later by trespassing into the Oba's sacred throne room. Indeed, were it not for the intervention of the young prince, Chester and Karimu would have paid with their lives for this great act of sacrilege.

The palace is a replica of Chester's dream vision and he is disappointed that he is not wanted there. He concludes that this palace cannot be the Holy Grail of his quest, especially as the king has shown his lack of confidence in his people by seeking medical attention in the very country from which Chester set out.

The debacle at the palace convinces Chester of the need for re-centering his quest, since he seems to be chasing an ever-moving mirage. At Karimu's urging, Chester relocates his quest to Jimoh's church. Karimu assures him that since dreams are the medium through which God communicates with human beings, Jimoh's church is indeed an appropriate place to pray for the revelation of the true meaning of his dream. Despite Chester's initial misgivings about the uninspiring church building, he acquiesces in the end. This house of worship is merely a shack with only four rows of planks that serve as pews and the only other item of furnishing in the church is a three-foot white wooden cross.

Before service begins, Mowunmi – Jimoh's wife – roasts and sells what she calls 'the corn of life' in the vicinity as a way of attracting converts to their congregation. However, at the appointed time, she dons her church vestments – a white robe – and is transformed there and then into a religious leader with the ecclesiastical name of Sister Marian. Thereafter, altar bell in hand, she harangues the people to repent: '*Chialianu*' (repent), she says again and again.

To boost Chester's flagging faith in the church, Karimu assures him that many people before him have come to them for the interpretation of their dreams. More importantly, he informs him that people often go mad when they are unable to realize their dreams. But this argument produces an undesired negative effect on Chester. Rather than make Chester more confident about the efficacy of their church's intervention, Chester begins to wonder whether he is not mad for continuing to rely on Jimoh and the members of his family in the face of Jimoh's failure to return his passport. Thus, Chester remains skeptical that his kingdom will be revealed in the church. In the end, Jimoh's church is unable to identify Chester's kingdom despite his many offerings and the congregation's prayers and speaking in tongues.

As a result of the failure of prophecy and the church, even Karimu acknowledges the need for yet another re-centering of the quest. In desperation, he suggests they try the Oba of Chamala. However, the outcome of the visit to this ruler's palace is by far worse than the experience in the two earlier sites. The surroundings of this Oba's palace are like a scaled down model of the palace of the Oba of Benin: 'a yard of reddish earth, with little huts along the walls. Women peered out from the huts, and from nearby came the sounds of children at play' (p. 136). Thus, the residence of this ruler is a smaller model of the palace of his dream.

Yet, the traditional perimeter structures merely camouflage a modern air-conditioned mansion, where the American-trained monarch lives. The reception room of this mansion is lavishly furnished with deep-pile wall-to-wall carpeting and an impressive throne. The Oba is amazed that Chester's dream vision is a replication of a popular local legend the king learnt as a child.

This ruler, who has the habit of grinding his teeth, epitomizes current Nigerian leadership: greedy and ostentatious. Although he is obviously wealthy, he continues to be grasping. Rather than be satisfied by Chester's gifts, he plans to rob these guests at gunpoint, but dies in the process. Incredibly, he is eulogized as an enlightened leader who was killed by armed robbers, but whose virtues will be sorely missed by his society.

After the traumatic experience of being shot at by the Oba armed robber, Chester relocates his quest back to the church. But the outcome of his return to the church ends almost tragically. Nevertheless, Chester's collapse and delirium triggered by a severe malarial attack are interpreted positively by the congregation as proof that the spirits have finally accepted Chester. However, the malarial attack precipitates his hurried departure from Benin and necessitates an immediate return to Lagos, where he can obtain adequate medical attention.

The events of this terrestrial journey from Benin back to Lagos are different from the initial journey to Benin. Chester is delirious during this return journey and his companions, who are members of the church, are dressed in their awesome ecclesiastical robes. Throughout this journey, they recite their protective incantations and constantly sprinkle on Chester the holy water from the River Niger. This ritual is efficacious in warding off even the predatory police, who readily grant them un-hindered passage through the numerous checkpoints on the way. Indeed, the church members are convinced that their ritual performance is responsible for Chester's eventual recovery, rather than the medicines that were administered to him in the Lagos hospital.

The aerial phase

The aerial phase of Chester's journey begins with Esther Willoughby's arrival in Lagos. However, her trip to Nigeria is not the homecoming of a diasporic sojourner; it is simply a rescue mission. She is convinced that

Africa is not the home of the Black diaspora any more. In her view, the diasporic sites are now the permanent homes of these Black people, who are making a tremendous impact on their neighbors through such cultural activities as the London Notting Hill Carnival.

Appropriately, before Esther and Chester leave Nigeria, they attend a farewell party that is organized in Chester's honor in the same Festac suburb where he spent his first night in Nigeria. Thereafter, the two offspring of the new and secondary diaspora return to Liverpool, England by air.

From the description above, the structure of Chester's quest in search of his African heritage may be represented as follows:

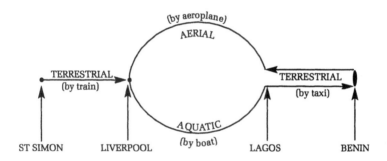

Chester's sojourn in Africa and his eventual return to England revisits one of the most contentious issues in African diasporic discourse: the issue of return to Mother Africa. This has been the subject of a passionate debate among Africans of the primary diaspora in the Americas; that is, those forebears have lived in the New World for the last three centuries. The two extreme positions were embodied in the persons of Marcus Garvey and W.E.B. du Bois.[5] Briefly, Marcus Garvey argued that the separation of the Black and White people was the only viable solution to the intractable racial problem of America. Hence, Africans in the diaspora should be encouraged to return voluntarily to the homeland of their ancestors. To this end, his Universal Negro Improvement Association began the Return to Africa Movement and inaugurated the Black Star shipping company in order to facilitate the transportation of those who wished to return to the motherland. The tremendous popularity of Garvey's movement among the masses of Black America demonstrates conclusively that Garvey's ideas were acceptable to a sizeable segment of his racial kinsmen. Equally vigorous was du Bois' opposing argument. Du Bois viewed America as the rightful home of the Black Americans. He was convinced that it was in the best interest of these Black people to evolve strategies for adapting successfully to that reality. The irony was that in the end, du Bois emigrated to Africa, where he lived the last days of his life, died and was buried, while Marcus Garvey remained in the Americas.

The unresolved argument above has been rekindled in recent times among the Africans of the new or secondary diaspora, that is, those who emigrated from Africa in the wake of the catastrophic collapse of the continent's post-independence economy. It must be admitted that the economies of many non-African states also declined at the same time. Indeed, globally, the collapse of the material wellbeing of the people of most non-Western nations has triggered a great migration of millions of people to the Western countries. In Africa, it has generated a phenomenal brain drain to the West. These African exiles of the secondary diaspora, who may or may not have naturalized in their new locations, have varying levels of identity problems. They wear African dresses on special occasions and like the Jewish singer of the psalm cited at the beginning of this article, these African exiles dream that they will return to their homeland some day. Not surprisingly, their identity problems are magnified in the lives of their offspring. Indeed, there is often a generational disconnection between the parents and their children.

Consequently, the dreams parents have for their offspring are usually at variance with the children's own dreams. The children may bear African names, but most do not speak any African language. Worse still, many of these young people have never visited the continent and know very little about African cultures. More importantly, it is doubtful if they even regard Africa as their homeland. Above all, the vexing and often unanswered question is: Are these youngsters Africans in the diaspora or are they indeed the New Tribe of the Western World?

This is the complex discourse that is portrayed in Buchi Emecheta's *The New Tribe*. In this novel, Chester belongs to the second generation of the secondary African diaspora; his mother left Nigeria as a child and has settled since then in England. His father is an African–American soldier, who is stationed in England, where Chester is born. All these factors complicate the issues of nationality and identity for the youngster.

The resolution of the crisis in *The New Tribe* would be problematic indeed if Chester's return to England were interpreted as his repudiation of Africa or his acceptance of Esther's argument that Africa is not the home of the Black people in diaspora any more. If it were so, the resolution of the novel would run counter to the end of similar diasporic journeys in various national literatures, as is exemplified in the following recapitulation of the journey in Jewish tradition – the source of the psalm cited at the beginning of this paper.

Briefly, Chapter 12 of the Book of Genesis records[6] that there is a famine soon after Abram, his brother, Lot, and his wife Sarah have relocated to the Promised Land. Consequently, they go to Egypt in search of food. In order to avoid being killed by their Egyptian hosts, Abram pretends that his wife is his sister. As a result, the Pharaoh takes over the attractive Sarah and treats Abram well on her account. This enables Abram and his brother to acquire tremendous resources: men servants, maidservants, asses, camels, cattle, gold and silver. Eventually, when God plagues the Pharaoh for taking Sarah, the king expels Abram from his country and Abram and his wife and brother return to the Promised Land, taking with them all their new acquisitions.

Two generations later, another famine devastates the land of Israel and again the descendants of Abram go to Egypt to procure their sustenance. This time, though, they live in the foreign land for a long time and their ancestor Jacob – who is also known as Israel – dies in exile. Before his death, however, he enjoins his offspring to repatriate his remains and bury them in his homeland:

> And he charged them, and said unto them, I am to be gathered unto my people: Bury me with my fathers in the cave that is in the field of Ephron the Hittite. (Genesis 49: 29)

In keeping with their father's will, the children of Israel carry the remains of their father back to his homeland and bury them in the cave bought earlier by their great grandfather, Abram himself.

Centuries later, the fortunes of the Israelites deteriorate dramatically in Egypt – their place of refuge. When their kinsman Joseph is in power, they are treated favorably. Sadly, with passage of time a new generation of Pharaohs comes to the throne and demotes the status of the Jewish immigrants to that of slaves. Thereafter, oppression and persecution mark the history of the Israelites in Egypt until the emergence of their leader, Moses.

The entire Book of Exodus records the birth of this hero and his preparation for the daunting task of leading his people from Egypt through the desert wilderness back to their homeland. Specifically, Exodus chronicles the spectacular confrontation between Moses and Pharaoh, the crossing of the Red Sea and the journey to the Sinai Mountain. Here two significant events occur. The first is the codification of a legal system for the Israelites, while the second is the establishment of a covenant between them and their God, which is followed by the erection of a tabernacle for his worship. Through these actions, Moses transforms an aggregation of previously disorganized groups of slaves into a theocratic nation.

Finally, he leads this covenant nation after forty years of migration onto the banks of the River Jordan, where he dies and is succeeded by Joshua, who spearheads the Jewish conquest of Canaan. Here, too, they bury the remains of Joseph, which they have carried with them all the way from Egypt. Thus, their diasporic journey ends in their homeland, where it began several centuries earlier.

The essential elements of the journey above are: a catastrophic event in the homeland, which necessitates an outward migration to a foreign land of a significant part of the population; the residence of these migrants in a diasporic site, which is a place of refuge; the acquisition from the place of refuge of the resources with which to mediate the devastation of the homeland; and a final return to the ancestral land.

Catherine Mba, Chester's mother, is Igbo; hence, Chester is an Igbo youngster in the diaspora. The Igbo people are great traders, who transact their business all over Nigeria. With the globalization of international trade, the Igbo have expanded their horizon worldwide. Consequently, they have now settled in various parts of the world. However, they have traditional festivals that are designed to entice those abroad to visit home regularly. Among these people, the tradition that enjoins the traveler or exile in foreign lands to return home is expressed in the aphorism: *Onye ije nwe una.* (The traveler must return home.) Recently, a rider has been added to indicate that the traveler or exile is obliged to come home either laden with the box of treasures acquired abroad or be brought home in a box (coffin).[7] This shows that the Igbo people believe that a sojourner has a duty to return home, no matter what.

Thus, the resolution of *The New Tribe* would indeed be problematic if Chester's departure from Africa were interpreted as his repudiation of the duty of the exile to return to the land of his ancestors. In any case, the internal evidence in the novel itself does not support such an interpretation. On the contrary, the resolution of the crisis that is portrayed in *The New Tribe* shows that the novel comes down on the side of Africa as the homeland of the Black diaspora and the authentic source of its invigoration. Although Chester's experience in Nigeria is in many ways an ordeal, it is redemptive in the end, since it transforms him fundamentally for the better:

> He had noticed that since his illness and recovery something had changed inside him. He no longer felt isolated and adrift; his head had cleared. Perhaps Karimu was right, and the water from the River Niger had washed away all his confusion and headaches. (pp.147–8)

Admittedly, young Chester sets out for Nigeria in the quest of an illusory and idyllic utopia – a kingdom that he can call his own. This quest – that is centered primarily in three sites in Benin, namely, the palace of the Oba of Benin, Jimoh's church, and the palace of the Oba of Chamala – totally immerses the young man into Nigerian life and culture, warts and all. None the less, it does not yield the physical kingdom of his dream. Rather, it gives him something even more valuable: a deep understanding of the kingdom within himself. By so doing, Nigeria has helped him to develop his true identity and right attitude to life. This emanates from his recently acquired knowledge that his kingdom is located wherever he happens to be; it does not matter whether he is in Africa or in the diaspora. As Mowunmi tells him: You do not need a palace to be happy. Armed with this understanding, he returns to England now secure in his identity and heritage. This is the conviction that he conveys to Esther in the following dialogue:

'Nigeria made me grow up quickly. I went there full of illusions, looking for something I expected to find.'
'You mean your kingdom. Did you find it?'
'No, and I don't think I'll find it in Africa either. But I did find more about myself, in a roundabout sort of way.' (p. 150)

Thus, *The New Tribe* portrays the most controversial issue in African diasporic discourse: the concept of an eventual return to Mother Africa. Specifically, it portrays the physical and spiritual quest of an offspring of the diaspora for his identity. His perceptive and nurturing English adoptive mother has earlier given him the greatest gift in life – a passionate love for his people – that she has implanted so successfully in his subconscious mind that he imagines it to be a real dream vision. This consuming love propels Chester to journey to Africa in search of his kingdom. However, his quest does not unearth a material or physical domain; there is no kingdom for him to appropriate. Rather, his sojourn in Nigeria turns out to be a deep process of acculturation and maturation. Undoubtedly, he is exploited in various ways by some of his Nigerian hosts and guides. Still, the hardships and tribulations that he experiences only help to strengthen him, much in the same way as fire purifies gold. Through it all, Chester emerges as a more complex personality that is endowed with self-confidence and a deep sense of identification with his African heritage. It is true that he returns to England, which is one of the major diasporic sites, but he has been branded with the love of his ancestral homeland and a healthy understanding of his own identity. Thus, he returns to his diasporic location not as a member of the new Black British Tribe but as a British African. By so doing, he remains faithful to the meaning of his African name: *Iloefuna*: your community will not be extinct, since he perpetuates his African identity even as he lives in England. Fortified by the wisdom and life skills that he has acquired in Africa, Chester can now sing the Lord's song in a strange land with such dexterity that he does not offend the Lord of Hosts.

NOTES

1. *The Holy Bible. Authorized King James Version. Personal Size Giant Print.* Grand Rapids: Zondervan Publishing House, 1994, p. 891.
2. 'Oedipus The King' in *The Norton Anthology of World Masterpieces. Expanded Edition.* ed. Maynard Mack. New York: Norton, 1995, pp. 590–631.
3. Buchi Emecheta, *The New Tribe.* Oxford: Heinemann, 2000. All quotations are taken from this edition.
4. Clement Okafor, 'Igbo Cosmology and the Parameters of Individual Accomplishment in *Things Fall Apart,*' *The Literary Griot,* vol. 10.2, Fall 1998, pp. 34–47.
5. Marcus Garvey, 'Africa for the Africans,' (p. 974) and W.E.B. du Bois, 'The Souls of Black Folk' (p. 613), in *African American Literature.* ed. Henry L. Gates and Nellie Y. Mckay. New York: Norton, 1997, p. 974.
6. *The Holy Bible,* pp. 15–16.
7. Conversation with Onwuchekwa Jemie.

Iniobong Uko

Introduction

The phenomenon of sexual rebellion in this study is conceptualized as a deviation relating to sex, an abandonment of the usual roles performed by that sex, an ignominious regard for the general social expectation of every member of that sex to fit into certain socio-cultural frameworks. Sex is understood as a person's biological maleness or femaleness, while gender refers to the non-physiological aspect of sex, a group of attributes and/or behaviors, shaped by society and culture, which are defined as appropriate for the male or the female sex.

Sexual rebellion pre-supposes sex roles. Although the issue of sex roles has generated heated controversies in recent years as researchers try to prove its untenability in current socio-political realities, it is, however, safe to argue that whether or not some men and women recognize their roles as stipulated by tradition, the roles still exist and are being acknowledged and performed by many.

It is unrealistic for men or women to totally condemn as unjustifiable their traditional roles. This is because many of these roles enhance cohesion and balance between the sexes in society. The dominant socio-political structures that exist in contemporary African society are those that impede the full development of women's potential. It is evident that certain paradigms in society apply only to women to make them unable to attain self-realization and fulfillment.

These commence in the girl-child who is conditioned to stay home and do domestic work, enjoy almost no leisure, unlike her male counterpart who is free to play and associate. At adolescence, the essence of her life revolves around serving her father and brothers, and she is made to believe that these roles make and define ideal womanhood. At adulthood and in marriage, the woman is assumed to have been properly grounded in servitude, muteness, invisibility and dependence, with a natural acceptance of a corresponding male superiority and dominance. These factors indicate that the society has some expectations of and makes some demands on the woman. These demands ensure her backwardness and inferiority, and in contrast, male progression and superiority. It thus becomes imperative and urgent that she devise coping techniques and viable options to get on within the system.

Essentially, the woman only needs to make manifest her naturalness which is feminine, and which is not antagonistic to masculinity, rather, is complementary. The well-defined male/female social roles indicate that the relationship between man and woman is one of sexual hierarchization, in which the man is the master while the woman is reduced to the state of mere slave, at once man's pleasure-object and his narcissistic assurance of his own importance, value and power (Shoshona 1981: 23).

Generally, one or a combination of the following factors, among others has caused the problems facing the woman:

- the traditional secondary position of the woman in relation to her male counterpart,
- female complacence and acceptance of poor and sometimes inhuman treatment by society,
- the obnoxious traditional values that operate only on women,
- the natural attempt by men to lead women, and keep them in total subservience,
- the high level of ignorance among women and their subsequent inability to understand male deceit represented as traditional values; and
- other extraneous factors – such as the supernatural – designed by men to oppress women and perpetuate male dominance.

These issues are responsible for the seeming synonymy of masculinity and power, and the strangeness which occasions any female attempt to express self, realize her potential, and meaningfully contribute to the system. These underlie Aidoo's *Anowa*.

Many factors indicate Anowa as a rebellious character. She is firmly against trends in society that she regards as retrogressive. Prominent among these is parental choice in one's marriage. In describing her, Old Man in Prologue states that 'Anowa is not a girl to meet every day'(7), and Old Woman adds:

> That Anowa is something else!...
> She has refused to marry any of
> the sturdy men who have asked
> her hand in marriage. No one
> knows what is wrong with her.

OLD MAN: A child of several incarnations,
she listens only to her own tales,
laughs at her own jokes and
follows her own advice.

OLD WOMAN: Some of us think she just
allowed her unusual beauty

to cloud her vision of the world...
Others think that her mother
Badua has spoilt her shamefully...
Why should Anowa carry herself
so stiffly? Where is she taking
her 'I won't, I won't' to? Badua
should tell her daughter that the
sapling breaks with bending that
will not grow straight.
...
And the gods will surely punish
Abena Badua (Anowa's mother)
for refusing to let a born priestess
dance! (7–8)

These issues constitute a framework within which to appreciate Anowa, her obstinacy, her psychological advancement and her self-expressiveness. These strange traits are succinctly captured in the proverb cited above by old woman: 'the sapling breaks with bending that will not grow straight'. This is suggestive of Anowa's 'abnormality' which is likely to have disastrous consequences.

Significantly, Anowa's sexual rebellion is epiphenomenally targeted at some repugnant socio-political values and expectations of the woman. These include the facts that the African woman should not express self, should accept whoever is chosen for her by her parents for marriage, should be in total subservience to her husband, and economically dependent on him. Even though these issues are socio-political in nature, they are, however, directed at the woman, with no corresponding demands made on her male counterpart. Thus, Anowa is regarded as a type whose action and reaction represent those of many other women. Her rebellion is aimed at turning around abhorrent constructs against women in society.

Anowa's circumstances of birth indicate that she is expected to be a priestess, but supported by her mother, she rejects this fate and insists on marrying. Her mother contends:

I have said and I will say again and again!
I am not going to turn my only daughter
into a dancer priestess.
...
... in the end, they (priestesses) are
not people. They become too much like
the gods they interpret.
They counsel with spirits;
They read into other men's souls;
They swallow dog's eyes
Jump fires
Drink goats' blood
Sheep milk
Without flinching

Or vomiting
They do not feel as you or I,
They have no shame.

I want my child
to be a human woman
Marry a man,
Tend a farm
And be happy to see her
Peppers and her onions grow
A woman like her
Should bear children
Many children,
So she can afford to have
One or two die
Should she not take
Her place at meetings
Among the men and women of the clan?
And sit on my chair when
I am gone? And a captainship in the army,
Should not be beyond her
When time is ripe! (11–13).

These are Badua's sincere desires for her daughter, and she finds it difficult to accept that Anowa should function as a priestess. Badua's wishes above, in dissonance with Anowa's pre-destination, contribute largely to the incongruous relationship and subsequent tragedy in Aidoo's *Anowa*. This element is accounted for by the fact which Old Man articulates that 'from a very small age, Anowa had hot eyes and nimble feet of one born to dance for the gods' (20).

The status of the woman as priestess is highly regarded in African cosmology, and Acholonu's survey (1995) indicates that:

> Throughout the continent [of Africa], women in priestly or ritual positions have held sway over their communities. Gender is never a hindrance to their performance of these functions in African traditional religions ... [In some communities], ... priestesses, queen-mothers and queens retained very high political, religious and ritual offices in the land (33).

In spite of these, Anowa refuses to be a priestess, a mouthpiece of the gods. She wishes to attain self-fulfilment as a married woman, through shared love and fulfilment through procreation. Anowa in this way validates the contention that the African woman realizes the need for her male counterpart and seeks to relate to him on a complementary basis whereby neither is superior. In fact, she recognizes Steady's thesis on African feminism that stresses 'centrality, multiple mothering and kinship, female autonomy and co-operation' (35–56).

Anowa's action in this play clearly portrays her as an intellectual who is necessarily a revolutionary, whose intellect has developed far beyond the natural limits of her native intelligence, thus presenting her as a strange species among her people. Anowa is a non-conformist. Her strong character traits empower her to transcend the parochial limitations that characterize her world. This fact underlies her pronouncements to her parents:

> Mother, Father, I have met a man
> I want to marry.
> ...
> I say I have found the man I would like
> to marry
> ...
> Kofi Ako asked me to marry him
> and I said I will, too (14).

This is unprecedented in the community, but it is explicable by the fact that the non-conformist can be confrontational. Maduka observes that:

> ... the inner rhythm of the non-conforming character paces along outer forces to move at its own rate ... If the inner rhythm is stronger, the character eventually triumphs and becomes a hero having the image of what Hegel would call a world historical figure able to leave his mark on history. (1978: 13).

By implication, Anowa emerges as a heroine within this category. She successfully withstands the forces that work against her vision of a society that allows individual choice in marriage, and condemns the interference of the supernatural in human activities, and advocates hard work and result-orientedness.

Analysis of Anowa's character typology reveals that her strength of character motivates her opinion, perceptions, expectations and expressions to be markedly different from the society's. The various schisms operating in her mind are both complex and dynamic. The dynamics of Anowa's character entail different forms of strategies that she adopts in withstanding (or possibly overcoming) pressures from the stifling socio-political paradigm and value systems of the larger society. Her strong inner rhythms embolden her to do the unusual: to apply herself to hard work, to choose her husband herself, to defy every form of interference or imposition, and to seek self-fulfilment through procreation. When her mother warns her that '... marriage is like a piece of cloth ... its beauty passes away with wear and tear' (16), Anowa responds:

> I like mine and it is none of your business
> ...
> I do not care, Mother. Have I not told you that
> This is to be my marriage and not yours?
> ...
> He is mine and I like him (16).

Anowa determines to make her marriage successful and invalidate the belief that Nsona men (one of whom is Kofi Ako) do not make good husbands:

> You will be surprised to know that I am going
> to help him do something with his life.

...
Mother, I shall walk so well that I will not find
  my feet back here again.

...
We shall not be coming back here to Yebi. (8, 19)

She abandons her parents and home, and leaves with Kofi Ako for a strange land.

Realizing that Kofi cannot get her pregnant, and that she is not expected to work hard, but to use slaves, the conflict in the play escalates. Anowa's ideals are at variance with Kofi's. He wonders:

What is wrong with buying one or two
people to help us? They are cheap ... Everyone
does it . . .And things would be easier for us ...
Anowa, who told you that buying men is wrong?
... I like you and the way you are different.
I know I could not have started without you,
but after all, we all know you are a woman and
I am the man. (30)

This assertion is significant because as Mitchell argues, 'economically, women are the most highly exploited group; they are also the most psychically determined as inferior' (1973: 67). In many situations, men and their ideologies control women's reproductive and sexual capacities, and as a result, women are trapped by their men's reproductive anatomy, capability and by a dogma of compulsory heterosexuality (Smith 1986: 172).

Evidently, Anowa expresses strong objections to the social expectation that reduces the woman beyond human contexts. She is remarkably different from other women and she laments the fate of the woman as she states that 'in order for her man to be a man, the woman must not think, she must not talk' (52). But 'what I don't understand, Kofi, is why you want to have so many things your own way' (53). These are the areas of remarkable differences between Anowa and Kofi Ako which are hardly resolvable because Anowa refuses to 'be like other normal women' (53) as Kofi observes.

Kofi's impotence and subsequent inability to get Anowa pregnant increase Anowa's agitation, and make her frustrated:

Kofi, are you dead? ... is your manhood gone?
I mean, you are like a woman ... there is not
hope any more, is there? Kofi ... is that why I
must leave you? That you have exhausted
your masculinity acquiring slaves and wealth? (61)
Why didn't you want me to know? You could
have told me.
...
Now I know ... My husband is a woman now.
He is a corpse. He is dead wood. But less than

> dead wood because at least, that sometimes
> grows mushrooms ... (62)

In spite of the plethora of problems facing her, Anowa refuses to return to Yebi. She takes full responsibility of her earlier decision and action, and is consistent in not returning home to be ridiculed by everyone.

The metaphorical implication of Anowa's failed sexual rebellion

In describing Anowa's sexual rebellion as a failure, it is relevant to note that even though her rebellion does not come off, it has contributed immensely to evolving and developing a fresh consciousness among African women and a new dimension in inter-relationships. Anowa has debunked the western feminist fear of maternal engulfment that is a major consequence of marriage, which Anowa desires and attains. She recognizes the essence of the family unit while upholding individual choice. Indeed, Anowa is conscious of Shoshona's observation of the woman as:

> the tame, domesticated essence of domesticity and homeliness who turns out to be a deluded, murderous narcissistic fantasy which in reality represses femininity as difference, kills the real woman. (1981: 42)

Anowa determines that, to her, wifehood will be a conscious choice rather than a passive yielding to tradition. Thus, when she is faced with a labyrinth of problems and rejection by her husband, she is aware that her precarious situation is caused by the fact that with such a totally different orientation and set of ideals and aspirations within her peculiar matrimonial context, it is difficult for her to find common grounds with Kofi Ako either as husband (as he is impotent), or as work partner (as he requires slaves to do the work). This awareness constitutes a giant step toward the demystification of wifehood.

Underlying Anowa's obstinacy is a consciousness that in the society she finds herself, if she talks too much, it is considered 'uncouth and uncivilized' (Ojo-Ade 1983: 159). Thus, her action is rebellious since she knows that the true test for a woman continues to be the marriage institution – a closed-in arena in which every married woman has to fight her survival as an individual. (Chukwuma 1994: 5). Anowa's sexual rebellion reveals her effort at negating Marks' assertion that female experience, depending on one's theoretical perspective, was either marginalized, privatized and secret, or so repressed as to be invisible, unspoken and unwritten (1986: 182). Here, Anowa seeks to be heard, and to make an impact, not necessarily in consumption, but in production and reproduction. She understands that intrinsic to sexual exploitation is the perpetuation of female economic dependence on their male counterparts, thereby making the former insecure, humiliated and timid. But Anowa does not wish to be served; she demonstrates no superiority to the women who have no benefit of wages, who represent an important and neglected component of the labor reserve, the quintessential reserve in peripheral societies (Harrison 1991: 179).

In conclusion, Anowa's sexual rebellion is described as a failure literally because it does not pull through since Anowa is not alive to witness the positive results of her initiative. But metaphorically, this act is successful, and very much so because she has attained independence. Independence is construed here not as implying a shedding of social attachments, but is linked to a strong sense of interpersonal connectedness which Anowa attains in marriage. This is buttressed by the notion that African women still believe in the institution of marriage and are not demanding to relinquish their nurturing and procreative roles, which are not problematic (Achebe 1981: 9).

WORKS CITED

Primary source
Aidoo, Ama Ata. *Anowa*. London: Longman, 1970.

Secondary sources
Achebe, Christie C. 'Continuities, Changes and Challenges: Women's Role in Nigerian Society'. *Presence Africaine*. 120, 4th Quarterly, 1981: 3–16.
Acholonu, Catherine. *Motherism: The Afrocentric Alternative to Feminism*. Published under the Let's Help Humanitarian Project (LHHP). Women in Environmental Development Series, Vol 3, in collaboration with the Nigerian Institute of International Affairs (NIIA), 1995.
Chukwuma, Helen. Introduction: 'The Identity of Self'. *Feminism in African Literature*. Enugu: New Generation Books, 1994: ix–xxiv.
Harrison, Faye V. 'Women in Jamaica's Urban Informal Economy'. In C. T. Mohanty *et al.* (eds) *Third World Woman and the Politics of Feminism*. Bloomington & Indianapolis: Indiana University Press, 1991: 173–96.
James Adeola. 'Ama Ata Aidoo' *In Their Own Voices: African Women Writers Talk*. London: James Currey, 1990: 9–27.
Maduka, Chidi. 'Intellectuals and the Drama of Social Change: The Writer's Insight'. *Kiabara: Journal of the Humanities*. Vol.1. University of Port Harcourt, 1978: 40–58.
Marks, Elaine. 'Transgressing the (In)cont(in)ent Boundaries: The Body in Decline'. *Yale French Studies, Feminist Readings: French Texts/ American Contexts*. No.72, 1986.
Mitchell, Juliet. *Woman's Estate*. New York: Vintage Books, 1973.
Ojo-Ade, Femi. 'Female Writers, Male Critics'. In Eldred Jones (ed.) *African Literature Today*. No.13. London: James Currey, 1983: 151–79.
Shoshona, Felman. 'Rereading Femininity'. *Yale French Studies, Feminist Readings*: French Texts/American Contexts. No. 62, 1981: 19–44.
Smith, Barbara. 'Towards a Black Feminist Criticism'. In Elaine Showalter (ed.), *The New Feminist Criticism: Essays on Women, Literature and Theory*. London: Virago, 1986: 168–85.
Steady, Filomina. 'Black Woman Cross-Culturally: An Overview'. In *The Black Woman Cross-Culturally* (ed.) Filomina Chioma Steady. Cambridge, Mass.: Schenkman, 1981: 49–64.

'To Write Beyond the "Fact"'
Fictional Revisions
of Southern African Women in History
by Yvonne Vera & Lauretta Ngcobo

Margaret J. Daymond

In the early 1990s, Yvonne Vera and Lauretta Ngcobo published novels
which revisit some key events and figures in the long opposition to
colonial rule in their regions. They have both chosen to use rural women
as their protagonists, and they have radically revisioned the historical
agency of women by placing their protagonists at the centre of an indigenous resistance to the colonial and apartheid measures by which the land
was appropriated and controlled. The disruptive presence of a woman
protagonist and a gendered representation of events in Yvonne Vera's
poetic novel, *Nehanda* (1993), have been discussed by Nana Wilson-
Tagoe (2002); I wish to extend this discussion by placing Nehanda
alongside Lauretta Ngcobo's novel, *And They Didn't Die* (1990). This is
because while Ngcobo works in a very different narrative mode, that of
realism, I wish to suggest that in her gendered representation of events
she too draws attention to the larger transformative possibilities that are
released when the material and signifying functions of the customary
gender hierarchy[1] are exposed. Like Vera, Ngcobo raises the question of
what it means to try to be at home in one's world, and to take responsibility for the maintenance of one's home (with all its cultural as well as
economic functioning), when one's world is controlled by an alien
colonising power. These claims raise the much debated relationship of
fiction to written history and to daily life, and in particular whether the
relationship is different in realist fiction from that in other narrative
modes. The argument here will be in relation to Vera's poetic fiction but it
could equally be in relation to narcissistic, self-referential modes of
narrative metafiction. I suggest that all fictional modes are a reworking of
the world requiring the conditional mood of re-presentation – more
evident in some cases than in others – but I will also show that within
this overarching similarity, the different fictional modes chosen by
Ngcobo and Vera affect what they choose to represent of their subject
matter. Finally I suggest that the points of convergence and divergence
between *Nehanda* and *And They Didn't Die* highlight some of the ways in
which a gendered focus on the past may produce an epistemological

transformation (Attwell 1990: 97–8) in which new possibilities of understanding the present and envisaging the future are opened.

'Fiction' implies a 'distance between the reality as it is and as it may be
imagined' (Wilson-Tagoe 2002: 175) that more readily enables a novelist
to undertake a revisioning of the past: fiction's mode is speculative, within
its own historicity, rather than the objective and authoritative account to
which orthodox history aspires. As Wilson-Tagoe says, two aspects of
Bakhtin's theorising of the novel's dialogic mode underpin this claim: the
novel is polyphonic (using multiple points-of-view) whereas written
history, with its focus on objectivity and verifiable fact, works with a
single-voiced narration' (ibid.: 156)[2] and, because fiction views the past
from the inconclusive present, time may function differently and 'the
semantic stability of the object is lost; its sense and significance are
renewed and grow as the context continues to unfold' (Bakhtin 1981: 30).
As a result, within the 'fluidity' of temporal relations and of polyphony
that the novelist can use, 'space for debate, dissent and rupture' is created
(Wilson-Tagoe 2002: 157). This, I will suggest, may be true when the mode
of the fiction is realistic as it is in Ngcobo's novel, as well as in Vera's more
poetic mode. While neither Vera nor Ngcobo is engaged in pure invention,
both avail themselves of the freedom to speculate that is the special
domain of fiction; they write and ask to be read in the conditional mood of
possible worlds which allows fiction 'to project a meaning that derives
from yet transcends phenomenal reality and sensory experience' (Wilson-
Tagoe 2002: 156).[3]

Indicating what is involved in women writers using woman protagonists in order to challenge established views, Boehmer has argued that the
narratives (fictional as well as historical) which have served nationalist
movements in Africa exhibit 'a unitary, monological vision, a tendency to
authorise homogenising perceptions and social structures and to sup-
press plurality' (Boehmer 1991: 7). And, she points out, these movements
and their narratives also tend to ally themselves with the authority of
patriarchal power, resulting in their overlooking women's agency and a
gendered understanding of issues such as freedom and responsibility in
daily life. One important consequence for writers of the dominance of
patriarchy in the historical picture is, Boehmer suggests, that the motherland of Africa, which is the focus of nationalist endeavours, may not
'signify "home" and "source" to women' (ibid.: 5) in the same way that it
does to men. '[G]ender ... as a historical category' and the implicit failure
of the andocentric, normative thrust of orthodox history to recognise
gender has also been taken up by Wilson-Tagoe (2002: 159) who asks 'by
what process have men's acts become the norm of history' (ibid.: 156).[4]
She argues that in aspiring to establish the 'facts', history moves towards
'continuity and closure using a representation of events and people that is
'consolidating and totalising' and has the effect of 'reconcil[ing]
audiences to current social systems' (ibid.: 156). All of these differences

between gender and narrative in fiction and in history play into the choice
made by Vera and by Ngcobo to explore the possible historical agency of
their women protagonists.

Jezile Majola, Ngcobo's protagonist, is an ordinary rural woman who
takes part in the late 1950s campaigns in the Ixopo district of KwaZulu-
Natal against the Pass Laws[5] and against enforced cattle dipping and
culling. She is a wholly fictional but metonymic figure.[6] Yvonne Vera's
eponymous protagonist is the spirit-medium who was a key Shona figure
in the revolt of 1896–7 (the first *chimurenga*) against the colonial occupation of the central and eastern parts of present-day Zimbabwe. She is
based on an actual woman called Charwe before she became a Nehanda
medium; Nehanda was one of the greatest of the *mhondoro*, the royal
ancestor spirits who protected the land and who brought rain and crops to
the living. Her medium was revered by the people, and her actions were
extensively recorded by the colonial authorities because, once they had
captured her they were determined to execute her for her part in the revolt.
Research done by C. G. Chivanda in the 1960s[7] shows that Nehanda is also
remembered as an important figure in Shona oral accounts of that time;
subsequently she became an icon of resistance for the freedom fighters of
the 1960s and 1970s, the second *chimurenga*, and was invoked in many of
the songs, poems, plays and novels about the struggle.[8] She has also been
celebrated in women's praise poetry.[9] In addition, although Vera deliberately refused to draw on anti-colonial history when writing *Nehanda*
(Ranger 2002: 203), the importance of Nehanda's part in the nineteenth-
century revolt and her significance for the 1960s had been put forward by
the historian Terence Ranger (1967), and the anthropologist David Lan
(1985) has argued that in Dande, the part of the Zambezi valley bordering
on Mozambique which was an important entry route for freedom fighters
after the mid-1970s, a Nehanda medium was again instrumental to the
struggle.[10] She enabled the in-coming fighters to gain the support of the
villagers to whom they would otherwise have seemed as threatening as
the Rhodesian government forces, and she advised the insurgents about
safe routes and strategy, as well as the rituals they should perform in
relation to the land and its protective spirits (Tungamirai 1995: 41–2).[11]

The non-fictional original of Nehanda and the comparatively full,
written and popular record of her existence might suggest that Vera would
have taken up the material and stylistic methods of documentary realism
for her narrative, while Ngcobo, with her imagined protagonist and generic
rural setting, might have availed herself of a greater freedom in relation to
the established record. But in the event, it is Ngcobo who, in placing her
protagonist within recorded events, gives attention to the impact of actual
documents and events on Jezile as she awakens to political action during
her first visit to Durban, the city where her husband is working:

> She picked up the previous day's newspaper *Ilanga Lase Natal*. Spread on the
> front page was a picture of a crowd of women, wielding heavy sticks and

chasing after some men. ... She read on, 'Clinics not beer halls' the headline read ... Jezile laughed to herself, at once feeling a bond with these city women – how similar their situations were. (1999: 30)

In keeping with this emphasis on actuality, the novel is written in the mode of conventional realism, and in its narration Jezile's consciousness becomes increasingly important as she understands more about the forces that shape her world. Vera, on the other hand, side-steps the written and the photographic record. She has said that she knew from school history the photograph of Nehanda which was taken in 1898 while the medium was in custody, awaiting execution. But, she says, she 'wanted to write beyond the photograph ... that frozen image, beyond the date, beyond the 'fact' of her dying' (1998b: 77). In wishing to counteract the meaning that the colonial authorities had given to the photograph of Nehanda,[12] in order to get beyond the 'fact' of Nehanda's dying, Vera creates 'another consciousness of feeling, of touching, of the body' (ibid.). For this her narrative style is allusive, lyrical and vatic rather than realistic. She uses no dates, no place names, very few character names and almost none of the signals by which a novelist usually enables readers to orient themselves in relation to the world of the narrative. She abjures an explanatory cause and effect approach to the cultural and military conflict and introduces another way of understanding history itself. It is a style which is summoned by her subject matter and her vision; it can also be thought of as emerging from the long-standing popular knowledge of Nehanda's story.

Besides wishing to counter the colonial record, Vera has indicated that she strove to reach back to a way of life, and to a way of relating to the land in particular, that was not comprehended in the colonial written record and is now no longer available to her people. She has chosen to reach back to this moment through the perceptions of a woman, and this suggests that she herself found an affinity between the hitherto neglected signifying potential of a woman protagonist's gendered point of view and a lost mode of being. It may be because both lie outside the accepted record that the occluded one, the comparatively unknown consciousness of a woman (which is both her subject matter and her strategy), can be used as a vehicle to recover an inwardness with the other, now lost, subject matter – an understanding of the land as sacred and to be held in trust for its guardian spirits. Vera has said of the 'mythic consciousness' and the relation to the land that she sought to create, that it was

part of a value system: it was a belief that the land was protected by the ancestors, that ... the departed – not the dead but the departed – were the guardians of the soil. ... They were the ancestral shelter for the land and they themselves were being taken care of by the land, by the ancestors. (1998b: 76)

This consciousness that does not see land as property to be owned is one which, she says, 'perhaps our people had had before they claimed the land as something belonging to them' but which, in the 'transformation of consciousness' forced on them by colonisation, they were compelled to abandon. Ironically, because they had to use the concept of privately owned property when contesting the colonists' claims to land, her people lost their vision because of 'their effort to resist the takeover by the British settlers' (1998b: 76).[13] Vera's recreation of a past relatedness to the land means that her poetic, avowedly non-realistic narrative is, somewhat paradoxically, being created for mimetic purposes – like realism, it has its imagined referent as it invites a reader to imagine how it might have been to live in such a way.

The relationship of Ngcobo's novel to the written record might suggest that it is to be read, as J. M. Coetzee has put it, as a 'supplement' to history which gives a 'dense realisation of the texture of life [and] the individual experience of historical time, particularly the time of crisis ... [that] orthodox history ... [has not] the formal means to explore' (Coetzee 1988: 2) because it seeks a more objective account of events, their causes and effects. Vera's writing on the other hand would seem to 'rival' (ibid.: 5) history in that her desire to get beyond the colonial 'facts' leads her to use another mode of thinking ... [and to produce a] ... novel that operates in terms of its own procedures and issues in its own conclusions [which are not] ... checkable by history' (ibid.: 3). Coetzee does remind us that all fiction is a 'game' in that (realistic or poetic) it can only be made meaningful by utilizing a specific set of rules or conventions which are not those of everyday life, but he implies that the realistic novel will usually more readily be taken up as the handmaiden of history because it does not declare its fictionality as overtly as do other modes. But there are at least two reasons why the poetic and the realistic modes no longer seem to give the novels I am discussing a home in opposed camps: firstly, as David Attwell has suggested there has always been a third possibility of relation, that of 'complementarity' (Attwell 1990: 107); and secondly because in their focus on gender matters, neither novel is subservient to orthodox history. The gendered focus of both novels issues in a re-conceptualising of events and people which can now be seen to be disruptive of our expectations and especially of the classifications that we might deploy as guides to the seriousness and effect of the fiction we read. In this argument, the context of reading is as important as that of writing.

As Michael Green has pointed out, Coetzee himself draws our attention to the particular context of his comments, stressing the 'historicity of history' (Green 1997: 20) when he identifies the polarisation of the options he sees for fiction with the specific socio-political climate of the 1980s.[14] In this decade in South Africa it was considered vital to recover and make acceptable the history of the freedom struggle, and this produced great pressure on writers directly and overtly to serve a political cause. Since then many changes have begun to take place in South Africa and the new dispensation has, while it is too early to say that a choice to supplement or to rival history will prove to have been limited to the 1980s, released fresh options to writers as well as to a re-reading of earlier texts. The trajectory in Zimbabwe has been somewhat different and will be taken up when I discuss the historicity of each writer as it affects the ending of her novel.

Vera's narrated time is the moment at which African cultures in Zimbabwe were just beginning to feel the cold winds of colonialism and to wither before its alien modes of thought. Ngcobo's time frame, on the other hand, is that of a more fully developed modernity which has, even in the countryside, only the remnants of a once coherent indigenous socio-political and religious system with which to compete. Her protagonists live by beliefs and customs which have not become the common heritage of all South Africans, but she is able to represent as familiar matters such as apartheid's destruction of the consensual rule of established chiefs. But the point of view of a rural woman on circumstances and events did not enter the colonial (apartheid) record, nor had it (in 1990) entered the memory of those who resisted colonisation, and nor has it been established in fiction. On the matter of a rural perspective, it should be remembered that although in South Africa the passing of the Natives' Land Act of 1913 has been seen as probably the single most destructive piece of legislation for African life, both rural and urban, and although it 'brought into being, for the first time, organised black protest of an intellectual kind .... stirr[ing] into existence the newly-founded South African Native National Congress ... and gave voice to a new class, a black elite educated for the most part by missionaries in the British liberal tradition' (Head 1982: ix), urban issues remained the rallying point for most organised resistance and, so far, for fictional and historical accounts of resistance. Govan Mbeki's history is an exception; it is subtitled *The Peasants' Revolt*[15] and surveys the 1959 to 1960 countrywide uprisings over land. Mbeki concludes that the urban focus of the ANC's resistance was mistaken because:

> [t]he Pondo movement accomplish[ed] what discussion had failed to do in a generation – convincing the leadership of the importance of the peasants in the reserves to the entire national struggle ... a struggle based on the reserves had a much greater capacity to absorb the shocks of government repression and was therefore capable of being sustained for a much longer time than a struggle based on the urban locations. (1973: 130)

From Tom Lodge's account of resistance politics it can be inferred that this recognition was, however, put into effect by the ANC only in the Transkei (now the Eastern Cape). He says that 'Congress during the 1950s could do little to exploit [rural tensions] ... Its organisational vulnerability apart, its social and ideological orientation ... helped to distance it from rural culture' (1983: 290).

Black writers of fiction in English have also neglected the plight of rural people. Several important autobiographies, such as those by women like Ellen Kuzwayo, Phyllis Ntantala and Sindiwe Magona, begin with scenes of a rural childhood but then move with their narrators into urban life. Similarly, while the move of peasant men to towns in search of jobs and the constraints imposed by the Pass Laws on their efforts have been extensively represented in fiction, this has, from R.R.R. Dhlomo's *An African Tragedy* (1928) onwards, usually been done from an urban perspective. From this angle, rural life comes to stand for age-old traditions, often seen by the protagonist in the gilded glow of nostalgia. What has not been represented is the experience from the point of view of those whom the job-seekers left behind – old people, the wives and the children.

Of the many points at which these two fictional projects converge and then diverge, three will allow me to demonstrate that despite Vera's re-creating an actual woman and then side-stepping the record, and Ngcobo's creating a fictional figure but placing her in actual events, these novels work in complementary ways to disturb established history, 'the certain kind of story that people agree to tell each other' (Coetzee: 1988: 5), and to affect thinking about the present and the future. The first point is the degree of analytical grasp of the forces which shape her world that each novelist has chosen for her protagonist; this is a choice which is conveyed in the narrative technique of each novel, setting in motion the novelists' analysis of her character's relation to power and authority. The second is the novelists' scenic representation of the profound rupture to an indigenous people's religious or customary relationship to the land, to their feeling at home there and to their ability to sustain a home and family on the land. As each novelist represents what happens when a hostile force erodes a people's sense of continuity and purpose, she is writing in and for the present. As understanding this rupture is dependent on a penetrating grasp of circumstances, I will discuss these two points together. The third is each novelist's writing for the future and her desire to promise eventual victory despite the historical record's showing that each of these resistance movements ended in defeat. Here both novelists are in a complementary relationship to history, and it will also be evident that their chosen styles enable each to draw fundamentally different matters into focus.

In creating the 'mythic consciousness' of Nehanda's day, Vera works, in the main, from inside her character's consciousness, but this consciousness does not stand alone. It is set within a polyphonic matrix, a choric expression by women of their world view and their actions[16] and this goes some way to answer the complex question raised by Maurice Vambe (2002: 128) of how Nehanda can be understood as both a mythic figure (eternal, outside of time in her meaning) and an agent of socio-political change who operates in the temporal realm of daily life. The continuity and interaction that the narration establishes between what 'ordinary' women think and say and what the spirit-medium thinks and says is what serves to contain and unite the medium's two functions. As the women chosen to herald Nehanda's birth sit with the mother in labour and the midwife, Vatete, one of them reflects on a journey she has recently undertaken and on her encounter with the 'stranger' whose threatening actions are incomprehensible but who is gradually being understood as a 'sign in the form of a human being' (Vera 1993: 10) that means death. The story of her journey that is also a dream unfolds in an elliptical mode of speech that Nehanda too will use, and it is punctuated by questions and comments from her listeners that enable the story-teller to present, simultaneously, both the immediacy of her own encounter and the meaning the colonisers' arrival is, over time, taking on for the whole community. In a later scene, which is filled with anxiety about the language that has to be used to relate events, Vatete tells Nehanda about the terrible drought that her people gradually came to understand as a sign of the gods' anger with them for allowing the strangers to desecrate the land, and of her peoples' attempts to propitiate the gods. She stresses the difficulty of speech in such circumstances.[17]

> No, we did not fear death. ... If they had killed us, we would not have had to be the bearers of such disturbing news to our village. Where would we find the mouth with which to tell what we had to tell? It is a hard thing to see strangers on your land. It is even harder to find a stranger dancing on your sacred ground. What mouth can carry a sight such as that? (ibid.: 23)

This is where Vera's narrative is at its most metafictional, inviting a reader to be conscious of her responsibility in re-creating an oral culture and of their shared responsibility for 'completing the communicative circuit' (Attwell 1990: 107) in which the text operates. Vatete's question also indicates that these are the challenges that Nehanda too will face when her role as medium has been accepted by her people. It is important therefore to recognise that Vera places it as one with which all of her women have grappled. Ordinary women have, themselves, created the discourse within which Nehanda's prophetic visions will one day be uttered. These links are articulated more directly later in the narrative, when Vera has Nehanda tell her people, 'You too have been chosen to tell this story, to accompany the story-teller on the journey which may not be embarked upon alone' (Vera 1993: 60) and they in turn 'listen to the unmasking of their destiny' (ibid.: 61). Because Nehanda is both an ordinary woman and one who becomes a 'passive' conduit (Lan 1985: 65) for the deity, and because in her later role she still speaks the dialect of the women, her place in a living community can be suggested to contemporary readers even while her world-view is registered as one which has now passed.

One of the first images of temporality and transcendence that Vera deploys to indicate the powers that her language is trying to reach is of the calabash, a sacred and an ordinary vessel:

> The calabash, which holds memories of the future, carries signs of lasting beauty. Forgetting is not easy for those who travel in both directions of time. (1993: 3)

Nehanda's way of being in space and time is signalled as both congruent with that of the women and different; so too are her sense perceptions.

They are those of a social being, a woman, and they are fused with the natural world which, for her, is portent as much as environment. This means that all dimensions of being and all sensations are strangely fluid, and in order to convey this the narrative takes a cyclical course, beginning and ending with the sensations of Nehanda's death which is simultaneously a re-birth:

> Ants pull carcasses into a hole, and she is not surprised. Pain sears the lines on her palms, and she turns her eyes to her hands in wonder. Rivers and trees cover her palms; the trees are lifeless and the rivers dry. She feels that gaping wound, everywhere. It is red like embers but soft like water. The wound has been shifting all over her body and she can no longer find it.
>
> The grass has abandoned the soil and sprouts triumphantly from her very feet. It is a grass with tendrils that violently claim the earth. Her arms feel boneless to her spirit. The earth moves. She feels her body turn to water. Insects sing in and out of her armpits. She looks up in surprise and her body has changed from water to stone. (1993: 1)

As Nehanda's corporeality first melts then sets, and the causal powers of the ancestors are made manifest, so the mythical consciousness created in this lyrical, 'oratorical' (Innes and Rooney 1997: 210) prose extends beyond the operations of time and place that have been made familiar in western narrative modes.[18] And it is in enabling this consciousness to converge with that of 'ordinary' women, and then diverge, that the gendered dialect of the women is crucial.

As the idea that time is a continuum to be travelled in either direction suggests, the past is an important dimension in Nehanda and her people's consciousness, but it is present to them as a living force, not as a separate and remote realm which can be remembered or recreated, studied and analysed. At the same time, however, Vera's narrative has to deal with a violent and puzzling rupture in this continuity which only Nehanda is able to grasp. The full meaning of the seizure and settlement of the land by alien people has not been understood by the Shona themselves and they are disoriented, unable to comprehend the disintegration of their world. They see the calamitous drought and outbreak of rinderpest which coincides with the invasion as a sign that the ancestors are displeased, but do not know how to interpret and propitiate such anger. Vera gives many aspects to their bewilderment. They cannot place the origins of the gods' anger because when the colonists first arrived, their actions were hospitable according to their custom and beliefs. They are also helpless against land-grabbing because they do not conceive of personal ownership and so cannot name the theft in order to organise against it. Having allowed the strangers in, they can only lament that: 'our kindness [will] ... be our death' (1993: 10). When they *are* in a position to draw on experience, as in the matter of trade, the people are again wrong-footed because the Portuguese, who had been trading for gold since the early seventeenth century, had always been content to withdraw with their loot and so for the Shona it has been impossible to imagine that the newcomers who seek gold might want to settle on the land. Finally, the people do not trust the paper, the written treaty, with which the invaders claim to legitimate and regulate their presence. This is not because the bogus nature of such agreements is apparent but for the more profound reason that the idea of turning speech into writing is alien and unthinkable:

> Our elders have taught us the power of words. Words must be kept alive. They must always be spoken ... How can words be made still, without turning into silence? ... Silence is more to be feared than the agitation of voices. (1993: 42–3)

Through her visionary powers Nehanda understands what is still so obscure to her people, and what she is shown to do is to seek a way to 'give [them] ... a future by giving them back a past' (Ranger 2000). In putting them in touch with the will of the *mhondoro*, she has to stir them to extricate themselves and to fight in order to restore their 'old selves and clarity' (Vera 1993: 64). Once the fighting begins, Nehanda's role is to give her people a belief that they will 'survive the retaliation of the stranger'. To this end she advises:

> Do not take anything that belongs to the stranger Take only the guns. If you touch anything else that belongs to him, even the spirits shall be offended ... It is the envying eye that will destroy us, that will change us entirely. We can become stronger and whole if we believe in our own traditions. (1993: 79)[19]

Vera gives her woman protagonist an unprecedented role in instigating and leading armed resistance against the strangers, and her representation of Kaguvi, the male medium who worked with Nehanda, gives him a lesser role than that allocated in the official record. The effect of these choices is, as Wilson-Tagoe has argued, to invite us to imagine 'a possible re-constitution of leadership, authority and the social order' (2002: 163).

As Ngcobo represents her protagonist, Jezile Majola, she is comparable not to Nehanda, but to the bewildered Shona people, for, like them, she lacks the understanding of her changing world that would enable her to believe that she could intervene in its processes, and she cannot, at first, grasp the connections between one event and another. She is a young wife, living in a remote valley in KwaZulu-Natal where a so-called 'betterment' scheme is being implemented by agents of the white government. Intended to 'control land use and soil management' (Walker 1991: 232) and imposed without consultation, this scheme demanded the culling of livestock as well as the regular dipping of cattle. In a strategy that exposes Jezile's limited understanding of these matters, the narrative opens inside the consciousness of the white agricultural officer responsible for implementing the scheme;[20] he thinks with irritation and some fear of women who are not disciplined by their men and who understand so little of their real needs that they blindly resist measures that seem to him so obviously beneficial. In this way, his masculine assurance and his racial power are immediately posted as the two factors against which Jezile and the other women will have to struggle. Then Ngcobo has

Jezile take the lead, somewhat impulsively, as a group of women empty one of the hated dipping-tanks. Shortly after, she visits her husband in Durban where he works, and there she witnesses urban African women's demonstrations against their husbands' drinking in the municipal beer halls because these white-controlled institutions robbed them of the chance to make a living by selling their home-brewed beer (La Hausse 1996). Once back in her village, Jezile is drawn into even more serious demonstrations, this time against the *dompas* which the government was attempting to impose on all women in order to control their mobility and earning capacities.

Jezile does not at first understand that all the government's means of economic control converge in the issue of passes. It is only when a woman doctor[21] who is working temporarily in a nearby town comes to a meeting to explain the full historical context of what is happening and the women's plight is connected to the measures (such as taxation and the control of beer production) which have forced their husbands to seek work in the cities, that Jezile begins to understand what is at stake and can begin to choose to act. But the prospect of creating a change, which opens the women to thoughts of the future in ways that are comparable to the scope established in *Nehanda*, is not represented as an easy step for any of them:

> [They] ... looked at one another like strangers. They knew vaguely about the rest of the world and [now] ... Tokozile had brought that unreal world and laid it at their feet. She had even implied that they had a lot in common with that world. It was a dimension that they had hitherto found hard to grasp ... In all their daily chat, for years now, they had concerned themselves only about the past and the present – never asked about the future; it was as though the security of the past ensured the certainty of the future. And never having asked about the future, they now did not know how to. (Ngcobo 1999: 48–50)

In this way, Ngcobo indicates that the women who contend with oppression do not share a common dialect and it can be inferred that this is why she does not begin her narrative from within their speech and why the narration has not yet entered Jezile's consciousness, as it will do later (and, more briefly, that of her husband, Siyalo). As with Vera's depiction of the beginnings of oppressive rule, these subject peoples are rendered powerless to act partly because they do not have access to a complete picture of what is happening. But at this point the novels also diverge, for in Vera's it is the ancestors who use their spirit-medium to restore a visionary, trans-historical sense of continuity and the power to resist, while in Ngcobo's novel it is the analysis of the present, within human temporality, which enables people to act.

Vera's lyrical writing from within Nehanda's mystic, visionary apprehensions tends, in what could be understood as a voluntarily incurred cost, to take attention away from the dimension of a spirit-medium's customary socio-political function and, apart from one scene in which the local chief is present but does not speak, Vera does not represent her medium's relationship with chiefly authority. Here she seems to ignore what oral history might have supplied, for the anthropologist David Lan found that during the guerrilla war in the Zambezi valley, and before, the spirit mediums were intricately woven into the socio-political system of the people as well as fundamental to their mythology and religion. He says that when a spirit first indicated its desire to inhabit a particular person who would become its medium, the choice had to be ritually approved by other mediums, then by the people and, above all, by the chief. A medium had to retain social (what westerners would call secular) approval and the degree of control it implies, otherwise he or she would be cast out. Conversely, because the *mhondoro* was the spirit of a great departed chief, it was in the interests of the present chief and the future role he would play as an ancestor, to cooperate with the medium. This meant that the medium's revelations had socio-political import as well as religious meaning and that they were given in a context of reciprocal control: the Shona equivalents of Church and State were not separated. As Vera's narrative engages by implication, rather than explicitly, with the failure of the male chiefs to resist the colonists' invasion of their land, Nehanda's assuming leadership is, however suggestive of different possibilities it may be, presented as a personal act of heroism. The cost of serving the spirit world is fully registered in the narrative when the young Nehanda's grieving mother tells her family 'My daughter is not my daughter' (1993: 43), after her visions reveal her calling. But beyond this, a direct representation of how Nehanda could answer her peoples' needs from within their political (as well as their religious) structures is not undertaken.[22]

By contrast, Ngcobo presents in detail the ways in which Jezile negotiates the complex structures of secular power in which interacting colonial and patriarchal constraints shape her personal and social life as woman, wife, mother, and daughter-in-law. The agency that she, like other women in her rural community, has to learn to claim because of her husband's absence is, at this stage, the novel's most significant challenge to the historical record. But then Ngcobo takes a gendered understanding of rural issues into a further dimension by arranging events so that Siyalo alternates with Jezile as the person who sustains the home (as an idea as well as a social unit) and is responsible for the family. This is where the conventionally gendered responsibilities of men and women are, as Bakhtin puts it, mutually 'destabilised' and where visionary possibilities really enter the narrative. This comes about when Jezile, after her political awakening in Durban, joins the women presenting a petition to officials in Ixopo, the nearest country town to the Sabelweni valley. At the same time that Jezile is jailed for six months for her part in their demonstration, Siyalo is dismissed by his employer in Durban because of his political activities, and he arrives home just in time to take her place. Simultaneously his mother, MaBiyela, who has taken on patriarchal authority in his absence, yields her place to him, thus reminding him of what custom expects of him.[23] Ngcobo uses this now hollow authority to expose Siyalo in his full, feminised helplessness, for he is unable to earn money to feed his children. In desperation, he steals milk, is caught and sentenced to a hefty term in jail and husband and wife again swap gendered meanings when he is taken from home shortly after Jezile is released. (In this sequence of gendered exchanges, it is particularly interesting that it is the husband's legal defence which is conducted on political lines; these resources are not provided for the women.) The alternations in filling the gendered labour of the homestead indicates Ngcobo's wish not to represent the division between men and women as inescapable (just as she suggests that urban and rural people share a common political cause which should over-ride their differences) and it indicates that gender is always what is performed rather than being a fixed entity. At the same time, Siyalo's despair when he is unable to act either as the customary hierarchy expects of a man (earning money) or as a surrogate mother (providing milk) is being used to figure afresh the impossibility of a rural family's functioning as an economic, let alone a cultural, unit under apartheid.

Having brought their very different women protagonists into a re-imagined history as fighters rather than victims, both novelists choose to conclude their novels by heralding a future victory despite the recorded fact of defeat. This, the third of the points of convergence and divergence which I have chosen to discuss, draws into consideration the novelists' own historicity. Both suggest a positive future by drawing on repetitions, but they do so from different positions in history. In Vera's case the promised victory was well established when she was writing, for, after the failure of the first, the second *chimurenga* culminated in Zimbabwe's achieving self-rule in 1980. This is not written into her narrative; it is a text-external factor that she relies on the reader to utilize. What she does represent is a mixture of historical record as it had passed into legend and her own vision. Although the Shona had surprise and knowledge of the terrain on their side, they could not sustain their resistance and, even when the people had stopped fighting, the colonists hunted Nehanda ruthlessly, torturing the women and children left on the land to make them reveal her whereabouts. Vera has Nehanda give herself up, rather than being captured – as in some versions of events. The written records have it that she was charged with the murder of Native Commissioner Pollard (Ranger 1967: 309) and that after a trial in which her Irish defence lawyer contested the court's jurisdiction she was taken to the gallows, shouting defiance at her captors, and hanged (ibid.). Legend has it that Nehanda predicted a second, successful *chimurenga* in which her bones would return; oral history says that even when the rope tightened around her neck she was able to resist death until the source of her power was betrayed by two chiefs who should have been her guardians (Chivanda in Ranger ibid: 394). All of this 'information' constitutes the connection with the second *chimurenga*, the repetition, through which we can choose to read the last part of Vera's narrative. Vera indicates Nehanda's death but uses nothing of the trial or the recorded scene on the gallows, although she does have Nehanda refusing the conversion to Christianity which her colleague, Kaguvi, has accepted. Instead, remaining within her protagonist's consciousness, Vera evokes the images and stories through which Nehanda herself might have glimpsed the future. The process begins with a scene in a cave when Nehanda uses her will-power to defeat the shadow-bird which embodies her fears (Vera 1993: 82), and it is picked up again in the parable of the chameleon which slowly and patiently uses a dipping branch to cross a broad stream (ibid.: 91). Then the narrative returns to the portents with which it began. In the opening passage of the novel Nehanda foresees her own death and understands her visionary powers through the image of a whirlwind. At the end, this image returns as a promise of victory:

> In the future, the whirling centre of the wind, which is also herself, has collapsed, but that is only the beginning of another dimension of time. The collapse of the wind, which is also her own death, is also part of the beginning, and from the spiralling centre of the wind's superimposed circles another wind rises, larger and stronger. Hope for the nation is born out of the intensity of newly created memory. (ibid.: 111)

These images transcend time but they do not allow an explicit connection with future events; this is what her readers supply.

The successful outcome of the South African struggle for freedom is not something to which Ngcobo could allude, even had she wanted to, for she wrote her novel from exile in the years before the unbanning of opposition movements was announced in 1990. Instead she can convey only her faith in an eventual success. It is expressed from the outset in the wording of her title, *And They Didn't Die*, which can be understood as an indirectly reassuring response to the cry of a woman who was interviewed by *Drum* magazine during the Natal disturbances of 1959:

> We do not get enough food. Our husbands pay more than 2 [pounds] in taxes. The employers do not pay them anything. Our husbands are stuck at home. If husbands come home from Durban because of the sickness they cannot go back to Durban. Because of these things we are dying. (quoted in Walker 1991: 233)

The inclusiveness of 'they' in the title indicates the extent to which Jezile's final act of resistance can be read as signalling the eventual triumph of all.

The realistic conventions within which Ngcobo has chosen to work also allow her to express her faith in ultimate success by building explicit repetition into her linear plot, thus making it (after the earlier alternation of gendered roles) her chief indication that her fiction has an exploratory, questioning, complementary relationship to actuality. When the women's resistance to carrying passes fades because the land is being consumed by drought, Jezile is forced to leave home and work as a domestic in a white family. She is raped by her employer's husband and has to return home, pregnant, to disgrace. Her husband's family will not allow them to meet again and they take away her daughters. Some years later, her second daughter, who has joined the resistance fighters, visits the valley in secret. She is being hunted by the army and at night Jezile has to show her a safe route out. When Jezile gets home she finds a white soldier about to rape her eldest child and she 'recalled in an instant her own struggle with Potgieter and the memory stung her into action' (Ngcobo 1999: 242). This time she kills the rapist. Although Jezile is not a visionary figure, she, like Nehanda, is now liminal and, shaman-like, both have taken on the burdens of their community, finally sacrificing themselves for the sake of its future.

The writers' historicity calls up that of readers, and it is here that a discussion of what fiction, in its various modes, can accomplish in relation to history has to recognise that interpretations of both change with time, and it is here that the polyphony and intrinsic plurality of meanings of fictional narrative serve it well. I have already implied that Ngcobo's mode suggests the interventionist and instructive purposes of the late 1980s, but it is also evident that now that the South African struggle for equality and justice is officially over, and democracy looks reasonably well established, her picture of rural poverty turns a spotlight on women and gender in newly disruptive ways. As I write about this novel, the South African public is midway through a series of harrowing news reports that are being broadcast during a sixteen-day government campaign to stop violence against women and children. This, and the continuing poverty of rural women in particular (we hear daily that the gap between rich and poor is widening, not diminishing) may lead current readers to interpret the end of the novel in new ways. Once Jezile's endurance of her own rape and her refusal to let her daughter be raped, seemed a particularly relevant heroism; now, as not enough has changed as a result of actions such as hers, her self-sacrifice may have a more questionable value. As novelists do not bring their stories to an end in order to be right or wrong, both responses to the fiction would, unlike responses to representation in historical writing, be valid. Vera's novel is equally, if not more, likely to bring forward new responses in readers in Zimbabwe for the way in which long-standing questions of land ownership are now being acted on there suggests that her lyrical treatment of holding the land in trust is more than ever needed as a reminder of alternatives. Similarly, as the earlier system which contained the spirit-medium within the requirements of social order has been destroyed, it seems that, despite her iconic value during the second *chimurenga*, the spirit-medium embodies powers that are difficult for the State to control. At the time of independence in 1980 conflict between the new government of Zimbabwe and several spirit mediums had arisen; Ranger writes that at 'Great Zimbabwe a Nehanda medium gathered ex-guerrillas around her, declared that the war was not yet over because land had not yet been won back from the whites, and sent her fighting men out on missions to kill white farmers' (2000). Like her forebear, she was sentenced to death. And he adds that 'today there are still several rival claimants for possession by the Nehanda spirit, one of whom has become virtually the candidate of the regime and the other of whom is spokes-woman for opposition to resettlement schemes in the Zambezi valley' (2000). Now, with the land invasions by the 'war veterans', what may dominate interpretations of *Nehanda* may be Vera's representation of the principles (which take on a feminine quality) by which her people once decided how land should be controlled. In taking her readers into the cosmic system of another culture, or a lost culture, Vera is able to indicate just why the colonists' declared principles of 'order, culture ... and justice' (1993: 55) were so terrible at the time and now look so laughable. Perhaps her narrative will prompt readers to a similar scepticism about forms and uses of power today. These possibilities are all glimpses of the many ways in which the speculative mode of fiction, and in particular these two novels' disruptive focus on gender in history, can influence both an understanding of the present and actions for the future.

NOTES

1. Joan Scott has argued that 'gender is a constitutive element of social relationships [and] ... a primary ... way of signifying relationships of power' (Scott 1986: 1067).
2. See my discussion of the novelists' use of women's speech.
3. Wilson-Tagoe is quoting Alexander Gelley (1987: xi).
4. This is not to deny that many historians of Africa are revisiting questions of gender in the past, but one of the difficulties is that the 'archive' will not usually be the written record, but that of oral memory, making it somewhat more difficult for the historian to re-enter, re-read and so recover women's actions, unless the performer of the oral record has begun to do this too. This difficulty makes a fictional revisioning of possibilities ever more necessary.
5. These laws controlled the movement of people and had the effect of confining women to unproductive land in remote country areas while their husbands laboured in urban indus-tries.
6. Jezile is not a Lukacsian type, selected as embodying the full experience of an historical moment; rather she is one who stands as part of, but is a distinct individual within, her community.
7. This research has, as far as I can ascertain, remained unpublished in its own right. It is quoted in Ranger (1967).
8. One song sung by the fighters comes from a novel, *Feso* by Solomon Mutswairo, first published in 1957. It is: 'Where is our freedom, Nehanda? / Won't you come down and help us? / Our old men are treated like children / In the land you gave them, merciful creator' (quoted in Lan 1985: 6–7). Another song is quoted in Ranger: 'We are fighting for Freedom / In our Country. / Father have mercy on us / Listen to our cries/ Our continent of Africa / Has many riches / Nehanda represent us / So that we can be freed' (1967: 385).
9. A praise poem performed by Elizabeth Ncube in 1993 begins, 'Heroine Mbuya Nehanda / You finder of the nation being a woman / You stand for the nation being a woman / Open the way for us we are your orphans' (Hurst 1999).
10. As Lan explains it, there are two legitimate traditions of Nehanda in Zimbabwe and two different regions where she was revered, one in Dande in the Zimbabwe valley and one in Mazowe near Harare (1985: 6). The Nehanda of Vera's novel is from Mazowe. There are also two versions of her origin. In one she was a princess, daughter of the founding King of the Mwene Mutapa Empire; in the other she is a great rain-making spirit, dating from a period before chiefs and kings (Ranger 2000).

11. My thanks to Christopher Hurst for this reference.
12. A photograph is not pure or neutral evidence and its meaning is, like that of any other document, subject to interpretation. In Ngcobo's novel, for example, the photograph which so influences Jezile is understood by her in gendered terms, indicating that women can take an active role in public life. This means that it does not speak to her as an example of the brutality of urban life.
13. Beach (1986) does not give much weight to the violation of religious beliefs in the build-up to the first *chimurenga*. He discusses taxation, enforced labour and the loss of land as causes of unrest but does not consider the desecration of sacred sites and the conflict of beliefs. More recently, Ranger has corrected this omission. After a discussion of the meanings of the land to its indigenous inhabitants and to the invading white settlers, his account of the war in the Matopos hills (south of Bulawayo) begins 'In the 1890s the contradictions between white and black notions of environment and how to exploit it led to open violence' (1999: 27).
14. Coetzee's full wording is: 'in times of intense ideological pressure like the present, when the space in which the novel and history normally coexist like two cows on the same pasture, each minding its own business, is squeezed to almost nothing, the novel, it seems to me, has only two options: supplementary or rivalry' (1988: 2).
15. The other exception is Colin Bundy (1979). Ngcobo has confirmed, in conversation with me, that she had read Mbeki before writing her novel. See also Daymond (1999).
16. Vera has said that she listens to women's gossip in order to learn about the past (Ranger 2002: 205)
17. For an illuminating discussion of the possibilities of gender and language, and of 'braided voices' in Vera's novels, see Samuelson (2002: 19)
18. It is also different from the dramatising voice of folk narrative which selects its materials from a common store of 'functions' (Propp 1968) or 'core cliches' (Scheub 1975) and then mobilises them in established or in unique ways.
19. An implacable opposition to all things derived from colonisation, even apparent benefits such as dams and agricultural techniques, was true also of the spirit mediums of the second *chimurenga* (Lan 1985: 43).
20. The significance of this opening was pointed out in a graduate seminar in 2002 by Emma Louise Mackie.
21. This figure is based on Dr M. M. Chuene.
22. A similarly excluded matter is that in the 1896–7 *chimurenga*, it was not the Shona people alone who rose in revolt. Ranger (1967) gives a detailed account of the neighbouring Ndebele people's part in the uprising, and argues that the two groups can be understood as involved in a concerted anti-colonial resistance.
23. Ncgobo commented during a discussion with students in 2002 that while their men were migratory labourers in the city, women always ran the homesteads and disciplined the children 'in the name of the (absent) father'.

WORKS CITED

Attwell, David. 'The Problem of History in the Fiction of J. M. Coetzee'. In Trump, Martin (ed.), *Rendering Things Visible: Essays on South African Literary Culture*. Johannesburg: Ravan Press, 1990.

Bakhtin, M. M. *The Dialogic Imagination*. Austin: The University of Texas Press, 1981.

Beach, D. N. *War and Politics in Zimbabwe, 1840–1900*. Harare: Mambo Press, 1986.

—— *The Shona and Their Neighbours*. Oxford: Blackwell, 1994.

Boehmer, Elleke. 'Stories of Women and Mothers: Gender and Nationalism in the Early Fiction of Flora Nwapa'. In Nasta, Susheila (ed.) *Motherlands: Black Women's Writing from Africa, the Caribbean and South Asia*. London: The Women's Press, 1991: 3–23.

Bundy, Colin. *The Rise and Fall of the South African Peasantry*. London: Heinemann. 1979.

Coetzee, J. M. 'The Novel Today', *Upstream* 6 (1), 1988: 2–5.

—— 'Jerusalem Prize Acceptance Speech (1987)'. In *Doubling the Point: Essays and Interviews*. Harvard University Press, 1992: 96–9.

Daymond, M. J. Afterword. *And They Didn't Die* by Lauretta Ngcobo. New York: The Feminist Press, 1999: 247–73.

Dhlomo, R.R.R. *An African Tragedy*. Lovedale: Lovedale Institution Press, 1928.

Gelley, Alexander. *Narrative Crossings: Theory and Pragmatics of Prose Fiction*. Baltimore and London: Johns Hopkins University Press, 1987.

Green, Michael. *Novel Histories: Past, Present and Future in South African Fiction*. Johannesburg: Witwatersrand University Press, 1997.

Head, Bessie. Foreword to *Native Life in South Afri*ca by Sol Plaatje. Johannesburg: Ravan Press, 1982.

Hunter, Eva. '"We Have to Defend Ourselves": Women, Tradition, and Change in Lauretta Ngcobo's *And They Didn't Die*.' *Tulsa Studies in Women's Literature*. 13(1), 1994: 113–26.

Hurst, Christopher. 'Izimbongi, Images and Identity: Interpreting Two of the Later Praise Poems of Elizabeth Ncube.' *Current Writing* 11 (1), 1999: 1–19.

Innes, Lyn and Caroline Rooney. 'African Writing and Gender'. In Mpalive-Hangson, Msiska and Paul Hyland (eds) *Writing and Africa*. London & New York: Longman, 1997.

La Hausse, Paul. 'The Struggle for the City: Alcohol, the Ematsheni and Popular Culture in Durban, 1902–1936'. In Maylam, Paul and Iain Edwards (eds) *The People's City: African Life in Twentieth-Century Durban*. Pietermaritzburg: University of Natal Press; Portsmouth, NH: Heinemann, 1997: 33–66.

Lan, David. *Guns and Rain: Guerrillas and Spirit Mediums in Zimbabwe*. London: James Currey, 1985.

Lodge, Tom. *Black Politics in South Africa Since 1945*. London and New York: Longman, 1983.

Mbeki, Govan. *South Africa: The Peasants' Revolt*. Gloucester, M.A.: Peter Smith, 1973.

Muponde, Robert and Mandi Taruvinga (eds). *Sign and Taboo: Perspectives on the Poetic Fiction of Yvonne Vera*. Harare: Weaver Press; Oxford: James Currey, 2002.

Ngcobo, Lauretta. *Cross of Gold*. London: Longman Drumbeat, 1981.

—— *And They Didn't Die*. Johannesburg: Skotaville; London: Virago, 1990. (Republished 1999, New York: The Feminist Press.)

Plaatje, Sol T. *Native Life in South Africa*. Johannesburg: Ravan Press, 1982.

Propp, Vladimir. *Morphology of the Folktale*. Austin: Texas University Press, 1968.

Ranger, Terence. *Revolt in Southern Rhodesia, 1896–7*. London: Heinemann, 1967.

—— *Peasant Consciousness and Guerilla War in Zimbabwe*. London: James Currey, 1985.

—— *Voices from the Rocks: Nature, Culture and History in the Matopos Hills of Zimbabwe*. Oxford: James Currey; Harare: Baobab Books; Bloomington: Indiana University Press, 1999.

—— 'Nehanda.' Unpublished paper for the Women Writing Africa project, 2000.

—— 'History Has its Ceiling. The Pressure of the Past in *The Stone Virgins*'. In Muponde, Robert and Mandi Taruvinga (eds), *Sign and Taboo: Perspectives on the Poetic Fiction of Yvonne Vera*. Harare: Weaver Press; Oxford: James Currey, 2002: 203–16.

Samuelson, Meg. '"A River in My Mouth": Writing the Voice in *Under the Tongue*'. In Muponde, Robert and Mandi Taruvinga (eds), *Sign and Taboo: Perspectives on the Poetic Fiction of Yvonne Vera*. Harare: Weaver Press; Oxford: James Currey, 2002: 15–24.

Scheub, Harold. *The Xhosa Intsomi*. Oxford: Clarendon Press, 1975.

Schmidt, Elizabeth S. 'Ideology, Economics, and the Role of Shona Women in Southern Rhodesia, 1850–1939'. PhD Dissertation: University of Wisconsin-Madison, 1987.

Scott, Joan. 'Gender: A Useful Category of Historical Analysis'. *American Historical Review* 91 (5), 1986: 1053–75.

Tungamirai, Josiah. 'Recruitment to Zanla: Building Up a War Machine'. In Bhebe, Ngwabi and Terence Ranger (eds), *Soldiers in Zimbabwe's Liberation War*. London: James Currey; Portsmouth NH: Heinemann; Harare: University of Zimbabwe Publications, 1995.

Vambe, Maurice T. 'Spirit Possession and the Paradox of Post-colonial Resistance in Yvonne Vera's *Nehanda*'. In Muponde, Robert and Mandi Taruvinga (eds), *Sign and Taboo: Perspectives on the Poetic Fiction of Yvonne Vera*. Harare: Weaver Press; Oxford: James Currey, 2002: 127–38.

Vera, Yvonne. *Nehanda*. Harare: Baobab Books, 1993.

—— *Butterfly Burning*. Harare: Baobab Books, 1998a.

—— '"Shaping the Truth of the Struggle": An Interview' with Eva Hunter. *Current Writing* 10(1), 1998b: 75–86.

Walker, Cherryl. *Women and Resistance in South Africa*. Cape Town: David Philip, 1991. (First published, 1982.)

Wilson-Tagoe, Nana 'History, Gender and the Problem of Representation in the Novels of Yvonne Vera.' In Muponde, Robert and Mandi Taruvinga (eds), *Sign and Taboo: Perspectives on the Poetic Fiction of Yvonne Vera*. Harare: Weaver Press, Oxford: James Currey, 2002: 155–78.

Azubuike Iloeje

> In the dark womb where I began
> My mother's life made me a man.
> Through all the months of human birth
> Her beauty fed my common earth.
> I cannot see, nor breathe, nor stir,
> But through the death of some of her.
>   (John Masefield)

It may be too soon to figure out how literary/critical posterity would evaluate the vision, talent and achievements of Zulu Sofola (1935–1995). It is certain, though, that she was the first Nigerian female playwright to see both print and production and to attract critical attention of any serious sort. She occupies, therefore, a niche of honour in the annals of Nigerian literature and culture. Her plays, embodying, as Ayo Akinwale (1989) has pointed out, a comprehensive vision, contribute significantly to the discourse on the nature of her country's yesterday and its implications for her today.

A good deal of the evaluative response so far to the efforts of Zulu Sofola has been rather unsatisfying for its cynicism and truculence. Much of this has derived from the perceived disinclination of the playwright to be a soldier-writer with bold and emblazoned causes to champion and intransigent fortresses to assault. In the words of Olu Obafemi:

> We encounter in Sofola's plays, a simple and even simplistic plot all geared towards a thesis or advocating submission to the whims and caprices of age-old demigods or 'custodians' of bogus tradition (1989: 62).

Chikwenye Okonjo Ogunyemi berates Sofola for 'throwing sand into the feminist garri', and then concludes:

> Sofola cleverly raises numerous sexist issues to create an awareness in both men and women; however, she retreats to maintain the status quo (1988: 63).

Olu Obafemi, more strident in assailing Sofola's lack of revolutionary feminist fervour, would recommend a radical manifesto of art for her:

Rather than advocate the continued subjugation of the female folk in particular and humanity in general to old, out-dated lore and burdens, she should strive toward the emancipation of her sex in particular, and the liberation of humanity in general, from enslaving codes, icons and ideas (1989: 65).

A sense of the function of a contemporary invocative approach to history and culture is seemingly lost to both Obafemi and Ogunyemi. It certainly cannot do to dismiss Sofola's plays as churlishly as the former has done:

Most of her plays advocate a return to a past that could be reasonably regarded as decadent where magic, ritual and a certain overdose of the tyranny of age tower oppressively. (ibid.: 61)

Due regard should be accorded Ayo Akinwale's view expressed in an essay which suggests itself as a rejoinder to Obafemi's:

The world of her plays are [sic] always succinctly chosen, her prophetic eye and cosmic consciousness of the life of the society she is dealing with in each of her plays is handled with a clear understanding of that society (1989: 68).

He goes on to urge a contemporary relevance for Sofola's plays about our past, against the judgement of those he calls 'material-oriented ideologists':

If the past and the present are but one continuum, if the past can be used to examine the present so as to make projections into the future, then these plays serve a very relevant purpose (ibid.: 68).

The appositeness of the plays of Zulu Sofola could be grasped, then, within the context of Nigeria's search for codes and mores for collective and individual responses and postures, within the psychology of our self-imaging and myth-making in relation to what Echeruo (1981: 136) has described as 'the archetypal meaning derivable from the structure of ideas and action in a given work of art'. Sofola (1979) herself did insist on the dramatist's mythopoeic obligation to interrogate the human contingency through the envisaging of a 'living organic image', 'a collective corpus' of humankind construed as:

The articulator of group experiences from which ideas, philosophy and meta-physical thoughts are concretized and codified as the community attempts to make statements on life, the destiny of man, its social institutions and moral values, and the machinery through which they are maintained as well as how they may be modified or changed. (1979: 68–9)

King Emene: Tragedy of a Rebellion (1974) (*KE*), it could be said, has the honour of being Sofola's most intense work, possessing a degree of gravitas not noticeable in her other plays. It embodies the most profound formulation of her notion of our past and the crisis-ridden mores that sought to secure its self-definition. This position is advanced in spite of Adelugba's (1978: 208) rather tentative view that *King Emene* is 'not a very ambitious play'. Akinwale apprehends the play as 'constructed purely on the Aristotelian principle of drama' (1989: 69). The echoes in *King Emene*, of Sophocles' *Oedipus Rex* are noticeable. There is the murder of the legitimate king of which, at the onset of the action, the reigning king is unaware. There is also the hubris of an impetuous king who repudiates to his peril the wise counsel of his elders. In addition, we confront in both plays the trauma of the anagnorisis, the self-inflicted violence which marks the steeply arrived at resolution. Yet, as shall be seen later King Ogugua is a victim hero in a manner that King Oedipus is not. His sin is not bloodshed. Neither wittingly nor otherwise has he killed Chibueze; he has not even been privy to the plotting of that outrage. Indeed he does not usurp the throne; it is his mother who, unknown to her son, has usurped the place and honour of the queen mother. The king, nonetheless pays the ultimate price for the offences of his mother. Moreover, heedlessness, Ogugua's most obvious character flaw, is more in consonance with his youth than it is with Oedipus, the middle-aged king of Thebes as action opens in Sophocles play. Indeed, the impression can hardly be avoided that *King Emene,* like Shakespeare's *Romeo and Juliet* – a play which itself resonates in Sofola's *Wedlock of the Gods* (1972) – is the tragedy of sapling youth. Ogugua's death through suicide seems out of all proportion to the failings and misdoings for which, at his very tender age he could be held accountable.

Ogunyemi locates the other pole (apart from the character of the protagonist) in *King Emene* and perceives some Shakespearean influence:

> In *King Emene* [Sofola] traces in a Macbethian manner the tragedy of an ambitious queen mother. (1988: 63)

The resemblance of Nneobi to Lady Macbeth is graspable; yet the dissimilarities are far more insistent. The whole trajectory of the plot in Shakespeare's play is Macbeth's movement from apprenticeship in murder to a full mastery of it. Of course, his early mentor in the ignoble trade is his wife who bears a greater responsibility than her husband in the plotting of Duncan's assassination. The ambition of the two for the glories of the crown, however, coalesces as together they conspire and wade through blood to the throne of Scotland

In *King Emene* the king's mother, not his wife, is the sole villain. Nneobi has plotted alone; unlike Lady Macbeth who indeed is the poor cat in her own adage, she undertakes the secret murder that would pave the way for her unsuspecting son to accede to the throne. Unlike Macbeth, King Ogugua is ignorant of the dastardly hand of murder which has placed the crown upon his youthful head. Part of his brusqueness with his advisers arises from his conviction that he has come to royal rule through legitimate succession, not through deviance and malfeasance. Largely on account of this, he is persuaded that deviance and malevolence are the motivating attributes of his antagonists in the play. Since he has been neither initiator nor collaborator in the darksome murder of Chibueze, Ogugua is not burdened by the guilt which torments his own mother and also, Macbeth and his Lady, those 'infected minds' who to 'their pillows ... discharge their secrets'. His recourse to desperate self-destruction at the moment of full knowledge is a compulsive expiation of the ignominious deed that has made him king, an annulment of the doomed kingship that has been so abominably made. It is also wilful self-sacrifice, an atonement for the sins of the womb that has given him both birth and rule.

The position of this essay is that as a protagonist Ogugua is the victim of the umbilical cord, of the attachment of mother to son and son to mother. In avoiding pleading the ideological cause for women, Zulu Sofola has produced in *King Emene* an enduring evocation of the capacity of the womb which has created and nurtured to also ironically devour, through deadly ambition and greed, its own fruit. The tragic outcome is the destruction of the son and the remorseful anguish, but not the death, of the ambitious mother. The ruin of the mother in *King Emene* lies not in her own death but in the annihilation of her dream for herself as embodied in her royal dream for her son now deceased.

King Emene is set in the late nineteenth century in the ethnic Igbo part of what is now Delta State of Nigeria, Sofola's home area prior to her marriage into Yorubaland. There is no mention of the European colonial, missionary or commercial enterprise in this play; rather *King Emene* is a play on the tragic operation of the singular will to power in Oligbo, a traditional Igbo kingdom. In order for the temperament of allegiance and rebellion at work in *King Emene* to be comprehended, notice should be taken of the true nature of kingship among the west Niger Igbo who in the words of Kenneth Onwuka Dike 'have a society patterned after the semi-divine kingship of Benin' (1962: 26), their neighbour to the west and a source of noticeable cultural influence. However, as Afigbo (1986) has remarked, the *Obis* of this area

> never become even nearly half as powerful or as influential with their own peoples as the Oba of Benin or the Attah of Igala, no matter how flambouyantly and successfully they adopted the regalia and ceremonials associated with these two potentates (1986: 10).

Earlier, Elizabeth Isichei, herself west Niger Igbo by marriage, observed:

> These kings were regarded as sacred, and lived in ritual seclusion. But they were not absolute, and took decisions in conjunction with titled men, and representatives of other groups. Their decisions could be challenged, and their persons deposed. (1976: 23)

Even within the consciousness of solemn monarchy, royalty amongst the people represented in this Sofola's play has little real ascription of divinity; its power is effectively contained and limited. It is constrained at all times to consult and take into account the popular will; it is prevented from imperiously decreeing and proclaiming. To lose sight of this arrangement is also tragically to ignore, as Ogugua does in *King Emene*, the vulnerability of a monarch set against the common weal and collective will of a resolute people.

Oligbo, like most traditional Igbo communities is also a priest-controlled society. The 'priest-politician' as Amankulor has described him

> controlled ritual and religious matters, was responsible ... for fixing the village celebrations and festivals. Every social function was performed according to certain laid out principles, the strict performance of which enhanced the awe that surrounded the priestly functions and the invisible powers. (1980: 87)

A major aspect of the conflict situation in *King Emene* is the contest between the king representing a strand of the political class divorced from the goodwill of the people, and the priestly class fully enjoying the allegiance and confidence of the people of the kingdom. The conflict between the two classes centres around the ceremonial cleansing role of the latter during the week of peace. Within this suspicion-ridden crisis, Sofola works out her theme of murder and its expiation in a situation of envy, intrigue and struggle for succession and preferment in a polygamous royal household. The unravelling of the theme is anchored, as shall be established later, on the motif of the tragic umbilical cord.

The ritual/mythic significance of the week of peace as a season of rebirth, purification and reaffirmation of allegiance and loyalty to the superintending deity, has been memorably recorded in Achebe's *Things Fall Apart* (1958). The programme for the week is overseen by the members of the priestly class and the sacredness of the week denotes a communal search for peace, a restatement of the need and desire for it in a society of flawed, covetous, ambitious, mischievous and fractious men and women. This prayerful quest is announced quite early in *King Emene* in the supplications of both Nneobi and the Queen. The former, addressing 'the water of Life and Peace', asks first and foremost, for peace of mind: 'give our heart rest' (*KE:* 1). Thereafter, she prays for the blessing of her son and for the exclusion of evil from his realm. Her search for internal tranquillity indexes the turbulence in her innermost being; the guilt-ridden conscience of a murderer afflicted, not so much by remorse, as by the fear of exposure and retribution.

The queen, unhindered by hidden guilt, prays to 'the Goddess of Life and the God of All' first for her children, and then for her husband as the father of the realm: 'give him wisdom and strength to reign over his kingdom' (ibid.). The struggle between the two women for supremacy in relation to the necessary ritual processes suggests the mythic rivalry between wife and mother-in-law for the affection of the husband/son. But in this play, it is also a struggle between guilt and innocence in a context determined, in the words of Modupe Kolawole, by 'the inevitable tension as a woman tries to come to terms with the tensions of tradition' (1999: 30).

Nneobi is minded to take, albeit temporarily, control of the libation/cleansing rites at the palace for the duration of the peace week because she knows what the queen does not know – that she, Nneobi herself, has been the fountain head of the befoulment of the land, on the basis of which the oracle has already sent 'a frightening message'. Indeed, she does not pray for true peace in the realm. She would not, and cannot, pray for justice in the manner of anguished Obiageli, the mother of slain Chibueze. Nneobi's idea of peace arises from her maternal commitment to her son; it is the peace obtained through the discomfiture of Ogugua's opponents:

> Protect my son
> Guide my son
> Let the sun never set on his reign
> Let the New year see him tower among his peers
> Turn his foes into his footmat (*KE*: 8)

She has externalized evil, located it not within herself, but within others who would insist on her unmasking as the prerequisite for the enthronement of real peace. Unfortunately, her son the king, perceiving his political insecurity organizes his own responses along the lines of a similar pattern of externalization.

Possessing a limited knowledge of his past, and of the manner of his coming to royal sway, and even of the true nature of his own mother; king Ogugua would suspect no evil in his mother. He is unaware of any crime in the royal family and gives up the dire message from the oracle as spurious, imputing all to a malicious conspiracy by Olinzele members against him. His banishment of Omu from Oligbo is a political manoeuvre to neutralize the conceived threat from the Olinzele of which the Omu is a prominent member. It is an effort to control what indeed he cannot control for, as Ifemesia has observed in his study of Igbo society, the Omu, on account of her enormous ritual role and the sacredness of her being cannot be deposed (1979: 47).

King Ogugua professes an abiding confidence in the oracle. His appointment of Nwanu as a substitute for the Omu, with a charge to 'consult the oracle and deliver the message tomorrow' (*KE*: 6) is evidence of this. Having despatched his own emissary who is not a member of the Olinzele, he now expects a favourable message from the Oracle. His own sense of his noble programme of rule and promotion of the welfare of his people and realm is undiminished – 'I shall purge the kingdom and save myself and my innocent citizens' (*KE*: 6). This is the point of his irreversible alienation from the priestly class represented by Ezedibia, the palace medicine man, who unwilling now to further 'waste royal medicine on defiled kings' rescinds his allegiance in order eventually to lead the popular insurrection against the king.

Another factor in the confrontation between the king and the council presents itself in the play. Ogugua has a grievance against the Olinzele for having undone his father:

> I am not a child. I know how the Olinzele members killed my father with their deliberately planned evil advice. I know how the Omu in collaboration with Olinzele people colluded to kill my father (*KE*: 11)

The Olinzele, which allegedly ruined the previous king, is now perceived to have redeployed in order to also confound his son and successor:

> They have advised me to do what has never been done before in Oligbo. They have advised me against the week of peace and ushering in the new year and the Omu has foolishly allowed herself to be used as their mouth piece (*KE*: 11)

Ogugua's fight against the Olinzele is, therefore, a fight to save himself; it is also part of a perceived duty to a wronged father and the legacy that father has left behind.

Sofola traces with great care, the processes by which King Ogugua, held hostage at various levels by alienated modes of seeing, moves toward complete isolation and solitary death. His dismissal of the Omu, his brusque repudiation of his own godfather and his rejection of the appeal by Diokpa are but stations towards his tragic end. His encounter with Diokpa is particularly illuminating, showing the beleaguered king inclining himself to imagine that his own personal cause could be distinct from the cause of the people and the deities they worship and who protect them: 'What the oracle says or does not say is beyond your concern' (*KE*: 8), he wishes to inform Diokpa. Yet, this could not be, for the people of Oligbo are beleaguered too; the promise of their week of peace is a promise of their individual and collective tranquillity. The realm could be no more than a realm of people to whom the king must minister, 'We come not to insult the king but to appeal to him to act and save us' (*KE*: 19). Like the distraught chorus early in *Oedipus the King*, and the frightened women in Eliot's *Murder in the Cathedral*, the people of Oligbo have a presentiment of doom:

> Since your coronation, fears have rent our heart. Disaster and destruction knock at every door. We sleep in fear and rise in fear. The gods continue to warn us, we have come to touch a soft part in you for our sake. But alas, we find a wall of unyielding rock. (*KE*: 20)

An unpliable king, in the context, could, like the unbending priest in Achebe's *Arrow of God*, be the ruin of his own people. Reminiscent of the inhabitants of Umuaro in Achebe's novel, the people of Oligbo in *King Emene* reject their king in order to save themselves, their hopes and their dreams as a community.

The encounter in Act II Scene II between members of Olinzele and the king sets out in relief bolder than ever before what the line of dissonance is between the king and his advisers. Committed to the common weal the Olinzele members send their own emissaries to the oracle. The message brought back to the king is generally similar to Nwanu's. It pays tribute to 'the great heart and good intention [of the king] for your people' (*KE*: 24) – surprising, indeed, if the Olinzele has had insidious designs towards his majesty. For the first time, a definitive statement is made about what is required to restore the community to health:

> A certain member of the royal family has to make a vital public confession, and appropriate sacrifices have to be performed before your reign will bear fruit. It is also after this confession and sacrifices that you can enter the peace week. Anything other than this will bring doom to you and to all our people (*KE*: 24).

It should be noted that what are being stipulated are confession and rites of expurgation. The oracle demands neither the execution nor the banishment of the malefactor, nor indeed, the abdication of the king to whom the foul deed has given the crown. The king does not avail himself of the suggested avenues to social reconciliation and well-being; he still considers the message he has received to be of doubtful veracity, as part of the hostile plan of the members of the Olinzele. Odogwu's ominous outburst about Emene's father and immediate precedessor on the throne, adds a certain validity to King Ogugua's fears that his late father had been a victim of the Olinzele:

> We had enough of your father and we don't want any shit from you. (*KE*: 25)

The umbilical factor assumes a large dimension from the second act, before the king makes the ill-fated entry into the peace week. The king's godfather Ojei, ever seeking the good of his ward, consults the oracle himself and returns to make, before the king, more specific pronouncements about the health of the realm. He forthrightly names Nneobi as the evil genius in the palace and kingdom. Rather than soberly seek clarification, rather than respond with contemplation, the king rages out in stout defence of the womb that has given him birth:

> What! Do you realize what you have just said? You must be mad! You must really be mad, to be accusing my mother. (*KE*: 34)

To the fruit of a womb the indictment of that womb cannot but be unthinkable. The son compulsively claims his biological mother and effectively repudiates the godfather, the prudent surrogate father. Not even disconsolate Obiageli's tearful description of her awful dream of the wandering soul of Chibueze in need of pacification and rest would lead the king to comprehension.

In the last scene of Act II, the king is no longer totally insensible. He takes note of his mother's disquiet; her ill-health in the presence of Obiageli strikes him: 'Mother, something is wrong with you' (*KE*: 38). Yet, the cause of, and cure for, this loss of maternal well being, itself an echo of the community's loss of wholesomeness is unplumbed, unaddressed. Ogugua realizes the gravity of the allegations against her but asks his mother none of the vital questions which in the context, demand to be asked. He requests neither explanation nor confession and so does not proceed towards extracting an unbosoming and initiating the expiation demanded by the oracle. Overwhelmed by the umbilical force he submits to its egoistic appeal for mere protection:

> Son, don't listen to what evil plotters tell you. They want to kill you for me and you must not listen to them. Don't let them kill you for me. (*KE*: 38)

King Oedipus succumbs to the demand for the truth which would heal the realm. Ogugua in *King Emene*, succumbs, instead to the will of the physiological mother force whose interest lies in the concealment of the therapeutic truth society needs to regain its health. Rather than comfort his troubled subjects, rather than succour his realm, the king, as the lights fade at the end of Act II, comforts and consoles his guilt-ridden mother. In choosing in this manner, King Ogugua renounces his people, abdicates his responsibility to them and forfeits, implicitly, the moral right to rule over them and their community. In imagining that she is saving him from his antagonists who would be his assailants, Nneobi goads her son on to becoming his own antagonist and ultimately his own assailant. Ogugua has crept back into the womb of his exclusive biological mother and has disdained the behest of Mkpitime, the inclusive cultural mother figure unto whom the entire people of Oligbo, regardless of individual rank and station, are the children. Evil remains unconfessed in the appropriate manner, the gods unpropitiated. The physical mother of the king is protected; metaphysical mother earth is rejected and patently dared.

At the opening of Act III, Nneobi 'low in spirits' confronts the fact that 'the deed is known' (*KE*: 39). She wishes that Mkpitime would open 'her heart of grace and save my son' for she still thinks only in physiological maternal terms and could not understand that the fruit of her womb has acquired a meaning much larger than that which her mortal body alone could confer. She would not avail herself of the programme of public confession already determined as the only avenue through which any prayer of hers could be answered. By insisting on amelioration through half-hearted private penitence, by consistently wishing the redemption of her son, and not that of the collective realm that is Oligbo, she clings tragically to the umbilical bond and rejects the communal one. In the circumstance, it amounts to a betrayal of her son (to whom she does not confess her guilt until it is too late) and an affront to the gods and people of Oligbo. Mother and son paradoxically cling to each other in order, as it turns out, to secure a severance, through the death of the son, of the exclusive umbilical bond to which they have been so strongly and mutually dedicated.

When the obstinate king enters the shrine at the end, 'a dark circle' girdles the sun, symbolising that 'the gods are angry' (*KE*: 43) and that the community is in peril. It could also have amplified the situation which has existed even as action opens in this play: an evil mother has encircled and so is about to ruin her own son, the king and 'sun' of Oligbo. Ogugua, still blinded by his own will to mere power: 'I am king of Oligbo and must reign' (*KE*: 44) does not, even as he approaches the terminal point of action, realize that he has been the victim of his own mother and the great but sinister, force she embodies.

Nneobi, the tragic mother force in *King Emene* is, it should also be noted, herself a victim of the umbilical cord bonding her on to her own mother:

> I suffered in my childhood with a poor mother of twelve children. I saw my mother cry bitterly night and day when she had no food for her hungry children. I could not bear this, so I started praying very early for a better life. My prayers were answered. Your father married me. My fortune and that of my children changed. I promised myself then never to return to those days ... it happened that you were born the second son. This worried me very much. I decided that it was better to be the king than be the brother of a king. So I did the deed. Never did I foresee this. (*KE*: 44)

Nneobi's resort to murder in order to secure the throne for her son and the attendant honour and privileges for herself, is part of her programme to exorcise the ghost of penury and want which dogged her mother's marital existence and every moment of her own growing up. It is also a tribute to her attachment to the worth and condition of the womb that gave her her own life and womb, a manner of compensating her mother and also herself. The recognition that comes to Ogugua after the unburdening of self by his mother is swift. He still cannot lay murderous hands on his own mother even when he has come to know her as 'that accursed woman'. He willingly lays them instead on himself. The villain mother lives in agony and sorrow no doubt; her victim son dies repudiated by the gods and also by his own subjects.

In his essay on 'undermeanings' in Sofola's plays, Ayo Akinwale has posited the following regarding *King Emene*:

> Written shortly after the Nigerian Civil War, Sofola seems to be concerned not with kicking against tradition but *kicking against the voice of reason*. This was quite evident in the struggle between Ojukwu and Gowon, which eventually led to the Civil War. She probably saw how all the peace moves by concerned people all over were thwarted. She seems to be saying that history will always repeat itself. (96) (emphasis mine)

It is difficult to agree that in the play under discussion the dramatist has indeed been 'kicking against the voice of reason'. Moreover, it is not altogether true that *King Emene* was written after the Nigerian Civil War. An early version was written in 1967 and, according to Adelugba, acted at Ibadan in 1968 during that war and under his own directorship, assisted by the playwright herself (1978: 208). Of course, the scorning of opposing views applied to both sides during the 1966 crisis in Nigeria and hastened the advent of the shooting war itself in July the following year. The relative youth of the two military officers securely in control across the combat divide may have been a constituent in the pattern of initiative and response during those gruesome months. Beyond this, there is little parabolic alignment between the events, positions and personages that attended the Nigeria/Biafra war and the elements of plot, character and language which combine to confer meaning in *King Emene*. There is, for instance, in the play, no polarization of political contention around two personalities, each with considerable popular following and in command of consequential military force.

Akinwale continues:

> Of course, the king in question, Obi Osemene III, is still living. Hence, the play is a product of both history and the artist's own creative intuition. (1983: 69–70)

If indeed the monarch, who was a part of the late nineteenth-century historical events dramatised in the play, was still alive as late as 1989 when Akinwale's essay was written, who then could be his artistic double in the play? Is it Ogugua's father who dies even before his son accedes to royal rule? Is it Chibueze who is cheated out of both life and rule by being murdered in his youth? Could it be Ogugua himself who as king commits suicide as the final act of expiation for the sins of his mother? What indices in *King Emene* could link King Osemene III to the persons and events in it? It seems untenable to explain and establish this Sofola play as an historical drama of the sort that Akinwale has suggested.

Adelugba, while holding on to his view that *King Emene: Tragedy of Rebellion* has a 'narrow scope', accepts nonetheless that in it 'the artist has come close to perfection' (1970: 208). The plot is held together by the familiar themes of crime and punishment, of hidden guilt and of the tragic consequences of impulsive youth in a position of authority and power. Beyond these, this essay has argued, it is also a texting of the mythic capacity of an egoistic mother force to paradoxically prey upon its own seed. This, the transgressing mother force does by seeking to feed her own ego through the destruction of the fruit of the womb of another. Perhaps, the contribution of *King Emene* to Nigeria's discourse on due national mores, modes and temper is its suggestion that her people choose, to their utter peril, to affirm only primordial loyalties and abdicate, in so doing, their responsibilities to their contemporary collective selves. Martin Esslin has observed:

> The theatre is a place where a nation thinks in public in front of itself. And in the context all sorts of matters [no condescension intended] assume political importance. (1978: 101)

This is so because as Leslie Fiedler once noted, through 'the Mask of [the writer's] life and the manifold masks of his work', literary imagination 'expresses for a whole society the ritual meaning of its inarticulate selves' in order 'to redeem its unconscious' (1952: 273).

WORKS CITED

Adelugba, Dapo. 'Wale Ogunyemi, Zulu Sofola and Ola Rotimi: Three Dramatists in Search of a Language'. In Ogunba, Oyin and Abiola Irele (eds) *Theatre in Africa*. Ibadan: Ibadan University Press, 1978: 201–9.

Afigbo, A. E. *An Outline of Igbo History*. Owerri: RADA Publishing Company, 1986.

Akinwale, Ayo. 'Zulu Sofola: Her writings and their Undermeanings'. In Otokunefor, Henrietta and Obiageli Nwodo (eds) *Nigerian Female Writers: A Critical Perspective*. Lagos: Malthouse, 1989: 68 –73.

Amankulor, J. N. 'Festival Drama in Traditional Africa: An Essay in Dramatic Theory'. *Kiabara: Journal of the Humanities*. 3, 2 (Harmattan), 1980: 85–106.

Dike, Onwuka K. *Trade and Politics in the Niger Delta, 1830–1885: An Introduction to the Economic and Political History of Nigeria*. London: Oxford University Press, 1962.

Echeruo, M. J. C. 'The Dramatic Limits of Igbo Ritual'. In Ogunbiyi, Yemi (ed.) *Drama and Theatre in Nigeria: A Critical Source Book*. Lagos: Nigeria Magazine, 1981: 136–48.

Esslin, Martin. *An Anatomy of Drama*. London: Sphere, 1978.

Fiedler, Leslie. 'Archetype and Signature'. *The Swanee Review*. LX, (Spring), 1952: 253–73.

Ifemesia, Chieka. *Traditional Humane Living Among the Igbo: An Historical Perspective*. Enugu: Fourth Dimension, 1979.

Isichei, Elizabeth. *A History of the Igbo People*. London: Macmillan, 1976.

Kolawole, Modupe Mary E. 'Zulu Sofola's Cyclic Aesthetics: Rejecting De-womanization in the Search for a Lost Dream'. In Kolawole Modupe Mary (ed.) *Zulu Sofola: Her Life and Her Works*. Ibadan: Caltop Publications (Nigeria), 1999: 29–38.

Obafemi, Olu. 'Zulu Sofola's Theatre'. In Otokunefor Henrietta and Obiageli Nwodo (eds) *Nigerian Female Writers: A Critical Perspective*. Lagos: Malthouse, 1989: 60–67. An earlier version of this essay was published in Ogunbiyi, Yemi (ed.) *Perspectives on Nigerian Literature: 1700 to the Present*. Volume II. Lagos: Guardian Books (Nigeria) Ltd, 1988: 211–15.

Ogunyemi, Chikwenye Okonjo. 'Women and Nigerian Literature'. In Ogunbiyi, Yemi (ed.) *Perspectives on Nigerian Literature 1700 to the Present*, Volume I. Lagos: Guardian Books (Nigeria) Ltd, 1988: 60–7.

Sofola, Zulu. *King Emene: Tragedy of Rebellion*. London: Heineman Educational Books, 1974.

—— 'The Playwright and Theatrical Creation'. *Nigeria Magazine*, 128/129, 1979: 68–74.

Simiyu Barasa

Written poetry has often been seen as an elitist form. It has been seen to exclude people who do not conform to its norms in terms of race, class, and intellectual capacity and also as being individualistic and unrepresentative of the masses. A look at the South African poetry that is distinguished by its opposition to the apartheid system creates another question that poetry ought to answer – didn't women write poetry that stood against the racial crime that was apartheid? If they did write poetry, why was it not published? If the poetry was published, why was it in minute quantities? To answer these questions one may ask whether the poetry by southern African women was not committed enough to warrant acknowledgement and celebration as protest poetry.

The publication of Chipasula (eds) *Heinemann's Book of African Women's Poetry* in 1995 shows that there are numerous women poets in the African continent and more specifically southern Africa. The fact that this poetry does not receive the critical acclaim given to the work of Dennis Brutus, Augustinho Neto, Arthur Nortje or Es'kia Mphahlele has always been pegged on the claim that it was not committed enough to the anti-system cause. The existence of women poets like Lindiwe Mabuza, Zindzi Mandela, Gcina Mhlophe, Kristina Rungano among several others has now been recognised along with the acknowledgement of Noemia de Souza as a moderately committed female poet. The question, looking at the above poets, now turns to a statement that this chapter seeks to emphasize: that while female southern African poets have indeed produced committed works, these have been omitted from the critical literature. The main contention does not lie with the production of the poets themselves, but the reception that these gallant works have been given.

Commitment has been defined in various ways. One can sum it up in Chidi Amuta's words that it is art in eternal opposition to the dehumanisation of mankind. Theodor Adorno in 'Commitment' (1990) says 'A work of art that is committed strips the magic from a work of art that is content to be a fetish, an idle pastime for those who prefer to sleep through the deluge that threatens them in an apoliticism that is in fact deeply political'. In southern Africa, poets were obliged to stand up and be counted as being against foreign domination, class and racial injustice. They cried out, on behalf of fellow sufferers, against the scourge of apartheid that was indecent to all aspects of humanity, including its economic, political and military aspects as well as its cultural, and very importantly, psychological impacts. This writing has to take an oppositional stance. If protest literature has context as its basis, then the reception of southern African women's writing has contributed to its omission because it is analysed in the same terms as that of male poets, as if the conditions of production were similar.

Female poets protest against apartheid on three levels – on the wider racial level, on the more practical gender level with its domestic concerns and third, they make a very subtle insurrection against cultural patriarchal hegemony in the African traditions. For them, therefore, the cultivation of political identity and commitment, did not mean bleating along with what everyone else was already saying but saying what everyone wanted to say from a new angle, with new themes, in a new style, creating a new literature.

Much of southern African women's poetry is fueled by the sociopolitical pressure for freedom and written in the context of mass detentions by the authorities, the agonies of migrant labour and domestic servitude, and women coping as heads of households. Southern African poetry by women thus tends to feature personal feelings and pains. However, this speaks for the wider public for it may as well be viewed as a microcosm of the damaged, pained and disadvantaged black people.

The metaphor of love is used to show the dislocation of family units in a brutal system where interpersonal relationships were disrupted through detention, violence and murder. Lindiwe Mabuza's 'A Love Song' reminisces about a good time with a lover that was full of dreams of a better future, but death has brought about a terrible ache. Zindzi Mandela's 'I Waited for You Last Night' creates a feeling of loneliness where the heroine wonders what happened that her lover never came home the previous night. More anguish can be seen in Kristina Rungano's 'Mother', where a mother lies haunted by the memories of a father to her children who is waited for but 'Never came back again'.

This anguish and despair is a protest against the system that kills and detains without realizing the emotional anguish it causes to the nation as well as to lovers, condensing a national crisis to the personal level. The poetry is full of the use of a liminal voice as representational of the national narrative. It is poetry that narrates the nationhood. This is seen in other protest poets such as Dennis Brutus in his *Letters to Martha* (1968) and in *Stubborn Hope* (1978).

A running motif in the poetry is that of the womb, motherhood and fertility. The anguish of being surrounded by death brought out the feeling in women that even the sons they give birth to are destined to die in the struggle. The womb thus became symbolic as a generator of heroic sons and daughters who would rise to replace the dead. Lindiwe Mabuza in her poem 'Death to the Gold Mine', which was written in September 1973 after the South African police shot dead twelve striking workers in Carltonville, near Johannesburg, asserts:

> But there will be life.
> Forever the reservoir will generate fresh chords
> ...
> Of ripe blood (Chipasula 1995: 199)

The imagery of womb and pregnancy is a celebration of the continuity of the struggle through generations of heroes ('Birth of a new awakening'). It is no wonder then that all references in the work of Kristina Rungano and Gcina Mhlophe to the joys of birth, to the womb, or to lovemaking are juxtaposed with parallels of death, mourning and despair at the sight of violence. There were also feelings of giving birth to an already stigmatized infant as in Noemia de Souza's 'Poem of A Distant Childhood', about a child born into oppression.

Double protest was dynamited into the poetry. One theme was the domestic slavery that overburdened the maids and servants in colonial mansions where they were treated like dogs. Lindiwe Mabuza's 'Tired Lizi Tired' has a heroine who is tired of 'washing clothes for / forty years / ... sure fingers chafe and bleed...'. The body has been drained and battered. The men in the gold mines wrote about their weary bodies, and the poets working as nannies in the white-owned hell houses wrote of backbreaking labour.

As Pamela Ryan notes in her 'Singing in Prison: Women Writers and the Discourse of Resistance' (1998), another form of resistance was the attempt to see oneself as a valued person in a devalued occupation. This is a psychological refusal to relinquish control over self-definition, in an epoch when blacks were subjected to devaluation. It is no wonder that the heroine in 'Tired Lizi Tired' mourns that the white girl does not appreciate her job as a cleaner, trying to demean her as lazy when she is tired, hurt, bleeding and ageing. Echoes of the psychological assertion of a valued self, characteristic of Senghor's Negritude, reverberate here.

At another level the women had to have an insurrection against the traditional patriarchal pressures. Pamela Ryan is correct when she states that women were caught in traditional family and social patterns which were not foregrounded because colonialism and apartheid instituted a set of ideologies in which political ideologies overwhelmed gender considerations. Oppressive regimes enforce hierarchized and rigid distinctions between races and classes, colonized and colonizers and even resort to using already existing patriarchal structures that favour their own hegemonic practices.

Kristine Rungano's 'The Woman' tells of an overworked woman doing everything for her drunken promiscuous man who comes in demanding sex although he has also been tending to matters of the flesh outside. The pregnant woman suffers beatings and fears a miscarriage. This kind of treatment makes her feel weary, tired, used, full of hate and yet traditions say she should obey her 'Lord'.

The poetry also expresses the pain of exile, used to create nostalgic memories of home as well as an idea of the home they would like to see: a peaceful democratic home. Poets like Phumzile Zulu (South Africa) went into exile, while others like Kristina Rungano, Zindzi Mandela, Amelia Blossom Pegram and Lindiwe Mabuza went abroad to get education as well as to have more freedom to write about the motherland they envisaged. Others like Gcina Mhlophe used theatre right inside South Africa to highlight colonial wrongs at the renowned anti-apartheid Market Theatre. Through contact with other liberated nations they felt a yearning for the ideal country they wanted theirs to be and the means to do it. Lindiwe Mabuza's poem 'Tired Lizi Tired' talks of a young girl in America telling her South African mama how blacks are burning stores in America in fighting for freedom, a sentiment she the persona seems to love.

There are feelings of despair and desolation that creep in but these are countered by optimism, endurance and stoic acceptance of suffering. This is a common feature even in male poets, where the vicissitudes of the struggle and the deaths create a gloomy atmosphere and moments of self-doubt (very prevalent in Dennis Brutus and Arthur Nortje). However, and this can be seen as a significant contribution by female poets in Southern Africa, there was the ever-exuberant feeling of hope. Hope for a new future, hope for freedom, a hope for a black emancipation.

Lindiwe Mabuza's 'A Love Song' sings of death in the face of love, but some goodness comes because 'We sponged/the ache of each beat/with the blend of hope'. 'Death to the Gold Mine!' holds out the hope that the miners' death will not mean the end of life. Zindzi Mandela stoically refuses to have either the past or the future scare her in 'I have Tried', swearing she has yet another step to take. Noemia de Souza believes that one day 'the sun will flood life' in the poem, 'A Distant Childhood'. So does Jeni Couzyn have stubborn hope for a new life, once morning comes.

This poetry also transcends the personal wail into the cry of and for a people. When Noemia de Souza, in 'A Poem For Joao', has the heroine talk of Joao, we are told that though Joao is dead, he lives in the masses. Joao is me, is you, is us all. She cries out 'Let My People Go' in a poem that gives a personal voice an echo of the whole society.

This poetry is written in a very unique and fresh style that makes it worthy of our appreciation. Aesthetic brilliance is woven with an ingenuity in the expression of ideas and it is very different from male poetry in terms of style, a factor that perhaps hasn't always been recognized.

The major criticism of this poetry has been that it is not 'poetic' in terms of language, symbolism and imagery. This is partly due to the complexity seen in the work of male West African poets such as Wole Soyinka and Christopher Okigbo, who made poetry a highly esoteric art. The political exigencies in South Africa could not allow for such obscure forms, since urgency was needed in communication, hence the big chasm between the complex West African poets and the relatively straightforward poetry characteristic of Southern African male poets.

For the female poets, the language was even simpler, in line with theories of the gender politics of language. Using Lacanian psychoanalysis, Julia Kristeva combined linguistics, semiology and philosophy to show that language is basically the 'imaginary' in the prelinguistic undifferentiated sphere of a child. The 'symbolic order' comes with the acquisition of language where a child becomes aware of her sexual differentiation, and becomes a gendered subject. The symbolic thus is a patriarchal institution, an order that can be challenged. This can be through rejecting the use of symbolism in poetry, hence the lack of symbolism in women's writing, coupled with the foregrounding of semiotic signification. This consists of drives and impulses which traverse the body; oral and anal sensations to which the body responds by either submitting to or resisting (Kristeva, *Revolution in Poetic Language*, 1974 quoted in Sara Mills 1989). Southern African female poets often use simple, un-obscure language and also concentrate on body parts (wombs, mouth, lips etc.) and other oral–anal sensations e.g. of childbirth, kissing, eating, etc. The semiotic revolution against symbolism creates elements of rhythm, musicality, presence of voice and general smoothness in all the above-mentioned poetry. Some even go further to show disruption of syntax and typeface, as in Mabuza's 'Tired Lizi Tired'.

This poetry can also be seen as representative of two patterns: first the extended metaphor that is elaborated throughout the poem, for example in the birth in Kristina Rungano's 'Labour'. Second, they can consist of a series of related images which have an intensification of power through their combined associative potential, e.g. Lindiwe Mabuza's 'Dream cloud' that intensifies feelings of fertility through repeated use of related imagery: womb, pregnant, cloud, overdue relief, skies, rain, earth. This intensification can be done through correlative objectification or juxtaposition of different images as in, for example, Zindzi Mandela's 'Saviour' where the old and young are seen as wrinkled versus blossoming; the white polished child and the black deprived child, the old man versus young son, sorrowful in their prayer for a saviour to 'release these chains'.

The poetry is different from male poetry that is pastiche in nature and draws on past literary works like that of Brutus. It also lacks the highly literate and rhetorical registers associated with 'high' art because of the intra- and trans-class patriarchal prejudices against women as speakers. It thus has the private voice but which speaks for the public, a private sphere that serves the same political and rhetorical voice as male poets. Its use of metonymic and synecdochic tropes create 'a sense of dislocation between inner and outer experience' (Millard, 1989). Their body parts that are tortured, e.g. chapped hand in Mabuza's 'Tired Lizi Tired', represent the nation's torture, rape, pains, violence, exploitation.

It is clear therefore that southern African poetry as a whole derives meaning not only from its context, text, or style, but from its elements, which are greater than the sum total of its parts. Drawing out these poems by female poets of Southern Africa, then throwing them back to the context from which they arose (apartheid and colonialism), one sees that they were totally committed in the protest against inhumanity. They have been omitted yet they captured history, exposing a way of life as a reminder to future generations of the crimes of men. Committed they were.

WORKS CITED

Adorno, Theodor. 'Commitment'. In Dennis Walder (ed.) *Literature in the Modern World*. New York: Oxford University Press, 1990.

Amuta, Chidi. 'Poetry and politics: the dialectic of commitment'. *The Theory of African Literature*. London: Zed Books, 1989.

Brutus, Dennis. *Letters to Martha*. London: Heinemann, 1968.

—— *Stubborn Hope*. London: Heinemann, 1978.

Chipasula, Stella and Frank (eds) *Heinemann Book of African Women's Poetry*. London: Heinemann, 1995.

Millard, Ellaine. 'Frames of references: the reception of, and response to three women poets'. In David Murray (ed.) *Literary Theory and Poetry: Extending the Canon*. London: Batsford, 1989.

Mills, Sara. 'No poetry for ladies; Gertrude Stein, Julia Kristeva and modernism'. In David Murray (ed.) *Literary Theory and Poetry: Extending the Canon*. London: Batsford, 1989.

Ryan, Pamela. 'Singing in prison; women writers and the discourse of resistance'. In Obioma Nnaemeka (ed.) *Sisterhood: Feminism and Power*. New Jersey: Africa World Press, 1998.

Reviews

African stories

Stephen Gray (ed.) *The Picador Book of African Stories*
London: Picador, 2000, 282 pp., £9.99 pbk; £16.95 hbk

It is to be hoped that this excellent, well-presented collection will reach paperback so it can be more widely enjoyed. It includes fascinating stories from all parts of Africa, from Egypt to South Africa not excluding the islands off the west and east coasts, and it could prove a really good reading book in schools and universities both in Africa and beyond. If it were not so costly, I should prescribe it for my classes at once.

Professor Gray has found short stories composed not only in English (nineteen), but also in Arabic, French, Portuguese and Afrikaans which are presented here in translation. I found specially moving a little story translated from the Portuguese which had been written by Honwana in the basic language spoken by the disadvantaged in Mozambique. 'Rosita, until Death' might have seemed untranslatable but the author and translator have collaborated to produce the kind of tragic impact that powerful, inarticulate feelings can communicate.

The width of reference in the collection is notable and the presentation is excellent. The areas are geographically coherent, and within each section there is a chronological arrangement. The introductory notes about the author, and where needed the translator, are illuminating without being obtrusive.

Here indeed is a treasure house. The wealth and variety can simply be enjoyed by those wishing to pass a pleasant hour, or a story can provide an insight into the countries of the writers and into their feelings. There are stories to make one laugh, cry and puzzle over. There is also satire, sometimes, as in 'The Ceremony' by Dongala, overstated although genuine. One thing is certain: by the time you have finished this collection you will have been fascinated by the richness, the sophistication, and the illumination that these stories reveal. Stories may on occasion teach readers a little about problems they have not experienced. We can, for example, share the often-ignored problems of African women and there are stories, such as Ahdaf Soueif's 'Sandpiper', that reveal the difficulties of marriage between people from different cultures.

There is a particular pleasure in looking at stories which, while appealing to feelings we all share, put such feelings in settings which are new and unfamiliar. In Gray's collection, there are also stories which make readers understand something they may never have thought about: this happens in a horrifying tale, Albert Taieb's 'When a Dog is Worth Nine Children', in which the owners become aware that their dog is being made ill because it eats so much better than their servants. By use of incredible hyperbole, Ben Okri's horrific ' Prayer for the Living' makes a powerful point about starvation and external aid.

On another level, the collections contains rich material for a study of the short story as a genre and as a means of communication. The legitimate variety of this form is worth looking at and one is encouraged to ask: How far has the writer been influenced by his background or his narrative tradition? In 'If only the Gauls', Bebey makes a distinction between a story composed in the first instance for oral transmission and one prepared for a reading public, and produces a tale which combines both concepts. In 'Lice', Ama Ata Aidoo enjoys slipping from prose into poetry as it suits, and the switch is very effective. There is plenty of variety of mood in the collection which ranges from the pathos of 'Dolorosa' by Michele Rakotosin to the broad satire of 'Blood Feuds' in which Paul Zeleza effectively reveals the absurdity of baseless ethnic antagonisms. Gray's selection enables the reader to look at stories from well-known authors such as Ngugi wa Thiong'o, Nuruddin Farah and Aidoo, but theirs are not always the tales which make the greatest impact. 'The Blue Viper' by Tahr Ben Jelloun is almost a fabliau, and, from Nigeria, Tanure Ojaide, in 'God and his Medicine-men', uses an apparently straight-faced narrative to force the reader to see the satire.

It is significant, as the editor points out in his succinct introduction, that many of the authors represented in the collection find it necessary to write from outside their own countries. It would seem that African writers are not likely to descant merely on the beauty of the scenery but that they are prepared to fight for freedom of speech at considerable personal risk. In all this it is notable that there is no condescension to readers who are encouraged to make up their own minds. As we follow the progress of a mother who is taking her dying son to drown him, or as we discover the real status of Dom Pedro, we are expected to bring our brains to the reading of these stories. However, there is also plenty of wit and fun: for example, 'The Revolt of the Vowels' is a *tour de force,* maintaining the verbal comedy in a text translated from French to English, a real achievement. Next, as we move from the Comores to Mozambique, comes 'Rosita, until Death', which we have already mentioned. Honwana, like other contributors to this collection, writes in his spare time, and, since he is Director of the UNESCO Mission to Southern Africa, there can't be much of it. This is, however, not a collection from *dilettante litterateurs*, and no one could claim these authors, even those in exile, live in ivory towers. The dynamism with which they write is a major source of the pleasure they give. This reviewer does not usually enjoy short stories so the recommendation indicates the excellence of the collection.

Margaret Macpherson
Makerere University and Windermere

Francophone Africa

Véronique Tadjo, *As the Crow Flies* trans. Wangui wa Goro
Oxford: Heinemann Education, 2001,106 pp., £11.95, ISBN 0-435-92103-8

'Indeed, I too would have loved to write one of those serene stories with a beginning and an end'. Thus the Ivorian novelist Véronique Tadjo starts the disingenuous preface to this, her fourth novel. One wonders about the logic and sincerity of that sentence. In renouncing the supposed joys of an Aristotelian plot, Tadjo seems to claim that – very much against her inclinations – she is obeying some higher directive controlled, we can only suppose, by reality itself. A plot, according to this line of argument – well known to followers of the French *nouveau roman*, is an artificial construct. Life meanwhile is devious, or at least labyrinthine. A work of fiction that wishes to follow the tortuous course of human existence will therefore practise an equivalent indirectness.

There are philosophical and practical rejoinders to this point of view. Isn't *any* work of art an artificial construction? Fleeing the constraints of linear narrative, is a writer not likely to fall into the hands of another artistic programme, just as pre-conceived and superimposed, but more modish? The history of French and of Francophone fiction since 1945 – distinguished though that has been – tends to suggest just this.

Publishers' blurbs aside (where else should they be laid?), does *As the Crow Flies* resolve this interesting dilemma? Well, the first observation to be made is that it does possess a plot, though an oblique one. Across the cluster of short sections that compose its formal structure one glimpses – as in the *tesserae* of a broken mosaic pavement – the narrative of a lone woman, abandoned after an affair with a married man in Abidjan. She now considers her predicament whilst living overseas in a 'stone city' that bears some resemblance to Washington, DC (the place is once identified unambiguously as such). Sometimes this soulful waif presents herself in the first person, at other times in the third. She is at times addressed directly, both by the narrator and by herself. She appears deep, though she admires straightforward qualities: tall, strong-looking buildings and men. Her story is interleaved with episodes involving other suffering protagonists whose voices sometimes echo her own; these included: the death of a mother; the death of a mistress; the cancellation of a theatre production by a repressive government; an abortion in a ghetto clinic; a memory of child abuse, and a reversed adultery sequence in which it is the woman who is unfaithful. A series of chapters (X, XIII, XXXII, XLIII, and LXIII) involve beggars of different sorts, in various urban spaces. Two contiguous sections (LXIII and LXIV) are couched in allegorical mode. Chronology is left uncertain, though analepses do occur: section XXXIX, for example, happens immediately prior to the incidents described in section one. One chapter (LXXV) recreates a particular year, identifiable as 1988. Physical locations are usually more precise, though a passionate embrace in chapter XXXI takes place 'between the earth and sky', which must have been reassuring.

Images answer one another: the adhesion of adjacent bodily cells in one love passage (XLIX), for example, has already appeared in an earlier, complementary scene as the *separation* and individuation of cells (LXIV); at a still earlier stage the image had been of the forcible tearing apart of cells during the abortion (VIII). Stylistically the novel is dreamy. Indeed, through her translator Tadjo at times presents us with sentences – or sequences of sentences – that seem straight out of the disconcerting and mournful world of Marguerite Duras with its sometimes sententious profundities: 'You leave as one does. One always leaves' (XXVII). On other occasions a single direct sentence sweeps home, so that one thinks 'Yes, that is how life is.' One such runs 'His mother is dying and he wants to be there' (XLVIII). Certain moments possess a direct physicality that focuses the surrounding scene, as in Tadjo's description of the abortionist: 'The freshness of the harmattan has faded. The man's hands are moist and precise' (VIII). Oddly, the resulting sensation is almost erotic; an instance of a process of transference that is constantly recurring whereby the most extreme and opposite states actively recall one another.

Two sentences near the end, however, appear to be hostages to fortune: 'These stories are all very well, but not convincing' (LXIII), and 'I do not understand this musty story' (LXXVII). Both read like comments by some humourless Anglophone critic on the school of post-war French fiction represented by Alain Robbe-Grillet. True, Tadjo's book has a stronger affinity to this tradition than to anything in recent Francophone or Anglophone African fiction. Undeniably too, that very fact represents both its personality and its appeal. One would not exactly call this work original, but it has an undeniable atmosphere, consisting of a free-floating cloud of regret that hovers over successive persons and scenes.

The problem for this English version is that such diffuse and pervasive effects often read far more convincingly in French (indeed, even in the process of reviewing this fine text, one senses the restraining force of some pragmatic Anglo-Saxon hand). For the most part wa Goro manages magnificently, though one quibbles on the very first page at 'they met at the airport' when, as one subsequently discovers, the encounter was *by arrangement*. One's single strongest reservation involves the English title, which is not wa Goro's! The French original – *A vol d'oiseau* – is manifestly designed to convey the tacking, turning, zigzagging motion associated with a darting bird or, here, with the tergiversation of the narrative. A crow, by brutal contrast, flies dead straight, the very opposite of what the author intends. A more faithful effort might have been *On the Wing*. Cheekily, I am also tempted to suggest *Last Year in Abidjan*. This is a short book full of *longeurs*. It is also sad, and memorable. Read it.

Robert Fraser
Open University, UK

Ugandan literature

Moses Isegawa, *Abyssinian Chronicles*
London: Picador, 2000 in UK (First published in Amsterdam and New York),
462 pp., £16.00, ISBN 0330376659

Violet Barungi (ed.), *Words from a Granary: an anthology of short stories from Ugandan Women Writers*
Kampala: Femwrite Publications, 2001, 87 pp., £6.95, $11.95, ISBN 9970 700014
Distributed by African Books Collective, Unit 13, Kings Meadow, Ferry Hinksey Rd, Oxford OX2 0DP

Since the 1940s, when the film *Man of Two Worlds* was released, the changing face of what was once known as 'the dark continent' has been of increasing interest to writers. One could, of course, argue that the fascination goes back to *Heart of Darkness* but, as African countries moved to independence and the outside world realized the continent's market potential, there were writers to map the progress, the frustrations, the protests and sometimes the despair. The mother in Ngugi's *Black Hermit* complains that Uhuru made no difference to the plight of women. Baroka, the wily old chief in Soyinka's *Lion and the Jewel*, says he doesn't hate progress, only its nature that makes 'all places look the same'. But many writers end in the same situation as Chinua Achebe, in 1958, seeing 'things [falling] apart' as the strongest, such as Okonkwo, are unable to come to terms with the changes taking place, or, like Ngugi's young man does in *Weep not, Child*, responding with violence. Still the conflict continues. Still young men and women face the task of making sense of the chaos of modern living, where the natural hazards of climate are compounded by the increasing economic demands, the ambition of the power-hungry (both within and from outside the country), the friction of apparently warring religions, the constant erosion of those ideals which education (perhaps) has instilled and the increasingly complex demands of the flesh. The deteriorating conditions which may obtain produce the kind of despair which is mirrored both from outside, by such a writer as Barbara Kingsolver in *The Poisonwood Bible*, and from inside by Moses Isegawa in *Abyssinian Chronicles*.

The scope of this first novel is impressive. Isegawa covers the lives of three generations of the extended family of his narrator, Mugezi, from before Mugezi was born and moves through independence, the 1966 war, the overthrow of Obote by Amin, the expulsion of the Asians, the invasion from Tanzania which deposed Amin, the troubled period of successive governments which followed in the 1980s, and the hopes raised by the NRM take-over. Corruption seemed curbed but the situation was soon clouded by more exploitation, by the proliferation of religious sects, and by the increasing ugliness of AIDS. All the events are seen in relation to a single family among whose members are representatives of every problem. There is the conservative ex-chief grandfather, who is the nearest to anyone Mugezi admires, and his wife, a midwife who takes Mugezi with her to births in order to bring good luck. The narrator's father opts out of family responsibilities, but his horrifying, ex-nun of a mother, who was dismissed from her convent for cruelty, makes his life a misery. All the time, he responds to the varying influences of his relations, his friends and enemies. There is a very wide range of characters from the villagers Mugezi meets in his childhood to

Magdalen, whom he leaves at the end of the story when, in the Netherlands, she tries to possess him.

Events are seen through the eyes of the increasingly disillusioned Mugezi who leaves his village for the town with his parents and their growing family. We follow him through his school, and hear of the exploits of various members of his family. He discovers both at home, at school and at the seminary to which he is sent that he can get his own way by deceit, that he can manipulate events to suit himself. Eventually, he leaves the seminary for Makerere University where, unable to take the law course which he wanted, he has to settle to train as a teacher. Mugezi resolves to serve himself only, eventually leaving teaching for more lucrative employment. However, disappointment follows him.

Within Mugezi's family are those belonging to Catholic, Anglican and Muslim camps, and we follow the fortunes of his colourful relations as he grows up. The narrative purports to be told by Mugezi but, since it includes details of the parental courting from the viewpoint of his father and the dying thoughts of both his mother and his father (one killed by a crocodile and the other by a buffalo), liberties are taken. The author seems to want the immediacy of the autobiographical approach without any of its restrictions, and he sometimes strains credulity. To balance this, and the occasionally excessive sensationalism, the way in which Ugandan history following independence is presented as it affects a single family is stimulating. Moreover, the way in which the characters endure their battering by events and yet find the courage to bounce up again is convincing.

Isegawa's book is too long and would be more effective if the writer practised some verbal economy. There are points at which the reader becomes lost in the multiplicity of characters who appear and disappear again. Recurring references, such as the obsession with the sewing-machine bobbin with which Mugezi torments his mother and the use of the triangle image in the post-Amin period, are overused, and there are strange unevennesses. Compare, for example, the gang rape of Kawawo with her subsequent visit to the witchdoctor. While the sexual detail sometimes seems gratuitous, the presentation of the religious pressures upon young, ill-educated people, together with the way they are understood and misunderstood, is genuinely revealing. As increasing acceptance of all forms of corruption and self-seeking grows, the reader becomes aware that Mugezi has no genuine links with anyone. In view of this, the discovery of his grandfather's body is particularly poignant. However, any move towards a happy ending turns into nightmare with a death as a result of AIDS. Mugezi's survival techniques lead to disillusion before the 'escape' to Holland gives him some kind of solution. Or does it?

There is a shape to this overlong novel as we follow the life of this strangely tormented family through the Amin years, the 'liberation', Obote 2 and its terrible aftermath. Mugezi's father had said 'Uganda was a land of false bottoms where under every abyss there was another waiting to ensnare people, and that the historians had made a mistake: Abyssinia was not the ancient land of Ethiopia but modern Uganda'. And this seems to be true. After each major disaster we said, 'This must be the worst. Things can only get better' and yet there was another great drop: Amin to Obote 2, Aids to Ebola!

Laughter and tears, sex and cynicism, uprooting and hate, disillusionment eventually, about all authority. This impressively wide-ranging novel leaves the reader confused and exhausted, but not yet ready to give up. It ends neither with a whimper nor a bang but with a sense that the story isn't over yet.

A granary, the editor of *Words from a Granary* explains, is an essential feature of an African homestead and is never empty. It is therefore a symbol of hope. This is the second series of short stories published by Femwrite, the very energetic organisation encouraging women from all over Uganda to write. There has been a three-year programme of training workshops and this resulting anthology of fifteen stories has been selected from writers coming from all parts of the country and reflecting both rural and urban life. There is an excellent final session of notes on the authors, with interesting detail and, except for one writer, excellent photographs. The book is enticing and there is an intriguing cover illustration.

Femwrite is concerned at the lack of a wide reading public and wishes to encourage the habit of reading for pleasure by providing material of local relevance. Many of these stories will indeed furnish talking points and one hopes they will be read in schools. The editing has left the occasional clumsy phrase, just as the proof correction has not spotted every error ('taxdriver' not taxi), but in general the presentation is good and there are some interesting and individual stylists among the authors.

The stories show a predilection towards violence that can so easily descend into melodrama. This may be because Uganda has in recent years seen a great deal of violence. However, its presentation in fiction must convince. Truth is not enough. It is not enough for a writer to assert 'but this really happened' if the way the story has been told does not enable the reader to suspend disbelief. For example, could a woman keep secret for twenty-five years the fact that she was raped by the best man just before her wedding reception? And, how did a woman, even if called 'a leopardess', put a bomb in a rejected lover's car? If a story has been told from the point of view of one particular character who then dies before the end the reader may well wonder how we are supposed to know their inmost thoughts. In one case, 'Vengeance of the Gods', we are apparently encouraged to sympathise with Lalobo, who has killed her co-wife, only to find that when she reveals her guilt she is stoned by a horrified crowd. The finely expressed irony of the story of the young student killed on the way to the graduation ceremony could have been even more tragic if we had been securely looking at the event as a viewer. The viewpoint of the narrator can be an effective and economic technique, as in 'Rogue Male', where the employer who has become aware of her exploitation by an engaging ne'erdowell is used to underline the ironic denouement. One is left at the end of the story with a wry smile resulting from our response to what we have heard – a kind of audience participation. This is quite different from the simple 'Oh how sad' response asked for by the final very well told story, which has perhaps over-emphasized the truth that cruelty begets cruelty. In a short story it is especially important to decide how far the viewpoint of the narrative will contribute to the overall effect. Many of the writers represented in the collection are aware of the force of irony in the telling of a short story but could be less heavy-handed in its expression.

The tales raise serious issues. For example, what appears to be a simple love story of a girl discovering the young man to whom she is attracted has an illegitimate child makes one think of a wide range of points. Beside the obvious comments on moral issues, there is the need for openness in a relationship. In this instance, the generous conclusion raises a wide range of further issues. 'Esteri's Secret', again an effectively written story, takes up the theme of a secret which poisons a relationship but leaves the reader bothered that there is no conclusion and wondering why Esteri has not told the husband (who appears to love her) what happened on her wedding day. One ponders why she still can't talk to him directly after twenty-five years.

The collection is perhaps a little short on humour and the ordinary. One might single out, therefore, 'Floating Images' for its portrait of the student who comes to grips with her need for glasses despite her fear of their being unattractive and who finds the contrary. This is more effective than the somewhat exaggerated humour of 'Miss Nandutuu'.

For the ordinary reader there is a wide range of lively stories well worth reading. Many have an underlying theme about women needing to assert their independence and discovering that the right to say 'No' is part of finding how to become a full person. Indeed. Sociologists reading the collection might be aware of the continuing need for an assertion of the rights of women but, I think, they would also be aware of the need for stability in a fragmented and violent society with its extravagant differences between haves and have-nots (the keynote of the first tale) and its lack of any unifying factors.

Femwrite has also been concerned with the publication of a reference book for Uganda, a *Directory of Creative Writers,* supported by the Alliance Française in Kampala. This is a welcome beginning but it is only a beginning and leaves much to criticise. As a work of reference there are too many inconsistencies and absences. It has been inadequately researched and hastily compiled, as witnessed by the missing names, indeed many of those mentioned in Bukenya's introduction, such as Byron Kawadwa and Rose Mbowa, are omitted! While not wishing to negate the fine work of Susan Kiguli some mention could have been made of Grace Isharassa, and one would like to have seen entries for Nuwa Sentongo and Erisa Kironde. Surely, there should have been some record of the excellent compilations made by the Department of Literature of Makerere over the years? And, one wonders why, if such a full entry can be provided for Taban lo Liyong, who has somewhat tenuous Ugandan contacts, there is no entry for David Rubadiri who is at least fifty per cent a Ugandan creative writer. Mary Karooro Okurut claims in her introduction that the extracts of the writers' own choice from published or unpublished work that are included add to the excitement and entertainment of the directory. But these extracts are very patchy, and in any case, one normally uses a directory for reference rather than entertainment. The ease with which one can access the information one is looking for is important, and the layout is no help here. As a teaching aid, the excellent photographs where they appear are useful, and Bukenya's introduction is interesting and well worth studying carefully. However, the amount of information to be extracted about each author is inconsistent and a great deal of work remains to be done.

Margaret Macpherson
Makerere University and Windermere

Nigerian literature

Debo Kotun, *Abiku*
Pasadena, CA: Nepotist Books, 1998, 417 pp, $14.95, hbk
ISBN 0-9668772-8-4 (pbk); 0-9668772-7-6 (hbk)

> 'What's it like in Nigeria?'...
> 'Upside down.'
> 'What do you mean?'
> 'Just what I said, confused and sad. In the Third World , there's no such thing as government of the people as we have in America. There are only obsessed thieves in charge of the national treasury.' (p. 361)

Six years after Nigeria attained her independence from Britain, the Nigerian army took over the government. By the end of the century, military dictators had held the reins of power for almost thirty of the forty years of independence. Their legacy was of unbridled misrule, absolute degradation of human rights, pathetic deterioration of the quality of life of the citizenry, unprecedented anti-intellectualism, and the most scandalous looting of the national treasury. When the army left the scene on 29 May 1999, Nigeria had become the mockery of the civilised world. She was nicknamed the 'corruption capital of the world'.

First time novelist Debo Kotun feels compelled to tell the Nigerian story (using a title that requires explanation, *Abiku*) and does so in a gruesomely satirical manner that leaves the reader with a sour taste in the mouth. Animated by the nostalgia of a homeland once Africa's giant in word and deed, now ravished and devalued by lost hopes and squandered golden opportunities, Kotun portrays the foibles of Nigeria's leadership as only a Nigerian intellectual in exile can. In typical Nigerian military fashion, a journalist is assassinated in broad daylight. His house is burnt down in a bid to prevent publication of a sensitive document which contains a list of 'twenty Army Generals whose foreign-Swiss bank accounts add up to ten billion dollars'. The document also includes details of a deal struck between the head of state and 'officials of the Nigerian Oil Corporation to divert a total of two-point-eight billion naira (almost four million dollars) from the country's foreign reserves into a private account.' The elusive document leads to a bloody man-hunt across the Atlantic to New York where, in a manner that truly strains credulity, it implicates a wealthy white American industrialist and his wife (a PhD holder who is also white) in an unplanned trip to Nigeria in search of a witchcraft cure for their dangerously ill fifteen-month-old son, Jason, the sole heir to a multi-billion media empire. This treatment had been recommended by Chief of Staff, Dr William Doss Johnson, leading physician in one of the world's finest children's hospitals. Johnson had the extraordinary distinction of having served a 21-year apprenticeship under a master diviner in Abeokuta, Nigeria! He recommends the trip to Nigeria because he recognises that Jason is an 'abiku'. In Yoruba mythology an 'abiku' is an abnormal child, one who is born and dies in an endless cycle.

Taking off from the image of the 'abiku', the novel is woven into a saga of unparalleled treachery, intrigues, and all sorts of evil machinations by the Nigerian military. In this fictional depiction of army rule in Nigeria, Kotun has written a novel of immense socio-political relevance which is easy for many

Nigerians to identify with. Therein lies the strength as well as the liability of the work. In pursuit of social significance, *Abiku* degenerates to near farce and turns into an unwieldy story. Revealing and astonishing in its intricate details of intra-military intrigues, vibrant and insightful in places, *Abiku* generally lacks the finer artistic qualities of the novel. The phantom-like characters act out their human roles during the day and turn into ogres in the night as they criss-cross eerie clouds and traverse unchartable highways. Kotun mixes fact with fiction – he uses the names of actual people and places, and he adds fantasy to realism in disproportionate and unconvincing ways. The result is a tall tale that overstretches the reader's imagination.

The social value of *Abiku* is unmistakable, but its value as a work of art would have been enhanced if a balance had been struck between medium and message, between emotional impulse and imaginative control of subject matter. Some episodes are left hanging. Readers feel as if they are being served with two unrelated dishes lumped into one incongruous mish-mash. However, when all is considered, *Abiku* remains an important post-colonial, post-military Nigerian novel. For a long time, it may remain unsurpassed in its psychological study of the military mentality and the psychopathic personality of African dictators.

Ernest N.Emenyonu
University of Michigan-Flint

Abubakar Gimba, *Footprints*
Lagos: Malthouse, 1998, 370 pp., £7.50, $13.75, ISBN 978023688

Kris Obodumu, *Die a Little*
Lagos: Malthouse, 1997, 246 pp., £6.25, $10.00, ISBN 978260187X
Distributed by African Books Collective, Unit 13, Kings Meadow, Ferry Hinksey Rd, Oxford OX2 0DP

From the mid-1980s to the late 1990s, Nigeria was a continuous political drama, with a plot that in all aspects outran the weirdest imagination. Nigerian authors had to find a way of competing with it and the two novels under review here try to do just that. One, Abubakar Gimba's, takes an allegorical short cut with results that, I fear, are not happy.

Footprints is the story of the Jibran and Muhtar families living through a period of perpetual political turmoil in a country called 'Songhai'. Jibran and Muhtar were friends at university and, on graduation, Jibran became a teacher and Muhtar a civil servant. Jibran was drawn into union activities and rapidly rose to a position of leadership. But Muhtar, his unsuccessful rival in love, engineered his downfall and his early exit from the service. Muhtar exacts further vengeance in the next generation by making his son, Bakri, jilt Jibran's daughter, Farah. However, at the end of the novel reconciliation is on the way: Jibran's younger son, Haliyfah, is set to marry Muhtar's youngest daughter, Jameelah. In between, Jibran is twice detained by the security service because of Haliyfah's political activities, for Haliyfah himself, while still a schoolboy, leads a protest march of fellow pupils against the government. He is wounded by the police and on his return from hospital, dreams of his destiny: to rule Songhai. That is the final movement in a novel that is as dry as a government gazette and in which the characters talk straight out of a dictionary.

Even as allegories go, there really is no story in *Footprints*, only a series of pegs on which are hung endless perorations on the political situation in Songhai. These dilations are pedantic and abstract, situated neither in the real politics of a particular place and time, nor anchored in the experiences of the characters. Indeed, for these characters one would assume Gimba had no interest in human beings: the characters are blank sheets on which he writes what passes for political analysis. None of them has any life outside the tiresome disputations. Love is also a victim, pressed into the service of preaching a heavy-handed political sermon. It may be argued that politics has so pervaded everyday life that Nigerians talk about it endlessly, but faithful reflection of this pastime is neither a substitute for, nor a guarantee of, good fiction.

Footprints reflects the intrusive political climate, but it does so in an escapist manner. If the characters are blank sheets, the setting is, literally, nowhere. In the capital of Songhai, New Tymbuktu, there is a primary school called 'Azania International Primary School', and a university called 'Sankore University'. This brand of contrived pan-Africanism is off putting. One may presume that the discussions, designed to show off a presumed political sophistication and rhetorical power, are a distillation of the author's experiences during the 1980s and 1990s when he was a senior bureaucrat and banker. Those were the years when religion became the most divisive factor in the nation, when IMF-sponsored policies pauperised the middle and lower classes, and when the heads of state operated a 'breast-pocket' economy. These political and economic evils are proving impossible to undo, and may in fact ruin Nigeria. Yet none of them is alluded to in the novel.

The boredom caused by the lack of any real story or characters in *Footprints* and its ponderous political disquisition is compounded by the irritation caused by the poor expression. Here I pick a few examples at random: 'Haliyfah stood watching the vehicle moved down the road'; 'Haliyfah had began'; 'Then after a moment's silence he resolved to speaking'; 'he is aggrieved by his father'; 'if boys like him are dreaming to join the military'; 'people are happy to be relieved from ...'; 'Major Bakri immediately drove ... to intimate him about his finding'; 'A sizeable segment of the citizenry also believed so too'; 'She didn't expect Nashaa to be so emotive about it'; 'Haliyfah thought such stories were incredulous', and, some other time the same Haliyfah's 'low-spiritedness waned'. I simply had to stop noting half way through in order to finish the novel.

The novel is riddled with clichés in which language is completely divorced from reality. On one occasion, we are informed that the closure of the nation's universities made 'things a little difficult in getting the key officials *of the fraternities and sororities*' (my emphasis)! On another, one of the perpetually disputing characters spouts: 'I hope ... you are not saying that we cannot try something new in our bid to fashion out our political governance culture'. 'Governance' here gives the game away, for it was a chic, high-sounding term used *ad nauseam* in public speeches by the military dictators and their hangers-on in those years. Seminars and conferences on 'governance' also became an institutionalised substitute for real government. Here is another example of the speechifying that pervades the novel:

And that's the problem,' said Basil smiling. 'We are the engineers for the new destination and the road that leads to it, yet we show such remarkable lack of understanding of even the terrain across which our road would traverse. Or we deliberately don't want to understand: the road construction is bad, the signposts are lousy, the labels quite tawdry, signs of poor workmanship all over the place. What manner of destination are we going to give ourselves? I am quite apprehensive. (241)

This is supposedly a spontaneous outburst, and Basil is a teacher, not a politician. In this kind of pomposity – and there are many examples of it – one looks in vain for signs of irony.

Footprints parades an overblown rhetoric that is mistaken for eloquence, weightiness and profundity. I found the most glaring symptom of this in the author's overuse of the word 'however', and it is never preceded by a comma! Generously, one might suggest that this usage betrays the style of someone more used to memo writing than to composing narrative prose. Gimba has been writing for more than a decade now but, on the strength of this novel, a successful technocrat may not necessarily a good novelist make. As the blurb tells us, he was the 'National President of the Association of Nigerian Authors'. There is cause indeed for concern. Finally, *Footprints* is the kind of novel to be expected from a smug ruling class. The self-criticism which the characters engage in only masks self-flattery, its purpose being to affirm the interests of their class which, seeing itself as the state, has appropriated it and all its resources as of right. Its quarrels are family squabbles that must be patched up, and the sooner the better, so it can tighten its grip on the state.

Kris Obodumu's *Die a Little* is set during the same period as *Footprints*, but takes the humble approach of simply calling the urban underclass as witness. Where Gimba totally forgets this class, Obodumu focuses on it. He also reminds us that other classes exist, and are victims of the gross misgovernment created by Gimba's heroes.

Set in the time of the infamous Structural Adjustment Programmes (SAP) in Nigeria, *Die a Little* narrates the crushing of the urban underclass by that IMF-sponsored programme. Oche, a middle-aged father of two, has been out of work for two years. After his children have not eaten for two days, he takes a loan from Adama, a local government revenue collector, who diverts the taxes he collects into his own 'finance house'. This is the beginning of the family's inexorable slide into a moral and psychological hell. In desperation, Oche sells the paltry possessions he has acquired in all the years he worked to bribe the local council administrator for a job – which he never gets. At one point the iron bed on which he and his wife, Enole, sleep is carted away by the implacable and scheming Adama. Eventually, Oche is hired to work on the roof of a building. But he is not used to this: he falls off the roof and is badly injured. For three days, there is no money even to buy painkillers. Unable to bear her husband's pain and her own agony of helplessness, Enole finally agrees to sleep with Adama, who has been waging a war of economic attrition against the family all along with the object of securing her. However, in the hotel room, before he can commit the act, Adama dies, perhaps as the result of being struck on the back of his head by his wife earlier in the day. When the police come for Enole, everybody, Oche included of course, is shocked. This turn of events expresses Obodumu's bleak, ironic vision in the novel.

While mostly about Oche and Enole, *Die a Little* is also about two other couples, Ukwenya and Mary, and Adama and Onyeche. The varied marital tensions in the three families combine to give us a rounded picture of the effects of an economic policy (the Structural Adjustment Programme) that, formulated ostensibly to raise the entire society economically, actually has other results. One character in the novel re-interprets the acronym as having the effect of 'Steadily Accelerating Profits' for a minority, and 'Steadily Accelerating Poverty' for the majority. One key plank of the programme was the encouragement of the creation of private banks and finance houses. These institutions sprouted up everywhere, promising huge dividends on small investments. Naturally, they all collapsed quickly, though not before the 'bankers' and 'financiers' had made rich killings. Predictably, their 'investors' were left clutching waste paper. Adama embodies this economic policy and the new 'morality' it called into play, unconscionable opportunism and total cynicism. It found ready-made targets in the poorer but ever-optimistic segments of society. Adama never returns money to anybody who has 'invested' in his 'finance house' but a day's delay in paying the poll tax in the market is enough for him to dispossess the owners of their precious, hard-earned means of livelihood. Since the local government council itself has been turned into a finance house, it is no use lodging complaints there.

As with Adama, so with the big companies that were favoured by the programme. Oche got nothing from the firm he had worked for despite the fact that he had worked for them for ten years. Ukwenya learnt three trades, but neither his old employer nor any other company has use for them. He settles for teaching craft in a primary school, takes to *burukutu* (local beer) and vents his enormous frustration by beating his wife.

The women in the novel are portrayed as strong, resourceful and able to fight back, both against their abusive husbands and the system. Mary, the petty-trader, keeps her family in food and clothes, and pays the children's school fees. No sacrifice is too much for Enole to make for her family, and Onyeche refuses to yield to Adama's domineering machismo. There is also Baby, a petty trader, who stands up to Adama when he comes on his raids.

Mordant humour is a feature of the novel, and is clearly seen in the episodes in which Oche tries in vain to recover the bribe he has paid, and when he is caught in the loop of a rope meant to secure a bull. It is also present in the conversations, especially the pidgin exchanges in the *burukutu* bar and in Baby's altercations with Adama. The acid humour combines with the repeated references to the inclement harmattan to give a baleful dimension to the novel's central theme: a people are victimised by their own government and by nature. Those at the bottom are preyed on ruthlessly by those a little bit above them but none the less they remain human. There is an uncompromising realism to the narration, a steady confrontation with all the ugliness, cruelty and misery that has permeated Nigerian society, especially since the 1980s. The brutal realism, expressed in clear and trenchant language throughout, continues beyond the novel: the death of Adama brings more troubles for Oche and his family.

Obodumu's technique of characterisation combines dry wit with studied understatement, making even the horrid Adama convincing. Nigerians will recognise themselves as well as their social, political and economic woes of the last two decades in the desperate lives narrated in this novel. Indeed had it been published after 1998, one could have sworn that Adama's character, plus his ignoble death, were inspired by an all too real and all too eminent Nigerian.

The production values of the book fall below Malthouse's usual standards. Pages 27 and 28 are duplicated and the blurb tells us nothing about the writer.

Wole Ogundele
Obafemi Awolowo University, Ile-Ife

Four novels from Uganda

Mary Abago, *Sour Honey*
Kampala: Fountain, 1999, 122 pp., £5.95, $9.95, ISBN 9970 02 147 8

Anne Ayeta Wangusa, *Memoirs of a Mother*
Kampala: Femwrite, 1998, 73 pp., £3.50, $6.50, ISBN 9970 90 101X

Laury Lawrence Ocen, *The Alien Woman*
Kampala: Fountain, 1999, 145 pp., £6.95, $11.95, ISBN 9970 02 181 8

Mary Karooro Okurut, *The Invisible Weevil*
Kampala: Femrite, 1998, 206 pp., £5.95, $9.95, ISBN 9970 90 102 8

All titles distributed by African Books Collective, Unit 13, Kings Meadow, Ferry Hinksey Rd, Oxford OX2 0DP

Mary Abago's *Sour Honey* is essentially a story about betrayal, dejection and rejection. Set in Uganda, it traces the life of a family through three generations beginning with the story of Maria's grandparents and the brutal life of violence that Maria's grandmother endured at the hands of her husband. She died, miserably, with hoe in hand and baby on back. Only thirteen years old when his mother died, Oweka (Maria's father) tried his best to care for his brothers and sisters but, one by one, they died of hunger and disease and, at last, his father died too.

Almost mad with grief Oweka is slowly forsaken by all. He consults a soothsayer who advises him to 'chase the wind' which he does by disappearing into thin air. He is away for years and when he reappears is immensely wealthy. He marries Maria's mother, who bears him child after child who all die in infancy until Maria is born. Desperate for a son, he marries a woman who quickly bears him several sons. However, the sons are dull and Maria, who is brilliant at school, becomes the pride of her father.

However, when Maria succumbs to Jimmy, a Sugar Daddy, her father throws her out. She finds herself pregnant while slowly the love between her and Jimmy turns into hatred. She pins her hopes on the examination results, and when she finds she has passed well, she rushes to tell Jimmy the news, feeling that at last she has the strength to leave him and look towards a brighter future. But he has packed up and gone. This rejection hits her hard and she commits suicide, sparing only a brief thought for her unborn child.

Mary Abago writes powerful dialogue. Word by word, pause by pause, half finished sentence by half-finished sentence, all ring true to life, and the use of colloquial English with direct translation gives particular texture to the writing. The characters are well matched with the words she places in their mouths, and I suspect that the fast, tight dialogue would lend itself to a playscript or screenplay.

It is perhaps because the surface is so beguiling that the main characters do not develop much complexity; they lack the breadth and depth of three-dimensional characters. Maria's suicide, for example, is an astonishing surprise. At the end, Maria's story is, however, compelling because of the inevitability of it all, and because of its concern with the snares that are set for young girls. Snares that they fall into with eyes wide open. Maria brought a lot of her suffering onto herself, yet she has all our sympathy because she is a gifted young woman pitted against a hostile, male-dominated world. In such a society, a woman who crosses 'respectable lines' is judged harshly, treated with contempt and easily rejected, even by those she most relies on.

In *Memoirs of a Mother,* Elizabeth Sera finds herself pregnant and soon realises that her boyfriend Masaba will have nothing to do with their child, Mercy Khankwa. She decides to keep the baby but gradually finds the pressures are too great and parts with her. The story delicately portrays the challenges women face in attempting to conform to the stereotypical portrait of a woman that society demands while responding to the very real desire to fulfil their individuality. The results are often tragic, and in this instance very moving.

Sera's story is a touching one with a simple plot that moves convincingly. The character grows steadily and naturally following her transition from youth, to unexpected pregnancy and motherhood. Yet Sera does not really assert herself. For example, her survival during pregnancy stems from the advice of her friend, Edna, that she adopt Muslim attire in order to find work. Her decision to keep her baby despite a harsh father and hostile stepmother is, perhaps, the bravest decision she makes. Yet later, torn between her love for her child and the community's expectation that she will get married, she gives Mercy up, choosing to lose Mercy rather than her man. Astonishingly, she even agrees to look after a step-daughter!

Mercy grows up and, on the brink of marriage, is shocked to be told by Sera that the boy she intends to marry is related to her through Masaba. She blames her mother for having kept her father's identify secret and the tension between them leads to an estrangement with further pain for the long-suffering young woman. I confess that, after so much heartbreak, I was grateful for the eventual reconciliation between mother and daughter.

Anne Wangusa's use of Ugandan English sometimes creates ambiguities. For example, we read 'To prove their manhood they picked on young girls.' (p. 14). The conventional meaning of the phrase 'picked on' is to nag, find fault with, or select. Anne makes the phrase work hard to to do its duty (that of selection) while also making a feminist point (about sexual harassment). Generally, however, the book is written in a poetic register and Wangusa's meaning comes across clearly and powerfully.

Laury Ocen's *The Alien Woman* is a tale about how love conquers all. Set in Uganda, it is a compassionate story about the determination a young girl,

Margaret Nagawa, to win and keep the love of Obina. She has to do this although challenged by his conservative ideas about the sort of girl who is suitable for marriage.

In the first few chapters, Laury Ocen's narrative runs into hiccups as the author attempts to impress by using big words. Thus we have: 'A calyx of drooping flesh would screw his face with deep wrinkles' (p. 2) and 'cause him heinous turmoil' (p. 5). However, a few chapters on, after the marriage ceremony which is rather contrived to portray tradition, the story begins to flow freely and we become immersed in it.

From the perspective of Obina and his parents, Margaret is from the 'wrong' tribe, and far too well educated. In addition, Margaret does behave in the way Obina expects, for example she takes the initiative in their relationship by sending him a letter declaring her love, and refusing to take no for an answer. Eventually, she steals away from her family and presents herself at Obina's rural home, uninvited. She settles into a lengthy stay, enduring the rigours of a tough life. Through hard work, endurance and humility, she gradually wins the admiration of Obina's parents.

When Obina has to go to town to look for work, Margaret insists on staying behind. Soon after, Gorretti, Obina's betrothed, pours hot oil on her and we cannot help feeling that Margaret has pushed her luck too far. However even this attack works in her favour when she forgives Gorretti. In doing this, she melts away Obina's last resistance and that of his parents. They declare that no other girl would be fit for their son and acknowledge that, perhaps, he does not deserve her.

While Margaret is in Obina's village, her parents fear she has been abducted and a reward is offered to whoever can find her. Margaret asks Obina to go to report her whereabouts, and, at great peril to his life, he does so. One cannot help thinking that the young heroine took too much for granted and that her actions endangered the lives of the people she claimed to love. After all this, the ending is happy: Margaret's parents are ecstatic when they are reunited with her and they gladly give their consent to the marriage.

We are prompted to consider how much the young heroine used the power of her wealth and beauty to manipulate a hapless family. But the overall impression is that love conquers all and all is fair in love and war. This is not a story about Obina marrying a girl outside tradition, but, as we would say in Uganda, this is a story about Margaret getting her man against all expectations, for she was, in truth, as alien as alien could be.

The Invisible Weevil is an ambitious attempt by Mary Karooro Okurut to portray Uganda's history since independence through its impact on the personal and public lives of courageous heroines. The novel has a powerful opening which brings the reader into the presence of the dying Genesis as the plane carrying him and Nkwanzi, begins its descent towards Kaaro. The description of the view of the world below, the space surrounding their private anguished thoughts and the carefully chosen words they speak make us feel we are in the presence of the very secret of love, life and death. The gentle tension and fragile love between the woman and fatally-ill man almost recalls moments in Michael Ondaatje's *The English Patient,* and we are at once hooked into the story. We eagerly devour the past, desperate to learn how Genesis, one of the most powerful names I have ever come across in a novel, came to be so ill.

The story is a compelling narrative spanning three generations during a period which saw Uganda plagued by the terrorist regime of Idi Amin and then by the scourge of AIDS. When the book begins one may be inclined to think that it is a tale of girl meets boy, the gentle love story of Nkwanzi and Genesis and the strains upon the relationship exerted by customary and gender pressures. As the children move through adolescence and education, one is surprised when they join the Resistance Movement and are soon the people in power. We see the values that shaped Nkwanzi come into sharp focus and influence her actions, and yet we also see these same values are sharply mocked by circumstances beyond her control. They come to mean almost nothing when she is raped on her wedding night, and when she watches the final onslaught of the 'invisible weevil', the AIDS virus, on Genesis.

Reading the book, we wonder whether it was fate, or the curse of an uncle's word, that ruined their future. Perhaps in the end, the men have not changed and have not heeded the word of the uncle. The girls, however, transform themselves by shaving their heads before they go into combat, and, despite the advice of an influential aunt, by going to the police to report rape on their wedding night.

Okurut packs in twists and surprises that keep us reading to the end and wanting more when we close the book. Nkwanzi, we find, also took in her aunt's 'traditional' advice and credit is given to the aunt when, following her advice, Nkwanzi points her sharp *mpindu* at the Mafuta Mingi and knees Rex in the balls.

Atuki Turner
Prompt, Bristol

Critical essays on West African authors

Jacqueline Bardolph (ed.), Cross/Cultures 47, *Telling Stories: Postcolonial Short Fiction in English*
Amsterdam; Atlanta, GA: Rodopi, 2001, 477 pp.
$40, pbk, ISBN 90 420 1524 1, $136, hbk, ISBN: 90 420 1534 9

This review covers the chapter on West Africa, (pp. 231-277) containing essays on aspects of the work of Ayi Kwei Armah (Derek Wright), Chinua Achebe (Alain Séverac), Ken Saro-Wiwa (Jane Wilkinson), Ama Ata Aidoo (Christine Mbonyingingo), and Niyi Osundare (Christine Fioupou).

Derek Wright. 'Developing Agency: the Later Stories of Ayi Kwei Armah'
This essay calls attention to a shift in Ayi Kwei Armah's view of post-colonial Africa from the cynicism and pessimism of the early novels and short stories, to the satire and cautious optimism of his two later short stories: 'Halfway to Nirvana' (1984) and 'Doctor Kamikaze' (1989), [also published as 'The Development Agent' (1990)]. The emasculated, marginalized protagonist of the earlier work has given way to a female narrator; she is the modern, educated, professional African woman and it is her point of view that sets the agenda for Africa to come together, develop, and reconstruct itself culturally and socially.

Alain Séverac. 'Achebe's Short Stories: Their Intextextual Relationship to his Novels'
Séverac sets out to demonstrate how Achebe's few short stories relate to his novels. He argues that, just as the novels exhibit thematic and sociocultural ties, so do the short stories in their inter-connectedness on the one hand and their relationship to the novels on the other. Achebe's short stories, he suggests, anticipate the novels and complement them in that they elaborate not only on theme and characterisation but also on their socio-historical progression.

Jane Wilkinson. '"Second-New": Serialization and Circulation in Basi and Company by Ken Saro-Wiwa'
Basi and Company was originally a popular television series that ran from 1985–1990. Jane Wilkinson's essay considers how Saro-Wiwa transforms the traditional folktale and the act of storytelling into a television script and from this into a sequence of short stories. These individual stories echo the Yoruba / Shakespearean / Saro-Wiwan wisdom as reflected in the view that the world is indeed a market or a stage where life's episodes are continually being renegotiated and re-enacted. The discourse is of urban Nigeria, a densely woven fabric of ethnic and religious mix, where new ideas and influences are partly digested and reformulated but which lacks permanency. Adetola Street is like a temporary stopover, its dwellers drifting in and out.

Christine Mbonyingingo. 'Unanswered Questions. Unattended Quests: Ama Ata Aidoo's Short Stories'
This essay deals with the collection, *No Sweetness Here*, and is a review of the individual stories reflecting the 'harsh, unjust condition of women' in Africa. Ama Ata Aidoo's stories are seen as 'a testimony of loss, suffering, bitter hardship and moral starvation' (269). Unfortunately, Aidoo's other short story collection, *The Girl Who Can and Other Stories*, is not included in this review.

Christiane Fioupou. 'Poetry as a "metaphorical guillotine": in the Works of Niyi Osundare'
This is an in-depth study of Niyi Osundare's creative work that he himself refers to as of an 'alter-native' tradition in that it is an 'alternative' that fuses the 'native' oral tradition and 'alters' it. This new literature is discussed in terms of form and social commentary: as poetry, as short fiction or short faction – faction seen as not only the fusion of fact and fiction but also as a literary revolt that demands its own innovative form. This is narrative poetry that wields satire as a weapon: the 'metaphorical guillotine'. For the pen is the only means with which the people can fight the 'post-Independence self-proclaimed khaki kings' of Africa:

> When I become emperor I will slay the press
> And hang all editors by their itchy pens.

Kari Dako
Department of English, University of Ghana

Three collections of short stories

Little Drops I: an Anthology of Contemporary Nigerian Short Stories
Ibadan: Spectrum Books, 1999, 127 pp., $9.95, ISBN 978-029-153-9

Little Drops II: an Anthology of Contemporary Nigerian Short Stories
Ibadan: Spectrum Books, 2000, 181 pp., $11.95, ISBN 978-029-182-2

Both distributed by African Books Collective, Unit 13, Kings Meadow, Ferry Hinksey Rd, Oxford OX2 0DP

Sola Adeyemi (ed.), *Goddess of the Storm and Other Stories*
London: Smart Image, 1999, 150 pp., $9.95, ISBN 0 9535735 0 8

The African short story form is currently receiving a great boost: in 1999, a major prize focusing on the genre was inaugurated. Tagged 'The Caine Prize for African Writing', the award, worth $15,000, was established in honour of the memory of Sir Michael Caine, the late chairman of the management committee of the Booker Prize. The first award, announced during the 2000 Zimbabwe International Book Fair, was won by Leila Aboulela, a Sudanese writer for 'The Museum', published in *Opening Spaces* edited by Yvonne Vera.

Two or three years before the establishment of the Caine Prize, a major financial institution in Nigeria had initiated a short story competition. Restricted specifically to the citizens of the largest black country in the world, the competition has a 'star prize' of N50,000 ($500), a second prize of N30,000 ($300) and a third prize of N20,000 ($200). In introducing the contest, the management of the Liberty Merchant Bank claimed to have been propelled by the appalling situation of creative writing in Nigeria, by the lack of encouragement for writers, and by the absence of 'what may be considered a feeder team from our masters of yesteryears'. While this last point may be considered as rather exaggerated – especially with writers of the calibre of Iyayi, Omotoso, Osofisan, Sowande, Ofeimun, and Osundare forming the second generation of Nigerian writers, and Okri, Adesokan, Ndibe, Oguine, and Ifowodo forming the third generation – there is no doubt that the Bank's decision to inaugurate the prize was a good one.

The economic adversity that overtook Nigeria in the early 1980s has certainly had untoward effects on the country's literature. The lack of opportunities for educational advancement, the limited availability of gainful employment, and the absence of a basic infrastructure have resulted in stillborn hopes and abandoned plans. The charlatanism of some publishers represents a further source of frustration for those who try to defy the odds. The result of the situation is a worrying decline in literary productivity.

The Liberty Merchant Bank Short Story Series was first announced in October 1996. In less than two months, well over 500 entries were submitted to *Post Express* and *This Day*, the two national newspapers co-ordinating the contest. Out of this number, the three-member panel, made up of Harry Garuba, then of the University of Ibadan, Akachi Ezeigbo of the University of Lagos, and Nduka Otiono, editor of the *Post Express* Literary Series, shortlisted 60 stories. Further consideration led to the selection of 37 of these which have been published in *Little Drops Volumes I & II.*

There is relatively little on record about most of the writers represented in these two collections. Indeed of the seventeen published in Volume I, only Toyin Adewale-Nduka's name has enjoyed prominence in literary circles. It may be recalled that he wrote a collection of poems and edited two anthologies, one of short stories and the other of poems. In the second volume, can be found the names of M. S. C. Okolo, also an author of a collection of poetry, and Ike Oguine, 1997 winner of the Association of Nigerian Author's prose prize, whose novel *A Squatter's Tale* has been published by Heinemann, UK. It would appear that many of those represented in the publications were galvanised into writing by the prospects of winning a prize. That is understandable: a number of well-known writers began for the same reason.

Three very broad patterns of thematic engagements are discernible in the collections. The first has to do with issues of tradition, continuity, magical realism, and return; the second with the transformation of social, political and economic realities, and the third with love, matrimony and related crises. Two examples in the first category are Dave Chukwuji's 'The Dark Side of the Moon' which tells the story of a well-educated young man who abandons his legal practice in the United States together with his family in order to obey the summons of the gods. And Victoria Paul's 'The Combat' which dramatises a titanic spiritual battle between a young man and his vindictive father-in-law. In the second broad category can be found Victor Edward's 'My Mother's Motor Mouth', a story presented from the point of view of a child whose parents are forever engaged in violent quarrels, and Sidi Isiaka's 'Too Much, too Soon', which focuses on a middle-class woman involved in an extramarital affair with an up and coming young man. The strength of this story lies in the way the author has managed to work complex details into an otherwise familiar story-line, fully engaging the sympathy of the reader for the two principal characters and moving towards a very neat resolution.

The final category is large and varied. It includes Toni Kan Onwordi's realistic 'It was Christmas', Oma Mokoy's allegorical 'A Tale of a Church Mouse', M. S. C. Okolo's memory-piece 'Those Days', Boye Adefila's quasi-comical 'The Third "I"' and David Nnaemeka's profoundly tragic 'Daddy Went to Liberia'. They are united by being attempts to imaginatively re-work various aspects of day-to-day experiences in Nigeria.

From the prefatory note it would seem that the aim of issuing *Goddess of the Storm and other Stories,* edited by Sola Adeyemi, is to 'showcase the talents of yet to be acknowledged writers who have continued to produce outstanding works, undaunted by the prospect of not being published'. There is no doubt that the writers represented here are generally better known than those presented in *Little Drops I & II.* Wale Okediran, for example, is the Secretary General of the Association of Nigerian Authors (ANA) at the time of writing and has published at least two novels and two collections of short stories. Garuba, who has already been mentioned, has served on the executive of the same Association. Currently a senior lecturer at the Institute of African Studies, University of Cape Town, South Africa, his first collection of poetry was published in 1983. Of the remaining six contributors, Chukwuma Okoye-Nwajiaga, Kolapo Oyefeso and Sola Osofisan have also won annual awards offered by the Association of Nigerian Authors.

In stating this, there is no attempt to take anything away from the credit of providing an outlet for another set of Nigerian writers. However, by fore-grounding the experience and standing of the writers it becomes clear why they seem to be generally more sure-footed than those encountered in the earlier two volumes. Adeyemi is represented by a story that is presented as a dream sequence. Titled 'Blisterpack of Memories', the narration projects a persona who imagines himself dead and who then transmogrifies into the mourners' sub-conscious, revealing their true feelings. Kolapo Oyefeso's 'The Sign of the Crab' is structured like a diary, capturing a young woman's trans-formation from innocence to maturity.

These are challenging enough, but Garuba's 'Pleated Skirts' is even more daring. The story is based on the real life experience of a Nigerian journalist who was jailed in 1995 together with Olusegun Obasanjo, the current president of the country, on the trumped-up charge of plotting a coup. Garuba uses the actual first names of the journalist and that of his wife while the main action of the story is set in the actual prison where the journalist was held. Had it not been delicately handled, the story would have degenerated into melodrama. Garuba, however, proves himself to be a highly skilled narrator producing a story distinguished by a conclusion of rare pathos.

My reservations about *Goddess of the Storm* concern a matter of editorial judgement. In a book that purports to be presenting a new generation of Nigerian writers and which publishes a total of thirteen stories, it is difficult to understand why the editor included four stories by a single author, espe-cially when that author is not a major talent. Finally, the effect of the contri-butions of Chukwuma Okoye-Nwajiaga is to reduce the value of the collection considerably.

The situation regarding the editing of *Little Drops I and II* is also disconcert-ing. No editor is named, and there is no way of telling whether anyone looked at the stories after they had been selected by the panel. It would certainly have been helpful had the sponsors of the series realised that a panel of judges is not always at its best when it has a huge pile to select from and when it has a deadline to beat. There is, however, nothing extraordinary about the flaws that have so far been identified in the collections under review, and the uneven-ness is not surprising. In a sense, such unevenness should be expected in pub-lications presenting works by new writers. And the final point should be positive: in a society that has been almost completely overtaken by philistin-ism and crass materialism, it is a great achievement to stimulate a new set of people into taking up their pens. To provide some of them with a publication outlet is even more praise-worthy.

Wumi Raji
Bayreuth, and University of Ilorin

Ghanaian literature

Sam Aryeetey, *Home at Last*
Accra: Afram Publications, 2000, 446 pp., £7.95, $13.95, ISBN: 9964 70 214-0

Home at Last is a novel cast in the popular romantic genre, though it lacks the sensitivity of a love story. It is at times fantastic in its plots and subplots. True to expectation, in the end, the vulnerable female gets her tall, strong, handsome and successful man, and he will remain faithful to her forever.

The novel is set in London and Port Makra, Zombarland (Accra? Zombieland? Sombreland?). It tells the story of the young lawyer, Naana Sadlah, alias 'Oye Chuiche', daughter of a Zombari human rights martyr. She falls in love with Hilary Gilwah, alias 'John Bindou', son of the coup maker, Kamal Bindou, a murderer whose victims include Naana's father. But this is no Romeo and Juliet story. When, after the death of the aunt who brought her up, Naana discovers who Hilary is, she withdraws from him.

Naana now travels to Zombarland to look for her mother who has been in a psychiatric hospital since she witnessed the murder of her husband and was gang-raped by Bindou's men. On the plane, Naana meets Josh Farguh, a human rights lawyer, and the story ends with them getting married. Naana's mother is restored to good health and moves in with the couple who become parents.

Aryeetey's characterisation is not always convincing. Naana for instance, comes across as moody and unpredictable. Hilary changes completely from the initial scenes, when he meets and falls in love with Naana, to the final scenes, when his real name and parentage are revealed and he is abandoned by his new love, Akos, and commits suicide. One also wonders how familiar the author is with contemporary Britain, and therefore contemporary informal discourse. The choice of register falters at times.

The novel has unrealistic subplots. Relatively openly, through a British acquaintance, Naana is able to purchase bombs, and she gets malaria after only about four days in the tropics! Naana's mother, after twenty-three years, is miraculously healed of a mental illness and regains her speech! Naana gets justice in that Bindou collapses and dies when he is informed of his son's death! Throughout the narrative, the past reaches into the present and demands vengeance. The sins of the fathers are manifestly visited upon their children and the belief that 'good conquers all' appears to be the moral of the story.

The author does, however, allow his characters to discuss the problems of a developing country marked by coups and shaky civilian regimes. This is a discourse the writer is clearly very familiar with and this is where Aryeetey comes across at his strongest.

Kari Dako
University of Ghana

Stephanie Newell, *Ghanaian Popular Fiction: 'Thrilling Discoveries in Conjugal Life' & Other Tales*
Oxford: James Currey and Athens, Ohio: Ohio University Press, 2000, 180 pp., £14.95 pbk, ISBN 0-85255-556-3, £40.00 hbk, ISBN 0-85255-557-1

This book constitutes research into and an assessment of contemporary popular fiction in Ghana. 'Ghanaian Popular Fiction', as described by the author, is a product of 'migration and mimicry' seen in terms of post-colonial theory and not fiction spawned by the folk tale. Yet these 'mimicked' tales are fundamentally reinvented to create a space for themselves in their new environment. Stephanie Newell thus takes us into a world of Ghanaian fiction that has been given scant attention so far by academics. This new fiction is urban, it is written in English, and it creates a romantic tale, the indication of mimicry. This is because, as the author argues, well supported by socio-anthropological research findings and by her own field work in Ghana, the concept of romantic love, as reflected in the European romantic novel, is an alien concept in Ghanaian culture.

What then is 'popular fiction' and what qualifies a novel to be classified as 'serious' literature? Obviously creative art that has as its theme a male–female relationship – and the novel invariably has – cannot just be dismissed as 'popular' if it happens to deal with that relationship in terms of 'romantic love'. If it did then Ama Ata Aidoo's *Changes* would not qualify as 'serious' because the form of that novel is 'romantic' – and so is the theme to some extent. Essie, the protagonist, is definitely looking for 'something more' having fallen for the romantic male persona in the form of Ali. 'Popular literature' appears to be more a question of genre than literary merit. Asare Konadu, listed as author of *Don't Leave Me Mercy*, published as 'Asare Bediako' with Heinemann, and is an example of an author who obviously wore two caps and aimed at very different readerships. Newell refers to Linda Hutcheon (*A Theory of Parody*) who argues the popular novel in the West is 'insufficiently motivated', that by rehashing the plot of an earlier art form it has degenerated into 'pure convention'. Yes – but that 'pure convention' sells in the West as it does in Ghana and therefore obviously appeals to an emotional need.

How then is this 'mimicry' realised in Ghana? Newell gives an impressive overview of the historical development of this (dare I use the term?) 'art form'. She emphasises the utilitarian nature of this fiction, takes us through the didactic tale, comments on religious influence and draws attention to the cultural-contact phenomena behind these stories as they attempt to negotiate coping strategies to guide the reader through a confusing social 'modernisation' process and into the ideals and illusions of contemporary Ghana. Her identification of the themes and concerns that the authors so obviously have in common with their readership gives a valuable background to contemporary Ghana.

The chapter headings provide very useful indications as to the content of the book. After an excellent introduction that discusses the relevance of post-colonial theories in relation to West African popular fiction, Newell looks at the 'Proverbial Space in Ghanaian Popular Fiction'. She suggests the ways it invites interpretations, and how the reader/writer interaction functions. She provides a reader profile and an example of intertextuality, before commenting on 'The Book Famine' in West Africa, and providing a detailed discussion of the main themes of this fiction.

This is a book that will prove invaluable for anyone wanting to get a better understanding of the social dynamics of contemporary Ghana. Popular fiction is after all a mirror of how society wishes to view itself.

Kari Dako
University of Ghana

Kofi Anyidoho and James Gibbs (eds), *FonTomFrom: Contemporary Ghanaian Literature, Theatre and Film*
Amsterdam; Atlanta:, GA, Rodopi, 2000, 388 pp., pbk £20.85, hbk £63.25
ISBN 90-420-1273-0 (Double issue of *Matatu* (21–22))

> 'My brothers,
>   my people,
>   my brothers.
> I am sought,
>   I am sought because
> When you want to starve
>   the ocean,
> You paralyze
>   its source,
>   the river

Thus the Fontomfrom – the Ghanaian talking drums – were given voice by Atukwei Okai in his first collection dated 1971. Far from merely paying homage to ancestral culture and to one of its rhapsodies, the title of the volume edited by Anyidoho and Gibbs hints at the nurturing pervasiveness of traditional paradigms in contemporary Ghanaian cultural forms, three decades after the appearance of Okai's lines. As Anyidoho argues in his introductory essay, 'writers look to oral tradition for their most stimulating creative resources', and points at the mythical bird Sankofa (reaching back while moving onwards) as an emblematic 'expression of the nation's favourite guiding principle of development'.

Almost all the contributors of the volume seem inevitably faced with a similar issue. The value of *FonTomFrom*, though, resides mainly in the various cultural realms it analyses, and in the multiple generic approaches it takes. Some literary essays discuss foundational figures of Anglophone Ghanaian literature: the late Efua Sutherland is given a well-deserved tribute-cum-bibliography by the two editors, but contributors also construe works by Armah, Anyidoho and Laing, besides offering interviews with Ben-Abdallah and Marshall. Both essays on Aidoo's last novel *Changes* highlight its subtle, disturbing defiance of conventions and stereotypes; Odamtten's pages on her poetry (a part of her output often overlooked, as the author complained to me once) meet with a subject just as hard to pin down. One might notice, in the literary criticism of this volume, an overriding celebratory attitude, but this is counterbalanced by the more stinging reviews which close the publication, culminating in Ogede's ruthless mauling of Lorentzon's book on Armah.

Creative writing, constituting the other side of this volume, includes poems by Awoonor, Brew and Okai's 'Watu Wazuri', belonging to his uncollected productions of the past two decades, with its arresting inception:

> When all the blue is gone out
> of the sky,
> and the remaining hue is nothing
> to fly a kyte by

There are also lines from later poets such as Abena Busia and Opoku-Agyemang, who focus on contrasting themes: the effects of exile for the former, and, for Opoku-Agyemang, the consequence of the slave trade on the collective psyche of the African people who stayed on the continent. As he explains in his courageously unsettling essay included here: 'the place so savaged becomes a place of savages; it becomes the victim society ... a grim and conservative society, the people huddled together, furtive, subsisting by cunning, afraid even of the tremor lurking in the night.'

As for prose, Aidoo's feminist-futuristic short story 'She Who Would Be King' (from her latest collection *The Girl Who Can & Other Stories*, 1996) is included, and, in the field of drama, Efua Sutherland is represented by her previously unpublished short play 'Children of the Man-Made Lake'. *FonTomFrom* also has the merit of recovering the seminal (and hard to obtain) essay 'The Second Phase of the National Theatre Movement in Ghana' (1965), in which she lifted the lid off a series of issues that are still to be resolved by contemporary theatre practitioners. These include funding, the linguistic medium, activities in non-urban areas, and the need for creative material. It seems to me that a detailed account of some activities of her renowned village theatre Atwia Project – only mentioned in passing – would have perfectly completed the pages by and on Sutherland.

The one thing impossible to criticize, however, is the richness of the volume. To anyone interested in Ghanaian culture it is clear that video features have become one of the most relevant artistic forms, and *Fon-TomFrom* tackles this relatively recent development extensively, starting from Whyte's essay on the rapport between Armah and cinema. Esi Sutherland-Addy concentrates on the main themes of this 'video phenomenon', its ambivalent relationship with the ancestral dimension, and the director Kofi Yirenkyi's reshaping of traditional tales. The points touched by her apt and impressive study find further elaboration in Africanus Aveh's annotated filmography, Anyidoho's interview with director Kwah Ansah and his review of *Heritage Africa* and Gibbs' detailed review of the popular *Matters of the Heart*, 'a strange mixture' – he writes – 'of domestic melodrama, Indian movie and concert party'.

FonTomFrom's subtitle fails to do justice to its own multi-faceted nature: 'Literature, Theatre and Film' since it covers other fascinating fields of analysis, such as independent journalism, satirical columnists, the Ghana Dance Ensemble, choreography (and related Copyright Laws), popular musicians. Kwesi Yankah's contribution, for instance, trenchantly interprets the songs by the highlife artist Nana Ampadu as instances of protest discourse that constantly interact with Akan oral traditions. This runs through the whole history of independent Ghana until Rawlings's regime.

Other articles are devoted to the role of media and associations in the development of Ghanaian literature and to book publishing. At this point, spoilt by the generosity of the volume's contents, the reviewer might get more and more demanding, feel his appetite growing, ask for more, expect what only an encyclopedia – and a good one, to boot – could possibly contain. For example, I wonder why, while rightly arguing that 'Woeli Publishing Services has challenged the notion that Ghanaians are not writing', Dekutsey does not also discuss in depth the factors leading to the appalling scarcity of published books of creative literature in Ghana. I am concerned because in a period of five years during the 1990s, between my first and latest stay in the country, not a single text by a Ghanaian playwright was published. As evidence of this state of things, *FonTomFrom* includes a passage from Azasu's unpublished sequel to his novel, *The Stool*.

Following in this wake, other missing topics might come to the mind of the scholar and lover of Ghana, especially those far from his/her field of specialization. These might include the study of literature in Ghanaian languages, popular literature, or the contemporary state of the Concert Party. Anyidoho is the first to concede that 'the total corpus of Ghanaian literature emerges as a far more complex phenomenon than formal academic studies have so far indicated'. The complexities are suggested by the proliferation of churches with varying degrees of syncretism, which seem to be inexorably permeating all sectors of Ghanaian life, acting as a spectre behind the whole spectrum of writings offered by *FonTomFrom*. A scientific, non-proselytizing study of the phenomenon might end up discovering that even there, to quote again Okai's old poem:

> 'the faithful Fontomfrom
> Is sounding,
>   and sending
>   and sounding!'

Pietro Deandrea
University of Turin

Stephanie Newell, *Marita: or the Folly of Love,
A Novel by A. Native*
Leiden: Brill, 2002, 146 pp., $29.00, ISBN 1567-6951; 90 04 12186 2

The frontispiece of this volume includes the following: '*Marita: or the Folly of Love, A Novel by A. Native* by Stephanie Newell. At the time of the original publication, the authorship of *Marita* was indicated only as being 'by A. Native'. Newell has prepared the text for publication, performing various editorial tasks including providing some annotations. However, it will be suggested below that there are various layers of editorial intervention. It should be noted that at least one website links this book with both 'Native' and 'Newell' as author. This is not entirely inappropriate and issues of authorship will be raised in the discussion of this landmark (re-)publication.

> The introduction of christian marriage among us was a bane, coming as it did without those other requisites that alone could make it in some respects a

happy institution. An iron vessel is very good, certainly very strong but it is as liable to break as a clay vessel. (115)

The voice is that of the narrator of *Marita: or the Folly of Love.* 'Us' are the people of Cape Coast in the 1880s and the vessels referred to stand for church marriages and 'country marriages' respectively. The narrator's critical stance (note the use of lower case for 'christian'), the elements of disguise involved (Cape Coast is referred to throughout the novel as 'Dobblesie', Double C) and the use of an argument that works confidently through images – the vessels – introduces the as yet unidentified author who signed himself simply 'A. Native'. His fiction, now happily available in the African Sources for African History series, originally appeared in the Gold Coast press from 1886 and is yet another 'lost' literary text with abundant historical interest that has been recovered.

There are precedents for such 'recoveries'. About twenty-five years ago, nearly sixty years after it had been performed by the Cosmopolitan Club in Cape Coast ('Dobblesie' itself), Kobina Sekyi's *The Blinkards* was published by Rex Collings. Up till then students of Ghanaian drama in English had generally regarded J. B. Danquah and F. K. Fiawoo as the pioneering Gold Coast dramatists. Suddenly, thanks to investigative scholarship by J. Ayo Langley and others, they had a text and a playwright from an earlier generation. Since 1974 productions of *The Blinkards* have allowed audiences from West to South Africa to hear an early twentieth-century African dramatist, an artist who presented, in a trenchant and witty manner, the debates that were shaking the western educated community in Cape Coast in the first decades of the twentieth century.

Marita: or the Folly of Love, 'A Novel by A. Native', does for fiction what *The Blinkards* did for drama. It pushes back the mists of time, bringing a voice from the past into the present. It seems that the novel appeared in instalments in the *Gold Coast Western Echo* and *Gold Coast Echo* between January 1886 and 1888. Surprisingly, given the respect accorded to locally produced newspapers and to local writing, *Marita* was lost to view. Now, in the publication being reviewed, it has been put once again into the hands of lovers of Ghanaian literature.

The late Ray Jenkins seems to have been the first to be aware of and to write about *Marita* in recent times. In his 1985 thesis, he opted for the name 'J. E. Casely-Hayford' as the solution to the major mystery connected with the text: the identity of its author. Stephanie Newell, who provides an introduction and notes to the published text, points out that both Kofi Baku in a 1987 thesis and Roger Gocking, in *Facing Two Ways: Ghana's coastal communities under colonial rule* (1999), follow this lead.

But though *Marita* was known to historians, to Jenkins, Baku and Gocking, from the mid-1980s, it was not necessarily known to students of literature. In the words of Kofi Anyidoho, in *FonTomFrom*, the generally assumption was 'that Casely-Hayford's *Ethiopia Unbound* was the earliest work of fiction by a West African'. Anyidoho goes on to draw attention to the role of Bernth Lindfors in making copies of instalments of *Marita* available to students of Ghanaian literature, and, in the acknowledgements to the Brill publication, Newell also points in the direction of Austin, Texas. She writes: 'I am indebted to Bernth Lindfors for alerting me to the existence of *Marita: or The Folly of*

Love, and for giving me his photocopies of the story.' She adds 'Such enormous generosity will never be forgotten'. As Lindfors nears retirement from his academic post, it should be recorded that there are many, including myself, who have benefited from his serial generosity.

The text as we have it is incomplete. Newell's note at the end of the 'Prolegomena', preamble, indicates that 'the remainder of (the section) is missing, probably due to a printing error in the original' (42). However, my enquiries suggest that the loss may be due to a copying failure in Chicago rather than a printing error in Cape Coast. Reference to the copies held in the Balme Collection, Legon, might lead to the recovery of the missing portion.

The Prolegomena is followed by fourteen chapters of *Marita* laid out, in the Brill publication, in a way that clarifies the chapter structure, and retains indications of dates of publication. Newell assists with a few illegible sections and a non-sequiter that suggests a comment was omitted. The ending is abrupt, and Newell's note to the instalment she has reproduced from the *Gold Coast Echo*, 16th–31st January 1888 reads: 'There are no more extant issues of the *Gold Coast Echo* until 26th July, 1888, by which time *Marita or the Folly of Love* had come to an end' (144).

One can only hope that this confident assertion is proved wrong. It is clear from K. A. B. Jones Quartey's *History, Politics and the Early Press in Ghana* that while the Balme Library, at Legon, only had copies of the *Echo* for January 1888 and for July–December of the same year, Cape Coast University Library held microfilms of the publication for '1888'. Could that be for the whole of 1888? It is to be hoped that the publication of *Marita* will spur students and scholars to leave no archive unexamined in their search for copies of the *Gold Coast Echo* that contain later instalments. Cape Coast would seem to be the obvious first call.

While seeking additional parts of *Marita*, researchers may pursue further the identity of 'A. Native'. In the attempt to unmask 'A. Native', Newell lines up the suspects who fit the profile. For example, she looks for those taking 'a masculinist ideological line about the ill effects of church marriage upon African women'. She ushers into the frame the editor of *The Western Echo*, James Hutton Brew (1844–1915), and, with help, subjects him, J. E. Casely-Hayford, and other candidates to a 'forensic test'. That is to say, to stylistic analysis by computer. When this proves inconclusive, she ranks Casely-Hayford and Hutton Brew 'joint first' in the line up. In view of their relevant ages and their movements to and from England in the 1880s, the case for Brew is, I think, the stronger and I look forward to West African involvement in this investigation. As Sherlock Holmes might have said 'The game's afoot'.

Newell's consideration of the issue of authorship comes near the end of an 'Introduction' in which she provides a helpful context for the novel. She has valuable sections on 'Monogamous Marriage in Colonial West Africa'; 'Background to the Marriage Ordinance of 1884'; '"A. Native" and the Marriage Debate'; 'Women and the Marriage Ordinance'; 'Gold Coast Newspapers and their Readers', and 'Fiction as a Historical Source'. In preparing this material, she made use of the Methodist Missionary Society Archives, held in London, and of work by those, such as F.L. Bartels, Ray Jenkins, David Kimble, Margaret Priestley and Magnus Sampson, who have written about the coastal community. She includes an abundance of useful information including an explanation of the novel's title. She writes: "'Marita' is not used as a woman's name in the novel, like 'Martha' or 'Maria', but as an unconventional yet recognisable Latin word for 'wife': *marita* is the feminine form of *maritus* (husband)' (10). Incidentally, Newell's introduction makes the four-page 'Editors' Introduction' that precedes it look clumsy and redundant, an inept attempt to steal the scene.

The actual annotation of the text is curiously unpredictable: for example, the editor is clearly interested in language and society, but the starting points are not clear. One wonders why there is no translation of Latin expressions, such as '*Nolens, volens*' (62) or '*Deo Volente*', which are less familiar to readers of English than idioms such as 'up a gum tree' (121) and 'cat's paw' (124) that are explained? The editor neither translates French expressions, nor comments on the intriguing French influence on the vocabulary, apparent in the use of, for example, '*rencontre*' (129). Some of the surprising and surely significant, Scottish forms, such as '*guid*' are explained (132), but the editor's linguistic interest does not extend to a note on the form 'before we knew ourselves' (96) which may indicate the early appearance of a distinctive, and persistent, local usage. There is only partial coverage of the specifically Methodist vocabulary that is a feature of the text: 'class meeting' is explained; 'local preacher' and 'love feast' are not.

I suspect that what I have referred to as an unpredictable element may be the result of pressure of time and of the policy of the editorial board for the series in which the volume appears. The Board for African Sources for African History has strong links with the continent of Europe and their intended readership may have a 'better' knowledge of Latin vocabulary than of, say, idiomatic English.

Some of the footnotes explain or comment on classical and biblical allusions, others involve literary judgements or attempt to disentangle quotations. While often useful, there is again a certain inconsistency. The annotator helpfully prepares the reader for a Bunyanesque element in the narrative that is partly present through a 'fabulist' handling of material and through the names of characters, such as 'Mr and Mrs Littlemonie'. But when it is suggested that the name 'Sickaman', used for 'the West African country in which the story is set', conveys 'a sense of the moral sickness pervading society' one can only think that local resonances have been neglected. The possibility that Akan sources were involved should have been considered. In Akan 'sika' means 'gold', and the failure to introduce that possibility smacks of Eurocentrism.

In other instances, the annotator reaches too easily for the *Oxford English Dictionary* when other sources cry out to be consulted. For example, in commenting on the expression 'We will meet at Philippi', attention is drawn to the date and to the outcome of the Battle of Philippi (139). But there is no reference to Shakespeare's *Julius Caesar*, a play that has been very familiar to generations of Western-educated Ghanaians, where the line appears almost word for word. This oversight is the product of footnoting 'by numbers'; a more elastic approach is required.

It is to be hoped that the volume will be widely distributed in West Africa and that interested readers from all backgrounds and disciplines will be invited to comment in detail on the text. Newell acknowledges the need for further research in her introduction and this should involve not only West African informants as suggested above but also more access to archives and records. One of the areas of research that would benefit from intensive West African involvement is investigating possible links between the characters in the novel and members of the Cape Coast community. There is clearly scope for examination of *Marita* as a *roman à clef*. S. Tenkorang in writing about John Mensah Sarbah in the *Transactions of the Historical Society of Ghana* in 1973 is one of those who has provided useful points of departure for such an investigation and his references to Colonial Office papers in the Public Records Office identify a source that might help in establishing the relationship between fact and fiction. Unfortunately, Newell does not seem to have been able to exploit fully the PRO, or its equivalents in Accra and Cape Coast.

Incidentally, the most detailed section of Newell's 'Introduction' is on the salaries earned in the colonial service, and, briefly, the passage seems to bring the reader within hailing distance of the original Native. A footnote indicates that her source was the 'miscellaneous research notes of Michel R. Doortmont, University of Groningen' (24). Reference to the list of those on the Editorial Board of African Sources for African History indicates that Doortmont is one of the three. I recognise that it was probably generous of a member of the Editorial Board to make his notes available to Newell (if that is what happened), but for a really worthy volume Newell, whose admirable qualities as a researcher and writer are apparent from her book *Ghanaian Popular Fiction* (reviewed in this volume), should have been enabled to carry out properly-funded research herself, and to have been able to enlist the support of a Ghanaian team. One has to look no further than at the work of Ayo Langley on *The Blinkards* to appreciate the value of a local perspective.

It will be apparent that I have thought of the editor as Newell throughout but I suspect that there were several people involved, not only Newell but also Doortmont and others on the Editorial Board of African Sources for African History. I haven't subjected the different notes to a 'Forensic Test' but I have my suspicions about the whole process. In a sense I think the fact that there is already evidence of collaboration makes the suggested pooling of resources even more necessary.

Marita is not a gripping tale, but it is well written and that is much more significant than being 'well-made'. In assessing the achievement, one must recognise that 'A. Native's' fluency in English and his familiarity with English idioms did not mean that he was attempting to emulate British models. This should not surprise: the whole point of his argument is to show that Victorian ideas cannot be imposed on Fanti culture. This applies to the aesthetic ambitions regarding composition of a fictitious narrative as well as to marriage customs.

'A. Native' offers us a series of variations on a theme, an exercise in 'putting the same thing in different ways'. While aware of the advantage of a narrative core, the experiences of Mr Quaibu and of the 'country wife' of eight years whom he agrees to marry in church, Miss Wissah, A. Native is prepared to 'ring the changes'. His structure incorporates 'diversions' that relate to his central concerns with marriage, to Methodist hypocrisies, and to Fanti responses to Victorian institutions. The Bunyanesque element referred to, the story of the Allens, and the account of a 'tale' the narrator heard when 'at school in England' (112) are just three of the approaches he adopts, evidence of a literary composition that needs to be treated with respect and on its own terms.

But the book is far more than a fascinating exercise to be subjected to analysis by those interested in narratology: 'The Folly of Love' is very readable. Mr Quaibu, introduced as 'the hero', is admirably adept at manoeuvring his opponents into untenable positions, and he is frequently responsible for exposing the pompous in very entertaining ways. True, he sometimes fills the page with diatribes, but the discourse is relieved by rapid-fire exchanges and elevated by a breadth of vision. As in many African works of fiction, there are few descriptive passages, but there are dozens of observations that will fascinate anyone with the slightest curiosity about the evolution of society and ideas on the West African coast. At its core is a trenchant analysis of marriage *à la mode* in Dobblesie over a hundred years ago.

James Gibbs
University of the West of England

Books received

The publication of *Things Fall Apart* in the Penguin Classics series means that Chinua Achebe's 1958 novel now shares a livery, and a stable, with, Joseph Conrad's *Heart of Darkness,* one of the books with which it engages. Since some of Penguin's marketing practices, not least the use of orange in the covers, were used by Heinemann in establishing the African Writers' Series in which *Things Fall Apart* was number one, there is a certain poetic justice in this. However, ironies also abound. Not the least is the awareness of Penguin's reluctance to publish fiction by African authors, and the observation that even now the multi-national is being highly selective. With the canonical status of Achebe well established, it can't have been hard to convince the corporate accountants that the title would make a positive contribution to the company's finances.

In addition to *Things Fall Apart* (Introduction by Biyi Bandele), Penguin has brought out *Anthills of the Savannah* (Introduction by Maya Jaggi), and Ngugi wa Thiong'o's *The River Between* (Introduction by Jack Mapanje), *A Grain of Wheat* (Introduction by Abdulrazak Gurnah) and *Petals of Blood* (Introduction by Moses Isegawa). Heinemann will continue to distribute these titles in Africa.

James Gibbs
University of the West of England

Index

Abago, Mary 187-8; *Sour Honey* 187-8
Abdu, Saleh 15
Abdullahi, Hannatu Tukur 5-6, 14, 16-19, 19n; *She Talks, He Talks* 5, 16-19
Abeokuta 24, 182
Abidjan 176
Abioye, Temilola 19n
abortion 72, 110, 112
Aboulela, Leila 103n, 192; *The Museum* 103n
Abuja State 6, 19n
Achebe, Chinua 24, 43-4, 49, 54, 78, 87-8, 160, 178, 191; *Things Fall Apart* 49, 160, 178
Acholonu, Catherine 2, 55, 103, 133, 137
Adams, Gani 30
Adebayo, Aduke 69-70, 74, 76
Adefila, Boye 193
Adelugba, Dapo 157, 165-7
Adesokan, Akin 22, 192
Adewale-Nduka, Toyin 193
Adeyemi, Sola 192-4; *Goddess of the Storm and Other Stories* 192-4
Adorno, Theodor 168-9
Afigbo, A.E. 159
Ahmad, Nana Aishatu (Mogaji) 1, 5-6, 11-14, 19, 19n; *Vision of the Jewel* 1, 5, 11-12, 19, 19n; *Voice from the Kitchen* 5, 11-14, 19
Ahmadu Bello University 11
Aidoo, Ama Ata xii-xiii, 48, 56, 78, 92, 98, 105-7, 109-11, 114, 130-7, 175, 191, 196-8; *Anowa* 130-7; *Changes: A Love Story* 48, 105-7, 109-11, 114, 196-7; *No Sweetness Here* 191; *The Girl Who Can and Other Stories* 191, 198
AIDS 76, 178-9, 190
Ajadi, Gabriel 19n
Ajami language 18n
Ajima, Maria 6-10, 19; *Cycles* 6-9, 19; *Speaking of Wines* 7, 9, 19; *The Survivors* 6
Akan people 198, 202
Akande, Dorcas 58
Akinwale, Ayo 156-7, 165-7
Alkali, Zaynab 3-4, 19n, 24; *The Stillborn* 3; *Vultures in the Air* 4, 19n
Allurawa, Hawa M. 5; *The Weeping Heart* 5
Amadiume, Ifi 2, 77, 79-80, 86, 87n, 88
Amankulor, J.N. 160
Amin, Idi 178-9, 190
Ampadu, Nana 198

Ampah, Hadiza Lantana 6, 16; *Brides and New Brooms* 6
Amuta, Chidi 168, 173
Ansah, Kwah 198
Anyidoho, Kofi 197-9; *FonTomFrom* 197-9
apartheid 138, 143, 150, 168-73,
Arabic languages/tradition 2, 4, 18
Aristotle 157
Armah, Ayi Kwei 190, 197-8
Aryeetey, Sam 195; *Home at Last* 195
Asaba 24
Asante people 115; Asantehene of 115
Asmau, Nana 3, 18n
Association of Nigerian Authors 6, 15, 24, 185, 193; Cadbury Prize 25; Matatu Prize 25; NNDC Prose Prize 25; Okigbo Prize 25; Prose Prize 25, 193; Spectrum Prize 6, 25
Attwell, David 139, 142, 145, 154
Aveh, Africanus 198
Awoonor, Kofi 198
Azasu 199

Bâ, Mariama 56
Babangida, General Ibrahim 19n
Bakhtin, Mikhail 45, 87, 139, 149, 154
Baku, Kofi 200
Bamikunle, Aderemi 11, 19n
Bardolph, Jacqueline 190-1; *Cross/Cultures 47, Telling Stories* 190-1
Bartels, F.L. 201
Barungi, Violet 178, 180-1; *Words from a Granary* 178, 180-1
Bayero University 15
Bebey, 175
Bediako, Asare 196; *see also* Konadu, Asare
Ben-Abdallah, Mohammed 197
Benin 115, 118, 121-4, 128, 159; Oba of 115, 119, 122-3, 128, 159
Benue State 6, 11
Beyala, Calixthe 69-76, 86; *Amours sauvages* 69, 71, 76; *Assèze l'Africaine* 69, 73-6; *C'est le soleil qui m'a brûlée* 69-70, 72, 75-6; *Comment cuisiner son mari à l'africaine* 69, 71, 76; *La petite fille du réverbère* 69, 73, 75-6; *Le petit prince de Belleville* 69, 76; *Les honneurs perdus* 69, 71, 74-6; *Lettre d'une Africaine à ses soeurs occidentales* 69, 74, 76; *Lettre d'une Afro-française à ses compatriotes*

(vous aves dit racistes?) 69, 74, 76; *Maman a un amant* 69, 71, 75-6; *Seul le diable le savait* 69-70, 72, 75-6; *Tu t'appeleras Tanga* 69-70, 75-6
Biafra/Nigerian Civil War 24, 28, 30, 33, 63, 165-6
bisexuality 79, 83-4
Boehmer, Elleke 139, 154
Brew, Kwesi 198
Brown, Lloyd 3
Brussels 82-5
Brutus, Dennis 168-9, 173
Buba, Hafsa Muhammad xi, xiii; *Peeping into Destiny* xi, xiii
Bugul, Ken, 77-90; *Ashes and Embers* 78, 88; *La Folie et la Mort* 85, 88, 88n; *Le Baobab fou* 77-90; *Riwan ou le chemin de sable* 78, 88
Bukenya, Austin 181
Bunyan, John 202-3
Busia, Abena 198
Butler, Judith 78, 80, 86, 88

Calabar 24
Cambridge 25
Cameroon 69, 71, 75
Canada 69
Casely-Hayford, J. E. 200-1; *Ethiopia Unbound* 200
Césaire, Aimé 84, 86
Chalamanda, Fiona Johnson 53
Chamala 124, 128
Chaucer, Geoffrey 31
Cheney-Coker, Syl 48; *The Last Harmattan of Alusine Dunbar* 48
childbearing/motherhood 7, 10, 33, 38, 40, 64-5, 105, 107, 133, 149, 156-67, 188
Chinweizu 47
Chivanda, G.C. 140
Christianity 14, 30, 33, 38, 40-1, 118, 151, 179
Chukukere, Gloria 65
Chukwuji, Dave 193
class 29, 56, 70, 79, 81, 86, 92, 94, 96, 101, 112, 160-1, 185
Coetzee, J.M. 142, 154
Collectif Egalité 76
Collen, Lindsay 104, 106-13, 114; *Getting Rid of It* 104, 106-13, 114
colonialism 33, 41, 52, 55, 77-8, 81-2, 93, 97, 102, 138-55, 159, 170-1, 173
Concert Party (Ghanaian popular form) 198-9
Conrad, Joseph 178; *Heart of Darkness* 178
Constant, Paule 76; *White Spirit* 76
Coquery-Vidrovitch, C. 72
corruption 21, 29, 41, 60, 65-6, 121, 178-9, 182, 186
Courtes, J. 5
Craven, Margaret 49; *I Heard the Owl Call My Name* 49
Curtis, Lydia 81

Dana, Jean-Yves 83-4

Dangaremgba, Tsitsi 48; *Nervous Conditions* 48
Dankano, Bello Musa 5; *A Season of Locusts* 5
Danquah, J. B. 200
de Beauvoir, Simone 72
de Man, Paul 45
Dean, Tim 83, 86, 88n
deconstruction 43
Dekutsey, Woeli 199
Delphy, Christine 79-80
Delta State 159
Derrida, Jacques 45
Dhlomo, R.R.R. 144, 154
di Leonardo, Micaela 78
Diana, Princess of Wales 14
difference/otherness 78, 81, 107, 116, 150
Dike, Kenneth Onwuka 159
Dimka 30
domestic violence xii, 95, 105-10, 152, 171, 186-7
Dongala 174
Doortmont, Michael R. 203
Drum magazine 151
du Bois, W.E.B. 125-6, 129
Duras, Marguerite 177
Durban 140, 148, 149, 151

Echeruo, M.J.C. 157, 167
Edo State 19n
education 2, 18, 21-2, 30, 34, 56, 70, 93-7, 99-102, 105, 109, 178-9, 189
Edward, Victor 193
Egejuru, Phanuel 63
Egypt 115, 174
Eko, Ebele 14
Eliot, T.S. 162; *Murder in the Cathedral* 162
Elliot, Billy 83
Embaga, Nana 5
Emecheta, Buchi xii, 24, 56, 63, 78, 92, 115-29; *The New Tribe* xii-xiii, 115-29
Enugu 30
Erdich, Louise 49; *Love Medicine* 49
Esslin, Martin 166-7
ethnicity 2, 92, 112, 189
exclusion/invisibility/voicelessness 2, 4-5, 9, 25, 55, 64, 80, 92, 100, 104, 130, 136-7, 141
Ezeigbo, Akachi 23-42, 55, 57-63, 65-8, 192; *Children of the Eagle* 25-8, 30-5, 39, 42; *Echoes in the Mind* 57; *House of Symbols* 26, 28, 30, 32-5, 38, 42; *The Buried Treasure* 24; *The Last of the Strong Ones* 26-7, 30, 33, 40-2; *The Street Beggars* 25

Fall, Aminata Sow 3; *Le Revenant* 3
family 4, 32-3, 40, 63, 118-19, 136 144, 149-50
Fanti people 203
Farah, Nuruddin 175
feminism xii, xiii, 1, 13-14, 26, 34, 40, 47-8, 53, 55-6, 72-3, 75, 77-81, 86, 91, 97-8, 103, 109, 133, 156-7; Western xii, 26, 55-6, 72-3, 78

Femwrite 180-1
Festac 121, 125
Fiawoo, F. K. 200
Fiedler, Leslie 166-7
Fiji 82
Fioupou, Christiane 191
Flora Nwapa Prize 25
Fodio, Usman dan 3
Foucault, Michel 45, 79
francophone writers 69, 174, 176-7
Freetown 120
Freud, Sigmund 83, 86
Fulani people 2, 14, 18

Garuba, Harry 6, 11, 192-4; *Voices from the Fringe* 6
Garvey, Marcus 125-6, 129
Gary, Romain 76; *La vie devant soi* 76
gay sexuality 79-80
gender, African women on 56, 102; alternation of roles 149-51; bias of canonical male writers challenged 78, 138; binary thinking about 99; and colonialism 78; commoditization of 82; and consciousness 141, 146; cultural schizophrenia and 85; and daily life 138-9, 149, 152, 169; destabilisation of 149-50; as difference/otherness 78; discrimination 28, 59, 99; and equality 111-13; essentialist theories of 79-80; and freedom 139; and history 139-42, 146, 153; and identity politics 99-101; in Ezeigbo and Okekwe (contrasted) 28-9; intersection with racial, class, cultural, economic and political oppression 94, 97-102, 112, 170; and language 172; and marriage 100, 109, 112, 190; marginalisation of African women 92, 99; as mutual wild zone of misunderstanding 5; performance as basis of 77-82, 150-1; and political/social/cultural/economic change 78, 97-100; in postcolonial ideologies 77-8; postmodern view of 80; power relations 17-18, 59, 100-1, 112; and sexuality 130, 172; traditionalism and 65, 77-8, 80, 100-1, 108-9, 132; and violence 108, 152; womanism and 56, 67
gender, and marriage 190
Germany 25
Ghana 25, 106, 109, 120, 195-203; *see also* Akan people, Asante people, Fanti people
Ghana Dance Ensemble 198
Gibbs, James 197-9; *FonTomFrom* 197-9
Gimba, Abubakar 3, 183-5; *Footprints* 183-5
Giwa, Dele 8, 19n
globalization 40
Gocking, Roger 200
Gombe State 6, 11-12
Gordimer, Nadine xii, 92
Gowon, General 165
Gray, Stephen 174-5, *The Picador Book of African Stories* 174-5

Green, December 108, 112, 114
Green, Michael 142, 155
Griemas, A. J. 5
Guillaumin, Colette 79

Habila, Helon 22
Hassan-Tom, Fatima Usara 5; *A Flight Heavenwards* 5; *Eyes of Darkness* 5
Hausa people 2, 14, 18, 31
Head, Bessie 92
Hegel, G.W.F. 134
Heinemann African Writers series 21
homosexuality 78-80, 86, 113
Honwana, Luís Bernardo 174
Hove, Chenjerai 48
Hudson-Weems, Clenora 55, 57, 67n
human rights 58, 182, 195
Hutcheon, Linda 196
Hutton Brew, James 201
hybridity 31, 81

Ibadan 24, 30, 38, 61
Ibrahim, Jibrin 3
identity politics 78, 81, 83-6, 99-103, 115-19, 126, 128-9, 169
Idi-Aba 31
Idris, Aishatu Gidado 5; *Rabiat* 5
Idu, Prince of 119
Ifowodo 192
Igala, Attah of 159
Igbo Arts: Community and Cosmos 44, 54
Igbo people 19n, 23-4, 27, 30, 33-4, 44-7, 50, 58, 61-2, 77, 79-80, 87, 87n, 120, 128, 159, 165
Ige, Bola 31
Ikeja 31
Iloekunanwa, Ada *see* Okekwe, Promise
Imfeld, Al 4; *Vultures in the Air* 4, 19n
indigenous African languages xii, 47
Informart 5, 19n
Ipadeola, Tade 19n
Isegawa, Moses 178-80; *Abyssinian Chronicles* 178-80
Isharassa, Grace 181
Isiaka, Sidi 193
Isichei, Elizabeth 159
Islam xi, 14, 179
Iwuanyanwu, Obi 19n
Ixopo 140, 149
Iyayi, Festus 48, 192; *Court Martial* 48

Jaja, King 115
James, Henry 49
Janus 6
Japan 25
Jelloun, Tahr Ben 175
Jenkins, Ray 200-1
Jones Quartey, K. A. B. 201
Jordan 95
Jos State 6

Kaduna 1, 10, 24, 30
Kaduna State 1, 6, 14, 19n

Kagoro 14
Kaguvi 147, 151
Kaltho 30
Kanengoni, Chris 48
Kano State 6, 15
Kato, Cecilia 6, 14-15, 19; *Desires* 14, 19;
    Victims of Love 14, 19
Kaura 14
Kawadwa, Byron 181
Kiguli, Susan 181
Kimble, David 201
Kingsolver, Barbara 178; *The Poisonwood
    Bible* 178
Kironde, Erisa 181
Kogi State 18n
Kolawole, Mary 55-7, 63, 65, 67-8, 160
Konadu, Asare 196; *Don't Leave Me Mercy*
    196; *see also* Bediako, Asare
Kotun, Debo 182-3; *Abiku* 182-3
Kraft Books 24
Kristeva, Julia 85, 89, 172
Kuzwayo, Ellen 143
Kwara State 18n

Lacan, Jacques 45, 172
Lagos 24, 30-1, 118, 121-2, 124
Laing, Kojo 48, 197; *Major Gentl and the
    Achimota Wars* 48
Lan, David 140, 145, 149, 153n
Lancaster, Roger N. 78
land 138-46
Lane, Christopher 83, 86, 88n
Langley. J. Ayo 200, 203
lesbianism 79-80, 83
Liberty Merchant Bank Short Story Series
    192; *Little Drops I: an Anthology of
    Contemporary Nigerian Short Stories* 192-
    3; *Little Drops II: an Anthology of
    Contemporary Nigerian Short Stories* 192-
    3
Lindfors, Bernth 200-1
Lionnet, Françoise 113-14
Liverpool 118, 120
Lodge, Tom 143, 155
London 25
Lorentzon, Leif 197
Lusaka 98

Mabuza, Lindiwe 168-72
Maduakor, Obi 2
Maduka, Chidi 134, 137
magical realism 193
Magona, Sindiwe 143
Maiduguri State xi, 6, 11
Maiwada, Mu'azu 3
Makerere University 179, 181
Makurdi State 6
Makwemoisa, Anthonia 39
Malumfashi, Ibrahim 3, 5
Man of Two Worlds (film) 178
Mandela, Zindzi 168-9, 171-2
Mangut, Joseph 5

Marks, Elaine 136-7
marriage xii, 9-10, 29, 38-40, 72, 94-5, 98-100,
    104-13, 130-7, 149, 174, 188-9, 199-204
Marshall, Bill Okyere 197
Marxism 4, 79
Masefield, John 156
Mathieu, Nicole-Claude 79
Mbeki, Govan 143, 155
Mbonyingingo, Christine 191
Mbowa, Rose 181
Meena, Ruth 113-14
Mhlophe, Gcina 168
Michael Caine Prize 22, 103n, 192
Mill, John Stuart 87
Miller, Christopher 4
Mills, Sara 172-3
Minh-ha, Trinh T. 78, 87n, 89-90
Miri, Angela 6
modernity 33, 53, 58, 82, 143
Mohammed, Binta Salma 5-6, 14-16, 19, 19n;
    Contours of Life 5, 15-16, 19
Mohammed, Murtala 30
Mokoy, Oma 193
Molemodile, Vicky Sylvester 6
Morrison, Toni 49
Mozambique 174
Mphahlele, Es'kia 168
Mustapha, Farida 11

Nandan, Satendra 82, 88n
nationalism 10-12, 97-8, 139
NBC Short Story Competition 24
Ndibe, Okey 22, 192
Nehanda 140-1, 144-53
neo-colonialism 74, 78, 82, 84, 94-5
Neto, Augustinho 168
New Nigerian 5
Newell, Stephanie 196-7, 199-204; *Marita: or
    the Folly of Love, A Novel by A. Native*
    199-204
Nfah-Abbenyi, Juliana Makuchi 77-8, 89
Ngcobo, Lauretta 138-55
Ngugi wa Thiong'o 47, 78, 175, 178; *Black
    Hermit* 178; *Weep Not, Child* 178
Nigeria xi, xiii, 77, 115, 118-125, 128-9, 156-
    67, 182-3, 192-4; Civil War *see* Biafra;
    Northern 17-20, 21-42; *see also* Hausa,
    Igbo, Yoruba peoples
Njoku, Adaure 63-4, 68; *Withstand the Storm*
    64, 68
Nnaemeka, David 193
Nnaemeka, Obioma 56, 61, 68, 89
Nnolim, Charles 57, 68, 73, 76
Nortje, Arthur 168
Ntantala, Phyllis 143
Nwabunike, Uche 63
Nwankwo, Chimalum 53n; *The Womb in the
    Heart and Other Poems* 53n
Nwapa, Flora xii-xiii, 2, 49, 56, 63, 78, 92;
    Conversations xiii; *Efuru* xii, 49; *Idu* 49;
    The First Lady xii; *The Sychophants* xii;
    Two Women in Conversation xii

Nwosu, Maik 24
Nyanya, Kekelwa 91-103; *Hearthstones* 95-103

Oakely, Ann 79, 87n, 89
Obafemi, Olu 3, 18n, 156-7, 167
Obasanjo, General Olesugun 30, 194
Obodumu, Kris, 183, 185-7; *Die a Little* 183, 185-7
Obote, Milton 178-9
Ocen, Laury Lawrence 187-9; *The Alien Woman* 187-9
Odamtten, V. 197
Ofeimun, Odia 192
Ofowodo, Ogaga 24
Ogbomoso 19n
Ogede, O.S. 197
Ogot, Grace 78, 104, 114; *The Promised Land* 104, 114
Oguine, Ike 192-3; *A Squatter's Tale* 193
Ogundipe, Phabean 2
Ogundipe-Leslie, Omolara 2, 55
Ogunyemi, Chikwenye Okonjo 55-9, 62, 67n, 68, 73, 156-7, 167; *Africa Wo/Man Palava* 57
Ojaide, Tanure 175
Ojo-Ade, Femi xi, xiii
Ojukwu, Lt-Col Chukwuemeka 165
Okafor, Grace 58, 65, 67n
Okai, Atukwei 197-8
Okapi 83
Okara, Gabriel 43; *The Voice* 43
Okechukwu, Chinwe 55, 57, 63-8; *When Rain Beat the Cow in the Eyes* 57, 63
Okediran, Wale 193
Okekwe, Promise 23-6, 28-32, 34, 36-42; *Fumes and Cymbals* 26, 28-30, 36, 38-9, 42; *Hall of Memories* 25-6, 28, 36, 40, 42; *Soul-Journey into the Night* 24; *Tomorrow's Yesterday* 26; *Zita-Zita* 26, 28-30, 37, 42
Okigbo, Christopher 25, 45-6, 54, 172; *Labyrinths* 54
Okolo, M.S.C. 193
Okome, Onookome 24
Okot p'Bitek 43
Okoye, Ifeoma 24
Okoye-Nwajiaga, Chukwuma 193-4
Okpewho, Isidore 48; *Tides* 48
Okri, Ben 48, 76, 175, 192; *The Famished Road* 48, 76
Okurut, Mary Karooru 181, 187, 189-90; *The Invisible Weevil* 187, 189-90
Omobowale, Emmanuel B. 3
Omotoso, Kole 192
Onobrakpeya, Bruce 31
Onus, Suzanna 5, 19n; *The Turning Wheel* 5; *Waves of Emotion* 5
Onwordi, Toni Kan 193
Opara, Chioma 56, 67n, 68
Opobo 115
Oshiomole, Adams 31
Osofisan, Femi 192

Osofisan, Sola 193
Osundare, Niyi 191-2
Otiono, Nduka 192
Oyedepo, Stella 3, 18n
Oyefeso, Kolapo 193-4
Oyekunle, Segun 18n
Oyono, Ferdinand 75; *Chemin d'Europe* 75

Paul, Victoria 193
Pegram, Amelia Blossom 171
Penguin 22
Pereira, Francesca Yetunde 2
Pietermaritzburg 25
postcolonial societies 77-8, 81, 85, 94, 190, 196
postmodernism 43, 77-81, 86
pre-colonial Africa 79, 82
Priestley, Margaret 201
prostitution 53, 66, 71, 75
protest poetry 168-73

Questions Féministes (QF) 79

Rabelais 31
racism 62-3, 69, 74, 81, 84, 94, 103, 112, 118
Raji, Remi 24
Rakotosin, Michele 175
Ranger, Terence 140, 152-3, 155
rape 106-7, 110, 151-2, 173, 179, 190
Rawlings, Jerry 198
Riley, Denise 80
Robbe-Grillet, Alain 177
Romania 25
Rubadiri, David 181
Rubin, Gayle 79, 87n, 89
Rungano, Kristina 168-72
Ryan, Pamela 170

Sambo, Hauwa M. 1, 5-6, 9-11, 14, 19, 19n; *Disaster in the House* 5; *The Genesis and Other Poems* 1, 5-6, 9-11, 19, 19n
Sampson, Magnus 201
Sani, Abba Aliyu 3, 11, 19n
Sarbah, John Mensah 203
Saro-Wiwa, Ken 25, 191; *Basi and Company* 191
Segun, Mabel 2, 18; *Conflict and Other Poems* 2, 18
Sekyi, Kobina 200; *The Blinkards* 200
Senegal 3-4, 77, 81-2, 85-6
Senghor, Léopold 170
Sentongo, Nuwa 181
Séverac, Alain 191
sexuality 4, 38-9, 53, 71, 75, 77-87, 87n, 93-5, 103, 109-10, 112-13, 130-1, 135-6, 179, 187-8
Shakespeare, William 158-9, 202; *Julius Caesar* 202; *Macbeth* 158-9; *Romeo and Juliet* 158
Sheme, Ibrahim 1, 5-6; *Brides and New Brooms* 6; *The Malam's Potion* 5
Sheu Musa Yar Adua Foundation 5

Shona people 140, 146
Showalter, Elaine 5, 19n
Sierra Leone 120
slavery 104, 131, 135-6, 170, 198
Sofola, Zulu xii-xiii, 24, 156-67; *King Emene*
    156-67; *Wedlock of the Gods* 158
Sophocles 115, 157-8, 162, 164; *Oedipus the
    King* 115, 157-8, 162, 164
Soueif, Ahdaf 174
South Africa 25, 98, 138-55, 168-73, 174;
    African National Congress (ANC) 143;
    Natives' Land Act (1913) 143; South
    African Native National Congress 143
Souza, Noemia de, 168
Sowande, Bode 192
Soyinka, Wole 44-5, 54, 78, 172, 178; *The
    Lion and the Jewel* 178
Spain 25
Spectrum 4
stereotypes 65, 67, 93, 110, 188, 197
Stirling-Horden Publishing 6, 14
Stratton, Florence 78
Stratton, Jon 4
suicide 104, 106-11
Sule, Muhammed 3
Sutherland, Efua 197-8; Atwia Project 198
Sutherland-Addy, Esi 198

Taban lo Liyong 181
taboo subjects xi, 93
Tadjo, Véronique 176-7; *As the Crow Flies*
    176-7
Tahir, Ibrahim 3
Taieb, Albert 175
Takoradi 120
Tanzania 178
Tenkorang, S. 203
Togo 25
traditionalism 8-9, 13, 17, 23, 27-8, 32-3, 39-
    41, 52, 58-61, 77-81, 98-101, 105, 110,
    131, 144, 156-7, 160, 165, 189-90, 193
translation 43-54
Tristram Shandy 31
Tutuola, Amos 40

Ubah, Jib 3
Ugah, Adah 3
Uganda 178-81, 187-90; National Resistance
    Movement (NRM) 178, 190
Umar, Aishar 19n
Umuahia 19n
Umuga 27, 33

United States 25
University of Ibadan 24
University of Ilorin 19n
University of Jos 19n
University of Lagos 23
University of Maiduguri 11

Vambe, 144, 154
Vasanji, G.M. 48; *The Gunny Sack* 48
Vatsa, Mamman 3
veiling 3-5, 9
Vera, Yvonne 43-54, 105, 107-8, 111, 114,
    138-55; 192; *Butterfly Burning* 47-53,
    105, 107-8, 110-11, 114; *Open Spaces*
    192
video feature films 198
Vista Books 24

Wala, Mohammed Garba 5; *The Icons* 5
Walker, Alice 57
Walker, Keith 83, 90
Wangui wa Goro 176-7
Wangusa, Anne Ayeta 187-8; *Memoirs of a
    Mother* 187-8
war 33, 63-7
Washington, DC 176
Wilkinson, Jane 191
Wilson-Tagoe, Nana 128-9, 147, 155
Wilton, Tamsin 78, 90
Witting, Monique 79, 86, 90
Wolof people 77
womanism xiii, 26, 29, 34, 55-68, 73, 92
women's organisations 111
women's rights 33
WORDOC Short Story Competition 25
Wordsworth, William 10, 19n
Wright, Derek 190-1

Yaba-Akoka 31
Yankah, Kwesi 198
Yari, Labo 3, 5
Yirenkyi, Kofi 198
Yoruba people 18n, 31, 39, 182
Yorubaland 159

Zambia 95, 99-100
Zaria State 6, 11
Zeleza, Paul Tiyambe 48, 175
Zimbabwe 25, 138-55
Zulu people 140, 147
Zulu Sofola Prize 25
Zulu, Phumzile 171